MOON

Lisbon & Beyond

CARRIE-MARIE BRATLEY

Contents

Rua Augusta in Lisbon

Lisbon & Beyond

Consistently ranked among Europe's top destinations for tourism and quality of life, Lisbon is a thriving city packed with contemporary attractions that sit comfortably among its time-honored facets, a city that effortlessly manages to blend tradition with trendy. Add exciting cuisine, welcoming hospitality, and first-class accommodations, and you get a hugely appealing destination.

Follow the wonderfully scenic Marginal Road to the Portuguese Riviera for regal towns and some of the finest beaches in the region. Take a day trip to Sintra, a town whose whimsical buildings could be straight out of a children's storybook. Nearby, majestic Mafra, with its extravagant Baroque national palace and beautiful gardens, is easily paired with the surfy town of Ericeira. To the northeast lies Tomar, an enigmatic Portuguese city renowned for its medieval Templar Castle and monumental Convent of Christ.

Just across from Lisbon, you'll find sunny Costa da Caparica and the sea-salt-kissed Setúbal Peninsula, where wines and fresh fish are as abundant as vast golden beaches. Cross the Sado Estuary from Setúbal to the lesser-explored Troia Peninsula, gateway to colorful Alentejo hamlets. Finally, to the east in the deep Alentejo region is Évora, a fantastically preserved historic town with strong Roman ties.

A trip to Lisbon should be a priority for any European escapade—not only for the quintessentially Portuguese experience it provides, but for the opportunity it offers to explore a wealth of other incredible destinations, all within easy reach of the capital.

Costa da Caparica

9 TOP
EXPERIENCES

1 Getting 360-degree views of Lisbon from the towers of **São Jorge Castle** (page 62).

2 Touring the out-of-this-world **Pena Palace** in Sintra, with its colorful turrets and towers (page 150).

3 Getting immersed in Templar history at Tomar's spectacular **Convent of Christ** (page 178).

4 Strolling along Lisbon's tree-lined **Avenida da Liberdade,** past elegant shops and picturesque cafés (page 59).

5 Visiting the ancient, mysterious **Almendres Cromlech** outside Évora (page 253).

6 Relaxing on the **beaches** of the Portuguese Riviera (pages 130 and 139), Costa da Caparica (page 194), and coastal villages south of Setúbal (pages 224 and 231).

7 Seeing wild dolphins in the glistening **Sado Estuary** (page 209).

8 Taking in a soulful **fado** show in Lisbon's historical Alfama (page 109) or Bairro Alto (page 107) neighborhood.

9 Indulging in **regional delicacies** like delicious pastel de Belém (page 28).

Before You Go

WHEN TO GO

High Season

May-September offers the **best beach weather;** average temperatures for this time of year range from the mid-20s to the mid-30s Celsius (mid-70s to mid-90s Fahrenheit). **June-August** constitutes the peak of high season, when Portugal is at its busiest—and priciest. Most of the country's major events, such as the traditional **Popular Saints** festivities and **local festivals,** are held in summer. But don't feel obliged to visit Portugal when it's at its hottest; peak summer season can mean extremely busy monuments and beaches, packed hotels, and parking at a premium. Inland areas such as the **Évora** in Central Portugal can be sweltering (over 40°C/104°F) in summer and are much more enjoyable in **spring** or **autumn.** Just outside peak season—June and September, even October—are also beautiful times to visit, when the weather is milder and the pace is more relaxed.

Lisbon's famous Rua Augusta, connecting Comércio Square to Rossio

What You Need to Know

- **Currency:** Euro (€)

- **Conversion rate:** €1 = $1.11 USD; £0.87 GBP (at time of publication)

- **Entry requirements:** Currently, no visa needed for travelers from the US, Canada, UK, Europe, Australia, or New Zealand. South African nationals need to apply for a Portugal-Schengen visa. From mid-2025, people from over 60 visa-exempt countries, including the USA, UK, and Canada, will be required to have an ETIAS (European Travel Information and Authorization System) travel authorization to enter most European countries, including Portugal. For more information about the new requirements, visit the European Union travel requirements site (travel-europe. europa.eu).

- **Emergency number:** The common European emergency number is 112.

- **Time zone:** Western European Time (WET)

- **Electrical system:** 230-volt, 50-hertz electricity and type C or F sockets (the standard European round, two-prong plugs)

- **Opening hours:** Vary; most businesses open 9am-10am and close 6pm-7pm. Shops may close 1pm-3pm for lunch, but this is increasingly rare.

Low Season

Spring, autumn, and winter are mild and mostly sunny, with temperatures that can range from the mid-teens to mid-20s Celsius (mid-50s to low 70s Fahrenheit), although Portugal does have **rainy months, December** being the wettest; January is the coldest, when thermometers can sometimes dip to single digits (30s Fahrenheit), particularly at night. **Sintra, Tomar,** and **Évora** are **year-round** destinations. Hotels will again be close to full over Christmas and New Year, but outside that, low season in most of Portugal will mean fewer tourists and a more tranquil, relaxed pace of life.

GETTING THERE

From Europe

Traveling to Lisbon Airport from almost anywhere within Europe is quick and easy—and even better, it's now less expensive, thanks to the growing number of low-cost airlines. Gatwick, Stansted, Heathrow, and Luton in **London** usually have two or three daily flights to Lisbon on low-cost carriers such as **Ryanair** and **easyJet.** Flag carriers **TAP** and **British Airways** also fly direct to Lisbon from London.

    Bus and **train** services connect Portugal with Spain, France, Belgium, the Netherlands, and the United Kingdom. **Driving** to Lisbon from within Europe is also possible thanks to a good international road network and the EU open-borders policy.

From Outside Europe

There are **direct flights** from the **United States** to Lisbon from cities including New York, San Francisco, Miami, Boston, Washington DC, and Chicago, and from Toronto in **Canada.**

There are no direct flights between **South Africa** or **Australia** and Lisbon, but travel is possible on flights with main European carriers via other major European cities such as Madrid, London, Paris, Frankfurt, and Amsterdam, or via Dubai, Doha, and Luanda. There are direct flights between Lisbon and Dubai with Emirates and Doha with Qatar Airways.

Budgeting

- **Small espresso coffee:** €0.80
- **1.5-liter bottle of water:** €1
- **Sandwich:** €2
- **Local bus ticket:** €2
- **Museums:** €3-6
- **Small glass of wine or beer:** €1.50-2
- **Hotel room:** €60-100 d

GETTING AROUND

Thanks to its compact size and a good road network, Portugal is easily traveled by **car.** Renting a car also provides greater flexibility for exploring off the beaten track. But an efficient bus and train network also connects most major towns and cities. **Train travel** can often be more **scenic** and **cheaper** than the bus, but train stations can sometimes be located far outside the town centers. **Bus travel** is almost always **quicker** than the train.

Car

Portugal's road system is decent and major routes are kept in good condition, although the same cannot be said about smaller regional or municipal roads. Some are in urgent need of repair, particularly in rural areas, and on certain stretches signage could use updating.

Motorways are generally in good condition, although major motorways (autoestradas) have **tolls,** signaled by a black car on a white background with a blue border. Cars drive on the **right-hand** side of the road—the same as the rest of mainland Europe and the United States.

Train

Portugal's train service **Comboios de Portugal (CP)** (www.cp.pt/passageiros/en) is efficient and inexpensive but complex. Despite being

Lisbon's Oriente train station

comprehensive, the national rail network isn't as direct as bus services, and, oddly, some major cities have no train station, while many cities and towns have their train stations on the outskirts, requiring a taxi ride to the center. On the plus side, Portugal's trains tend to be spacious and clean on the inside, and offer cheaper second-class tickets and more privacy and comfort in first class, sometimes in private compartments.

Bus

There are many different bus companies in Portugal, including three major intercity long-distance ones; most of the regions in this book are serviced by national **Rede Expressos** (www.rede-expressos.pt). Local and regional buses link towns, villages, and parishes within municipalities. In Lisbon the local public transport company is **Carris,** which operates buses, trams, and funiculars. Lisbon also has a safe and efficient subway, the **Lisbon Metro,** whose four lines total 44 km (27.5 mi) of route and serve 56 stations. Bus travel in Portugal is inexpensive but not always the most comfortable, although long-distance express buses are mostly equipped with air-conditioning, TVs, toilets, and even onboard drinks and snacks.

TRAVEL DOCUMENTS

All travelers entering Portugal are required to have a **valid ID.**

As of mid-2025, nationals from over 60 visa-exempt countries, including the US, UK, and Canada, will be required to have an ETIAS (European Travel Information and Authorisation System) travel authorization to enter most European countries, including Portugal. The ETIAS is linked to a traveler's passport, valid for up to three years or until the passport expires, and is a fully electronic system (https://travel-europe. europa.eu/etias/what-etias_en). A valid ETIAS travel authorization allows multiple short-term entries into European countries, typically up to 90 days within a 180-day period. Entry is not guaranteed; border guards will check compulsory documents and ensure passengers meet entry conditions upon arrival.

At the time of writing, **European Union** nationals traveling within EU or Schengen states do not require a visa for entering Portugal for any length of stay. They do require a valid passport or official ID card. European citizens traveling between **Schengen Area** countries are not required to present an identity document or passport at border crossings, as an open-borders policy is in effect. However, it is recommended that travelers have ID documents with them, as they may be requested at any time by the authorities.

Citizens of the **United Kingdom** and **Ireland** must produce a passport to enter Portugal, valid for the duration of the proposed stay, and can stay for up to three months. Further documentation might be required post-Brexit.

People from **non-EU countries** always require a passport, valid for at least six months; some may require a visa. **Australian, Canadian,** and **US** travelers require a valid passport but do not need a visa for stays of up to 90 days in any six-month period. While it is not obligatory to have an onward or return ticket, it is advisable.

South African nationals need to apply for a Portugal-Schengen visa. This should be done three months before travel. Applicants must have a South African passport valid for six months beyond date of return with at least three blank pages.

WHAT TO PACK

Key items to pack include **mosquito repellent** and **sunblock** (sunblock can be expensive in Portugal) plus a **hat** for May-October, a **windbreaker** for all seasons (Portugal can be breezy year-round), and **warm sweaters,** a **jacket,** and a light **raincoat** for winter. **Comfortable shoes** for walking are advised if your trip is more than a beach holiday, and don't forget a **plug adapter** for chargers. Pack a **concealable pouch** to carry documents and cash while out and about exploring, and **never carry cash and documents together.**

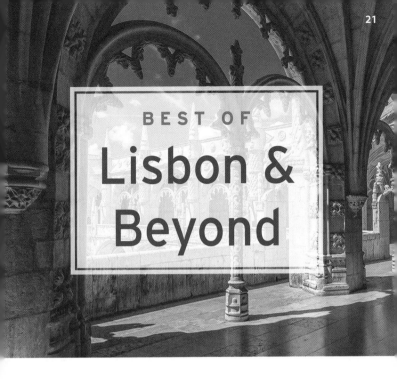

BEST OF
Lisbon & Beyond

Lisbon can get very busy and hot in summer, so a **hat, sunscreen, water,** and a healthy dose of patience are useful in warmer months. If you plan to visit in June, make sure you book well ahead, as this is the month in which the **Santo António Festival** causes the city to explode into party mode.

The Portuguese capital is also rather hilly, which can mean steep climbs. That said, **public transport** is pretty reliable, and all those hills mean amazing views from the many **miradouros** (viewpoints) dotting the city. If your feet get tired, the historical and famed **No. 28 tram** is one of the quirkiest ways to explore the city, trundling through authentic neighborhoods on the time-honored tracks.

After spending three days in the city, experience a few great day trips within a quick drive or train ride, from Lisbon's favorite **beach resorts** to the world-famous castles and palaces of **Sintra.**

Day 1

Spend the morning discovering downtown Lisbon, beginning at the main **Avenida da Liberdade,** exploring **Comércio Square's museums** and **landmarks.**

After lunch, take the tram to **Belém,** where you can visit the **Belém**

Where to Go from Lisbon

If You Want . . .	Destination	How Long to Stay
Beaches	Costa da Caparica (page 187)	1 day
	The Portuguese Riviera (page 122)	overnight
	Troia (page 220) and Comporta (page 229)	overnight
	Melides (page 235)	overnight
Palaces	Sintra (page 145)	1 day
	Mafra and Ericeira (page 159)	1 day
Historical villages	Tomar (page 174)	overnight
Nature	Setúbal Peninsula (page 200)	overnight
Rural Portugal	Évora (page 246)	1 day

Why Go	Getting There from Lisbon
spacious beaches; fun seaside feel; close to Lisbon	bus or car (25 minutes)
beautiful beaches; cool bars; glamorous hotels	car or train (40 minutes)
unspoiled, wild beaches with a touch of glamour; horseback riding	car (1.5 hours)
Alentejo village; endless golden-sand beaches	car (1.5 hours)
magical palaces and castles; shady woodland	car (30 minutes) or train (1 hour)
an extravagant royal palace within 15 minutes' drive of a beach; laid-back vibes	car (50 minutes)
the remnants of a Knights Templar stronghold; river-town charm	car (1.5 hours), train (2 hours), or bus (1 hour 45 minutes)
wild dolphins; unspoiled coastline; fresh fish	car (45 minutes) or bus/train (1 hour)
excellent wines; the thrilling Bone Church; a glimpse into rural life	car (1.5 hours) or bus/train (2 hours)

Moorish Castle

Tower and **Jerónimos Monastery** before indulging in a famous **pastel de Belém** custard tart.

Head back to Lisbon's **Chiado Square** for an afternoon refreshment before walking up to **Bairro Alto** for dinner and a show at a typical **fado restaurant.** After dinner, let loose in one of the many nearby bars.

Day 2

Today, explore the **Baixa, Alfama,** and **São Vicente** neighborhoods by Lisbon's famous **trams,** visiting sights such as the **National Pantheon,** the **Fado Museum, Lisbon Cathedral,** and the **Graça viewpoint.**

After all that walking, hop on the train toward **Park of Nations.** Here you can visit **riverfront gardens,** explore the **Lisbon Oceanarium,** and rest your feet on a scenic **cable car ride.**

End your day at one of the many **restaurants** and **bars** along the Park of Nations waterfront.

Day 3

Take the train to **Sintra,** a 40-minute ride from Lisbon, for a day of exploring the town's whimsical architecture. Give your legs a break and ride the tourist bus up Sintra's steep hills to top sights like **Pena Palace,** the **Moorish Castle,** and the **Regaleira Estate.**

Stop for lunch in town and be sure to grab a traditional baked pastry, queijadas de Sintra, before heading back to Lisbon for dinner.

Day 4

Enjoy some of Lisbon's quirkier sights today, starting with browsing the many stalls of the **LX Factory** in Alcântara.

From here, walk across the road to the futuristic-looking **MAAT— Museum of Art, Architecture and Technology;** be sure to take in the views from the rooftop.

Head toward the **25 de Abril Bridge,** where you can take the **Pillar 7 Experience,** a unique tour in, around, and up one of the pillars of this iconic bridge.

Finish your night with a sundowner at one of the many bars and lounges on the **Santo Amaro docks.**

Day 5

Do as the locals do and escape from the city for the day: Just a 40-minute train ride from Lisbon's Cais do Sodré station is the Portuguese Riviera, one of Lisbon's most popular beach resorts.

Stop first in **Estoril.** Spend the day on the **beach,** popping in to the famous **Pastelaria Garrett** for coffee and a sweet treat.

Stroll along the 3-km (2-mi) promenade to **Cascais,** enjoying the chic **boutiques,** and have dinner at one of the many **restaurants** on the marina.

Catch the train from Cascais for the 40-minute return to Lisbon.

MAAT—Museum of Art, Architecture and Technology designed by Amanda Levete Architects

Lisbon Beyond the Crowds

Venture off the beaten path to experience the quieter side of Lisbon and its nearby attractions.

Day 1

Start at the **Medeiros e Almeida House-Museum,** a private collection of historical Portuguese and international decorative artwork housed in a striking mansion.

After, stroll down the leafy **Avenida da Liberdade** to have lunch with the locals at Bonjardim, tucking into finger-licking delicious chicken piri-piri. From here, walk back up the Avenida (or jump on the Metro from Avenida to Praça da Espanha), heading north to the **Calouste Gulbenkian Museum** to check out its remarkable collection of artifacts, spanning from ancient Egypt to contemporary arts.

Take a half-hour walk west to the Gothic **Águas Livres Aqueduct** to round off the afternoon with a bird's-eye view of Lisbon. For dinner, treat yourself to an extravagant dining experience on the Avenida da Liberdade at fashionable **JNcQUOI Asia.**

Day 2

Take a half-day excursion to Queluz by train. Before setting off, make a stop at the **National Pantheon** in the São Vicente neighborhood, a 17th-century Baroque landmark overlooking the Tagus. From here it's a short 10-minute walk to the Santa Apolónia train station where you can make the approximate 40-minute train ride to the commuter suburb of Queluz. In Queluz, visit the beautiful **Queluz National Palace and Gardens.** On your return, enjoy dinner in Lisbon's atmospheric **Baixa** at the traditional Taberna da Baixa.

Day 3

Head to **Setúbal**—around an hour's journey south of Lisbon—by train or car. Set sail on a unique boat trip to the **Sado Estuary** to visit its resident pod of bottlenose dolphins. Alternatively, jump straight on the ferry from Setúbal to the chic **Troia peninsula** to soak up the sun on one of its pristine (and uncrowded) beaches. Savor a lazy seafood lunch at **El Cristo** with a view of the marina. On the return to Setúbal, stop at Adega Leo do Petisco in the town center and have some fried cuttlefish for dinner (a local specialty) before making your way back to Lisbon.

Queluz National Palace and Gardens

Regional Delicacies

- **Pastel de Belém:** These delicious eggy tartlets are made from freshly baked, crisp, buttery pastry filled with rich custard, usually enjoyed with a sprinkling of cinnamon. Not to be confused with pastel de nata, the country's iconic custard tart, **pastel de Belém** are found only in **Belém,** a short train ride west of central Lisbon (page 104).

- **Bacalhau:** Cod is Portugal's go-to fish, and the country is said to have as many recipes for cod dishes as there are days of the year. Lisbon has several restaurants dedicated solely to cod. Keep an eye out for popular dishes such as **bacalhau à Brás** (cod mashed with egg, potato, and onion, topped with crunchy matchstick fries), **bacalhau à Gomes de Sá** (flaked cod layered with sliced potato and egg and baked in the oven), **bacalhau espiritual** (like bacalhau á Bras but with grated carrot), and **pastéis de bacalhau** (cod fritters), usually a snack with cold beer. **Solar do Bacalhau** in Lisbon is one of the best spots for sampling cod dishes (page 92).

- **Queijadas:** Despite being made with fresh cheese, there is nothing cheesy about these sweet, stodgy, sticky delicacies. Many towns are renowned for their own versions of **queijadas,** but **Sintra**'s are especially famous (page 154).

- **Ginjinha:** An infusion of macerated morello cherries in aguardente

queijadas

alcohol, this sweet cherry liqueur is sometimes served in a chocolate cup, with or without a cherry. Dating to the 17th century, its original recipe is to this day a closely guarded secret, known only to a privileged few. That recipe is thought to have been first brewed by a friar—possibly with medicinal purposes, as ginja is a renowned digestive aid—and later local families would compete to see who could best replicate the recipe. Try ginja for yourself at award-winning **A Ginjinha** in Lisbon's Baixa neighborhood (page 105).

- **Canja de Carapau:** A fishy broth made from mackerel, **canja de carapau** is the trademark dish of **Costa da Caparica.** Ideally situated along the water, beachside restaurants use fish fresh from the market (page 196).

- **Peixe-Espada Preto:** The quaint fishing town of **Sesimbra** is renowned for its freshly caught black-scabbard fish—a fluffy, meaty piece of fish served simply, just charcoal-grilled (page 216).

- **Porco Preto:** A delicacy found widely throughout the Alentejo region, black pig pork meat is more moist and succulent than regular pork, and derives from acorn-fed pigs. You'll find most restaurants in **Évora**'s centro histórico serve the dish along with excellent regional wines (page 256).

Capes, Cliffs, and Viewpoints

Dramatically situated along Europe's most beautiful coastline, with many cities and towns famously set into picturesque hills, Portugal is a great place to get some altitude and take in awe-inspiring views of the sea. The following are some of the most jaw-dropping viewpoints, or miradouros, covered in this book.

- **Lisbon's Best Views:** Gorgeous miradouros abound in Lisbon, from the famous Graça viewpoint to the romantic Miradouro da Nossa Senhora do Monte (page 70).

- **Cabo da Roca:** Be amazed by the vastness of the Atlantic Ocean as you stand on the high cliffs of mainland Europe's westernmost point (page 137).

- **Cabo Espichel:** Walk paths where dinosaurs once roamed on the eerily remote and rugged Espichel cape (page 218).

Lisbon from Graça viewpoint

Fonte da Telha beach, Costa da Caparica

Day 4

Explore some of Lisbon's quieter neighborhoods with a leisurely stroll around affluent **Estrela** and **Lapa.** Family-friendly and lined with lovely mansions and green spaces, Estrela is home to historical sites such as the **British Cemetery** and the grandiose **Estrela Basílica.** Enjoy lunch at Restaurante XL, which serves haut international cuisine with views of Portugal's Parliament. Take a walk around the **Estrela gardens** before heading to Lapa, a short stroll from Estrela.

A wander along Lapa's well-heeled streets reveals beautiful buildings, many of which are home to embassies. Head back to Estrela for a low-key dinner at **Churrascaria o Lavrador,** which serves fresh meat and fish straight off the grill.

Day 5

Conclude your week venturing beyond Lisbon with a day trip to **Costa da Caparica.** Make the short drive (or direct bus trip) south across the Tagus. After arriving in Costa da Caparica, enjoy brunch or lunch at the highly-rated **A(mar)ia Café.** Afterward, take a walk through the atmospheric **Fishermen's Quarters** and promenade before jumping on the tourist train down the stunning stretch of coast to **Fonte da Telha beach.** If you're feeling energetic, explore the **Fossil Cliff Protected Landscape,** or simply enjoy the peace and space the beach affords. Make sure you don't miss the last train back to town, where you can toast to an enjoyable week with a fresh fish dinner and sunset views at the funky **Sentido do Mar beach** restaurant.

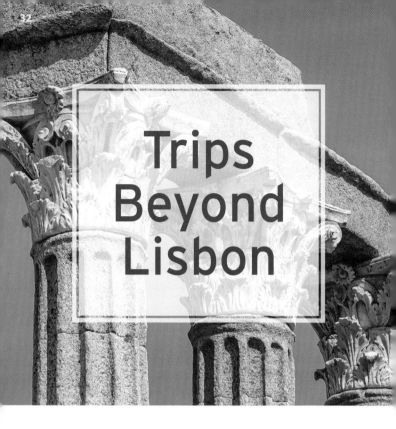

Trips Beyond Lisbon

The villages and cities in this guide make excellent day trips from Lisbon. For those with more time to settle in and explore a region in depth, here are some suggestions for creating longer excursions from Lisbon, with overnight stays outside of the city.

Lisbon and the Palaces
Number of Days: 5-6
LISBON

Start by spending at least a couple of days in Lisbon. Visit **São Jorge Castle,** which sits atop the former Royal Palace, and be sure to tour the **Museum of Decorative Arts** and the **National Museum of Ancient Art,** both housed inside former 17th-century palaces.

QUELUZ

For a half-day excursion, head 20 minutes northwest of downtown by train to **Queluz National Palace and Gardens,** the 18th-century summer palace of Portugal's royal family.

SINTRA

From Queluz, make the short train trip to Sintra, where you'll stay for at least two nights. You can visit the main palaces of Sintra, a fairytale forest town with whimsical architecture, in one full day, but with two days, you can see all the attractions.

MAFRA

Mafra's National Palace is a Baroque complex just an hour-long bus ride from Sintra, making it a perfect day trip.

Outdoor Adventure
Number of Days: 3-5
SETÚBAL PENINSULA AND ARRÁBBIDA NATIONAL PARK

The **Sado Estuary,** an hour south of Lisbon, is one of the best spots to see dolphins. For an adrenaline rush, Arrábbida National Park outfitters offer diving, mountain climbing, and other active experiences along the park's rugged coast.

Comporta Beach walkway

TROIA AND COMPORTA

A ferry connects Setúbal with up-and-coming Troia and Comporta. Troia and Setúbal city are the departure points for dolphin-watching trips on the Sado Estuary. In Comporta you can rent bikes or go horseback riding and explore the area's rice paddies and pine groves. Stay and take a well-earned rest on the white sand beaches.

MELIDES

With more time, extend your journey south to Melides, a seaside hamlet in the Alentejo region, with wild beaches and sand dunes.

Pastoral Sampler
Number of Days: 4-5

Escape the bustle of Lisbon with a few days in the countryside. You'll need a car to get to sights outside of Tomar and Évora.

TOMAR AND ALMOURAL CASTLE

Historical Tomar is home to fascinating Templar ruins, quaint streets, and traditional shops. Plan to spend a couple of days soaking up the area's history and wandering picturesque riverside walkways. Tomar is the ideal

Almourol Castle

megalithic ruins near Évora

base for a visit to **Almoural Castle,** the 12th-century castle only accessible via a boat ride across the Tagus River.

ÉVORA

Once the city of Portugal's kings, Évora is the place to be to get a sense of the history of the Alentejo. You'll want to spend a couple of nights in town, and plan to visit the nearby megalithic **ruins** and **Cartuxa Estate vineyard.**

Grand Tour Around Lisbon
Number of Days: 14

For the ultimate experience of Lisbon and its neighboring destinations, plan a grand tour around Lisbon, best done by car.

THE PORTUGUESE RIVIERA

After a few days exploring Lisbon, uncovering the hilly capital and its fascinating neighborhoods and monuments, head along the scenic marginal road to the glamorous coastal towns of **Estoril** and **Cascais**—collectively referred to as The Portuguese Riviera. You can walk the boardwalk or take a short train trip between them. Cascais makes an ideal base for one or two nights.

Cabo da Roca

SINTRA

From Cascais it's a short trip to magical Sintra. On your way you'll pass through the breezy **Cabo da Roca** landmark, mainland Europe's western-most point. Plan to spend at least one full day (preferably two) in Sintra to allow for the number of unique attractions (and huge crowds of visitors) that it hosts.

MAFRA AND TOMAR

From Sintra make your way to Mafra to see the staggering **National Palace.** From there, continue to Tomar. Plan to spend one night here. Tomar's beautiful river and captivating **Convent of Christ** make it well worth the trip.

ÉVORA

From there, head south to Évora, the "capital" of the Alentejo region. Allocate one to two nights there to explore its fascinating sights (such as the Roman Temple and eerie **Chapel of Bones**) and to sample famous regional wines, cured meats, and cheeses.

MELIDES AND THE TROIA PENINSULA

Return to Lisbon via trendy Comporta or nearby Melides, a quintessential Alentejo seaside hamlet and one of Alentejo's most characterful gems. Plan to stay the night to fully explore the windswept beaches by bike or on horseback. Continue up to the Troia Peninsula, a prime overnight beach destination that often flies under the radar.

SETÚBAL PENINSULA

From Troia, take the ferry across to the untouristed port city **Setúbal,** where a boat trip to see the Sado Estuary's bottlenose dolphins is a must. Rounding the beautiful Setúbal Peninsula, plan for a visit to **Sesimbra,** a former fishermen's village where the beaches and fresh fish draw in visitors. While around Sesimbra, stop at the blustery **Cabo Espichel** promontory to explore its deserted Sanctuary and dinosaur-trodden cliffs.

COSTA DA CAPARICA AND BACK TO LISBON

It's worth allocating a night to stay in Costa da Caparica to fully enjoy its beaches, traditional fishermen's quarters, and nightlife. From here, make your way back to Lisbon, ensuring you stop at the towering ***Christ the King monument*** in Almada on the south side of the Tagus River. Gazing over Lisbon with its arms outstretched, this is one of the capital's most iconic landmarks. Conclude a fantastic tour of Lisbon and beyond with one last night in the City of Seven Hills.

Christ the King monument

Lisbon

Portugal's magnificent capital is one of Europe's trendiest cities—vibrant and culturally rich, where the historical blends seamlessly with the cool and contemporary. At the mouth of the Tagus River (Rio Tejo), the "City of Seven Hills" is buzzing and cosmopolitan, home to melodic fado music and a vivid nightlife scene. Traditional tile-clad facades and redbrick roofs conceal a tangle of charming cobbled streets and elegant avenues that beckon to be explored.

Lisbon's impressive monuments, historical

Highlights

✪ **Carmo Convent:** Once the largest church in Lisbon, these ruins starkly show the devastation of the 1755 earthquake (page 54).

✪ **Avenida da Liberdade:** An appealing mix of historical and contemporary buildings, high-end boutiques, and tree-shaded cafés lines the country's most famous avenue (page 59).

✪ **São Jorge Castle:** On a hilltop in the heart of Lisbon, this imposing Moorish monument commands spectacular views of the historical city center and the Tagus River (page 62).

✪ **Jerónimos Monastery:** Home to the national archaeological and naval museums, Belém's stunning centerpiece is a marvel of ornate Manueline architecture and took the entire 16th century to construct (page 74).

✪ **Bairro Alto Nightlife:** Historical Bairro Alto has reinvented itself as the city's liveliest and coolest nocturnal hangout, with chic wine bars, historical fado houses, and renowned jazz clubs (page 106).

neighborhoods, and edgy vibe welcome visitors to drink in stunning bird's-eye views from many panoramic miradouros (viewpoints) or hip hotel rooftop bars. Stroll the chic boulevards with their many boutiques, admire striking riverfront monuments, explore the myriad museums, or for the classic Lisbon experience, take the famous tram 28 around the city's historical nooks and crannies before enjoying mesmerizing fado in one of the many original haunts in Alfama or Bairro Alto.

Less than an hour from the heart of the city are the upscale towns of Estoril and Cascais, as well as magical Sintra, which famously has a microclimate all its own.

ORIENTATION

Hilly Lisbon is divided into many neighborhoods and parishes, or

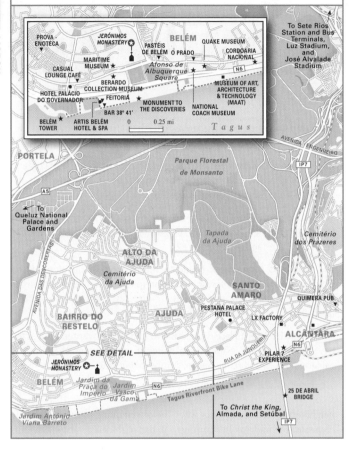

Lisbon

bairros. The heart of Lisbon's historical area is the **Baixa Pombalina,** often simply referred to as the Baixa; it's the main downtown commercial and banking area along the river. Baixa is immediately fringed by several of the city's other most famous neighborhoods: labyrinth-like **Alfama** and hilltop **São Vicente,** cultural and hip nighttime hangouts **Chiado**

and **Bairro Alto,** cool and arty **Cais do Sodré,** and chic **Estrela** and **Lapa. Alcântara,** a former docks area enjoying a hipster revival, is west of the downtown area.

Heading north from downtown is the **Avenida da Liberdade,** one of the city's most famous boulevards, surrounded by some excellent museums and historical monuments. On the western

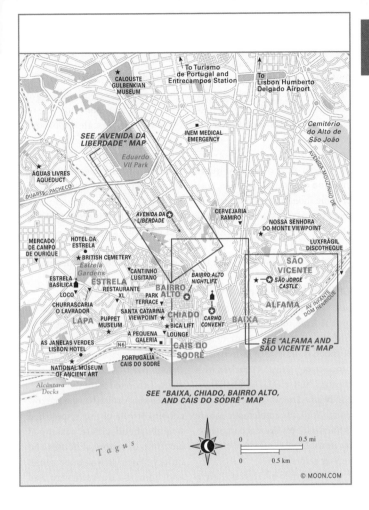

extremity of the heart of Lisbon is the culturally rich area of **Belém,** while at the opposite side, on the northeast, is the modern area of **Park of Nations (Parque das Nações),** dramatically developed for the 1998 World Exposition. And if you want visit a palace without venturing to Sintra just yet, only a 20-minute drive north is the commuter suburb of **Queluz,** home

to the beautiful **Queluz National Palace and Gardens.**

Baixa

Fronted by the Tagus River, the Baixa Pombalina (BYE-shah pom-bah-LEE-nah), or just Baixa or "downtown Lisbon," is the city's central shopping and banking district—and its tourist hub. The name derives from the distinctive

Portuguese Pombaline architectural style employed to rebuild the city after the 1755 earthquake, under the guidance of Sebastião José de Carvalho e Melo, the 1st Marquis of Pombal. Elegant neoclassical facades and patterned cobbled streets give the neighborhood an air of graceful uniformity. Two main streets, **Rua Augusta** and **Rua da Prata,** are laden with buzzing shops and restaurants. The main Metro stops in the Baixa area are Avenida, Restauradores, Rossio, Baixa-Chiado, and Terreiro do Paço, on the Green and Blue Lines.

Chiado and Bairro Alto

Just northwest of Baixa, centered on the **Luis de Camões Square,** Chiado (SHEE-aah-doo) neighborhood is the core of Lisbon's cultural scene—a district packed with theaters, museums, and galleries. Sandwiched between the Baixa and Bairro Alto, the emblematic square is lined with traditional commerce, fashionable boutiques, and cultural venues galore.

A bit further northwest, Bairro Alto (BYE-rroo AL-too) has long been Lisbon's bohemian hangout, a favorite haunt for artists and writers. In the evenings, its grid of steep streets echoes with melancholic fado. Visit after 11pm, when the innumerable **small bars** and **colorful nightspots** really start to hit their stride. The neighborhood's historical significance dates to its expansion in the 16th century to accommodate the city's booming economic and social transformation.

Avenida da Liberdade

This broad, leafy boulevard above the main Baixa is home to some of Lisbon's most upscale shops and priciest real estate. Walking distance from downtown, the Avenida terminates in **Marquês de Pombal Square,** with the towering statue of the Marquis of Pombal guarding the entrance to **Eduardo VII Park,** and is surrounded by some of the city's best museums, such as the **Calouste Gulbenkian Museum.**

Alfama

Alfama (al-FAH-mah), just east of Baixa, is Lisbon's oldest and most soulful neighborhood and claims to be the birthplace of fado, although Bairro Alto also makes this claim. Inhabited from the 5th century by the Visigoths, the narrow cobbled streets of this unpolished neighborhood create a stepped labyrinth of historical houses and quirky shops. It was once rough and home to dockworkers and seafarers. As the city's port prospered, so did Alfama, although its rugged charisma remains. Alfama boasts monuments, traditional **fado houses,** and many fabulous **viewpoints** along its slopes.

The northern part of Alfama, the stately and traditional area around **São Jorge Castle,** is known as Lisbon's birthplace and often called **Castelo.** One of the city's finest neighborhoods, it has fabulous views from almost every street corner.

São Vicente

Two major monuments, the **National Pantheon** and the **São Vicente de Fora Church,** are in São Vicente (sown vee-SENT), among a cascade of historical homes on the hillside toward the Tagus just east of Alfama. Peaceful and poised most of the week, São Vicente comes alive every Saturday morning for the famous **Feira da Ladra** flea market, next to the National Pantheon.

Cais do Sodré

Fronting Lisbon's downtown to the west is Cais do Sodré—or the Sodré Docks—a trendy, underrated part of Lisbon on the riverside. Historically important and one of the city's busiest areas for nightlife, Cais do Sodré is also the location of one of the main **ferry terminals** for crossing the Tagus, as well as the train terminus for the **Lisbon-Cascais train line.** Because of this, the area sees heavy footfall of students, commuters, and tourists passing through daily.

Estrela and Lapa

Northwest of Cais do Sodré, with **grand properties** and **elegant streets,** peaceful Estrela (eesh-TREH-lah) was settled by the well-heeled during the city's expansion in the 1700s and remains one of Lisbon's most affluent areas. The

adjoining Lapa (LAH-pah) neighborhood is home to many **foreign embassies.**

Alcântara

Wedged halfway between downtown Lisbon (Baixa) and Belém, directly beneath the **25 de Abril Bridge,** is Alcântara (al-KHAAN-ta-ra), a riverside area of significant urban revival, popular among locals. Said to take its name from the Arabic word for "bridge," the former port and industrial area is today one of the city's busiest **nightlife** spots, its old warehouses having given way to hip bars and restaurants. With a growing art scene, it is one of Lisbon's liveliest areas.

Across the 25 de Abril Bridge, technically in the town of Almada, is the the **Christ the King** statue, whose outstretched arms dominate the skyline of the Tagus's west bank.

Belém

Just west of downtown in bright and breezy Belém (beh-LAYN), iconic landmarks such as the **Jerónimos Monastery** and **Belém Tower** pay tribute to key chapters in Portugal's history, sharing a riverside location with modern museums, cafés, and gardens. During the Age of Discoveries, this is where ships set off to explore the globe. Belém, home of the famous pastel de Belém tart, can be uncomfortably busy, particularly in the heat of summer; expect long queues.

Park of Nations

Northeast of Lisbon, Park of Nations, or Parque das Nações (park dazh nah-SSOYNS), is an über-modern riverside neighborhood developed for the 1998 World Exposition, with mirrored high-rise apartment blocks and twin sail-shaped skyscrapers. It is linked to the south side of the Tagus River by the sinewy, 17-km-long (10.6-mi-long) **Vasco da Gama Bridge,** Europe's longest. Family attractions such as the **Altice concert arena** and the **Lisbon Oceanarium** are here, along with cosmopolitan restaurants and bars.

SAFETY

As with many tourist destinations, Lisbon is afflicted by petty and opportunistic crime. Take basic precautions such as not walking along dark streets alone at night, not leaving valuables in rental vehicles, and not carrying large amounts of cash. Pickpockets are an issue, so make sure backpacks are worn in front in crowded areas and on public transport. Better still, use concealed pouches and never keep cash and documents in the same pouch. Call the **PSP tourist police** (tel. 213 421 623) or visit the nearest police station. In an **emergency,** call **112.**

PLANNING YOUR TIME

Much of Lisbon's city center can be covered in a day, but it's worth allocating at least two or three days. A great way to cover the must-sees is either a **hop-on hop-off bus** that stops at all main attractions and landmarks, or the famous **tram 28,** which circumnavigates Lisbon's main neighborhoods. Other good options to explore include a neatly organized **subway,** nifty **tuk-tuk carts,** and a **hop-on hop-off ferryboat circuit.** Set aside more days to explore the many day trips within a few hours' drive of the city. While in Lisbon, an absolute must is dinner at a **fado restaurant** in Bairro Alto. Make reservations well in advance, as these are popular attractions.

In mid-June the traditional **Santo António festivities,** dedicated to the city's patron saint, explode into party mode. In December **Christmas** trimmings and roasted chestnuts bring warmth to the city. June, July, and August can get very hot, and even though many residents head south for summer vacation, Lisbon is still packed with tourists. **Summer** and **New Year** are tourism high seasons, when hotel prices soar and the city is full of visitors. Good times to visit are **March-May** and **September-October,** when the weather is pleasant and the hotels less expensive.

Itinerary Ideas

DAY 1: BAIXA AND BAIRRO ALTO

1 Spend the morning discovering downtown Lisbon. Begin by walking the main **Avenida da Liberdade,** heading south toward the Tagus River. Peruse the glamorous window displays, and stop for a mid-morning coffee at one of the picturesque cafés.

2 In the main downtown area, explore famous **Comércio Square** and its museums and landmarks—they're all within walking distance. Make sure you climb to the top of the Triumphal Arch on Rua Augusta.

3 A few streets back from the main square is the **Santa Justa Elevator,** also called the Carmo Lift. This historical contraption transports passengers from downtown up to the famous Bairro Alto neighborhood. Hop on the elevator and admire how the old-fashioned machinery comes to life, taking you to the viewing platform at the top.

4 Once up in Bairro Alto, visit the **Carmo Convent,** the eerily beautiful medieval skeleton of a 14th-century Gothic church that is a striking reminder of the city's history.

5 For lunch, hop on the Metro (from Baixa-Chiado to Cais do Sodré) or take a 20-minute walk west to the bustling **Time Out Market Lisboa,** set back from the Cais do Sodré quay. This eclectic food hall showcases the finest Portuguese products.

6 Head back to downtown Lisbon via tram, bus, or taxi, stopping at Chiado Square to enjoy a late afternoon cocktail on a panoramic terrace. The **Hotel Mundial Rooftop Bar & Lounge,** just off Chiado Square, is a good choice.

7 From here, it's a 20-minute stroll west to Bairro Alto for dinner at the typical fado restaurant **O Faia.** After dinner, let loose in one of the many nearby bars.

DAY 2: ALFAMA AND PARK OF NATIONS

1 From Lisbon's Baixa, head to the historic Alfama and São Vicente neighborhoods on one of the city's emblematic trams (no. 12 or 28). Spend a few hours ambling Alfama's maze of ancient cobbled streets, visiting sights including the **Lisbon Cathedral.**

2 Don't miss the **Graça viewpoint,** a short 15-minute walk north from the Cathedral.

Itinerary Ideas

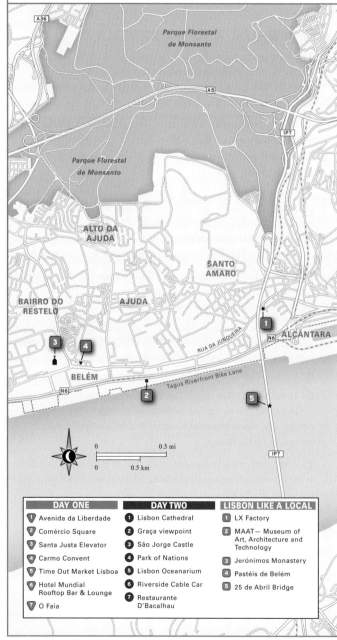

DAY ONE	DAY TWO	LISBON LIKE A LOCAL
1 Avenida da Liberdade	1 Lisbon Cathedral	1 LX Factory
2 Comércio Square	2 Graça viewpoint	2 MAAT— Museum of Art, Architecture and Technology
3 Santa Justa Elevator	3 São Jorge Castle	
4 Carmo Convent	4 Park of Nations	3 Jerónimos Monastery
5 Time Out Market Lisboa	5 Lisbon Oceanarium	4 Pastéis de Belém
6 Hotel Mundial Rooftop Bar & Lounge	6 Riverside Cable Car	5 25 de Abril Bridge
7 O Faia	7 Restaurante D'Bacalhau	

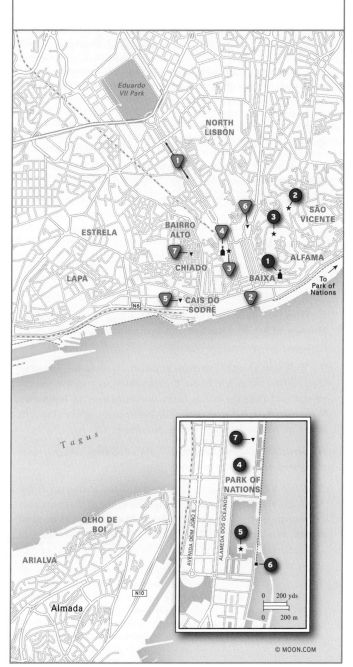

Eduardo VII Park

NORTH LISBON

SÃO VICENTE

ESTRELA

BAIRRO ALTO

CHIADO

LAPA

ALFAMA

BAIXA

CAIS DO SODRÉ

To Park of Nations

N6

Tagus

OLHO DE BOI

ARIALVA

N10

Almada

PARK OF NATIONS

AVENIDA DOM JOÃO II

ALAMEDA DOS OCEANOS

0   200 yds
0   200 m

© MOON.COM

3 Make your way toward **São Jorge Castle** for a spot of lunch with a view.

4 After lunch walk northeast toward the river to the Santa Apolónia train station. Jump on a train for a 10-minute journey north toward **Park of Nations** (Azambuja line; trains run every 15 minutes). Exit at modernist Oriente station. Here you can spend the afternoon walking the riverfront gardens.

5 Kids of all ages will enjoy exploring the **Lisbon Oceanarium.**

6 Follow this up with a fun ride on the scenic **Riverside Cable Car.**

7 End the day with a meal at **Restaurante D'Bacalhau,** along the Park of Nations waterfront, maybe followed by a boogie in one of the many bars nearby, before heading back to your hotel in a cab or rideshare.

LISBON LIKE A LOCAL

1 For a slower-paced day in the city, start by heading to the **LX Factory** in Alcântara (halfway between Baixa and Belém) for a leisurely browse of the stalls, enjoying a spot of brunch.

2 From here, walk across the road to the futuristic-looking **MAAT— Museum of Art, Architecture and Technology;** take in the views from the rooftop.

3 Walk west along the riverside to Belém, enjoying the sights and cafés on the way, or rent one of the many bicycles or electric scooters scattered along the stretch. Find a shady spot near the **Jerónimos Monastery** to sit and relax for a while, before enjoying a late lunch in one of the many restaurants located just behind it.

4 Now it's time to visit the famous **Pastéis de Belém** bakery to sample a pastel de Belém custard tart.

5 Catch a train back into downtown Lisbon, getting off at the Alcântara-Mar stop, to enjoy a sundowner at one of the many bars and lounges on the Santo Amaro docks underneath the **25 de Abril Bridge.** Don't miss the Pillar 7 Experience while you're here—a unique tour in, around, and up one of the pillars of the iconic bridge.

Sights

TRAMS OF LISBON

One of the most novel and enjoyable ways to explore Lisbon is aboard one of its iconic trams. Originally designed to provide access to harder-to-reach neighborhoods with challenging hilly terrain and narrow streets, trams have become a sought-after tourist attraction in their own right, thanks to scenic routes and nostalgic charm. They offer travelers an up-close, warts-and-all view of some of Lisbon's most charismatic areas. An instantly recognizable symbol of the city's identity and heritage, trams retain their original designs and give tourists a unique experience, as well as still playing an important role in local daily life. All trams and funiculars are covered under the Lisboa Card and the 24-hour transport pass.

No. 28

Lisbon's most famous tram, the No. 28, is a vintage yellow tram that rattles through some of the city's main neighborhoods, including Alfama, downtown Baixa, Chiado, and Estrela, passing by important landmarks and some of the best viewpoints en route. At approximately 7 km (4 mi) long, this point-to-point route, which starts in the **Martim Moniz hub** near Alfama and

tram 28

Lisbon's Best Restaurants

✪ **Café Nicola:** Frequented by poet Manuel du Bocage, this art deco landmark epitomizes European coffee culture (page 92).

✪ **Solar do Bacalhau:** This is one of the best spots to enjoy the Portuguese specialty bacalhau (page 92).

✪ **Cervejaria Trindade:** This beautiful brewery and banquet hall dates from the mid-1800s, when it was the place of choice for writers, poets, and politicians (page 96).

✪ **Chapitô à Mesa:** This restaurant is part of a famous circus arts school, so expect a fun and fanciful meal (page 98).

✪ **Cervejaria Ramiro:** Expect long queues at this famed institution where a steak sandwich replaces dessert (page 100).

✪ **Time Out Market Lisboa:** Hundreds of gastronomic goodies are under one roof (page 101).

✪ **Pastéis de Belém:** No visit to Lisbon is complete without a stop at this birthplace of Portugal's famous pastel de Belém tart (page 103).

✪ **O Faia:** At one of Lisbon's oldest and most charismatic Fado houses, the food is as typical as the music (page 107).

terminates in the neighborhood of **Campo de Ourique** west of the city, offers the chance to soak up plenty of the city's authentic atmosphere. Other main boarding points for tram 28 are near Rossio Square (Praça da Figueira), Chiado Square, and by the main Sé Cathedral. Due to its distinction, this route is almost always busy. The best times to experience it are early morning or after the afternoon rush hour—but expect tram 28 to be crowded at most times, meaning it could be standing-room only.

Tickets for tram 28 cost €3.10 one-way, bought from the driver or from vending machines at the stops. The ride is also covered by the Lisboa Card and the 24-hour public transport pass, sold at any metro station (€6.80).

No. 15

Tram 15, between the Baixa's main **Praça da Figueira square** and **Belém** (it terminates in the parish of Algés), is another popular route. The journey usually takes roughly 30-40 minutes, passing through historical neighborhoods like Alcântara, and past landmarks such as the LX Factory and National Coach Museum on the way.

Lisbon's Best Accommodations

✪ **Yes! Lisbon Hostel:** This hostel has it all: excellent location, fantastic service, and budget-friendly prices (page 113).

✪ **Hotel Mundial:** The rooftop bar at this four-star hotel has one of the best views in Lisbon (page 113).

✪ **Bairro Alto Hotel:** This grand 18th-century hotel enjoys a dominant position on the main square, within walking distance of shops and restaurants (page 114).

✪ **Solar do Castelo:** Sleep in medieval-contemporary style at this eco-retreat within the walls of the São Jorge Castle (page 114).

✪ **Memmo Alfama Design Hotel:** This chic urban retreat blends in with the historical Alfama neighborhood (page 114).

✪ **Hotel Palácio do Governador:** Located in the 16th-century Governor's Palace is an oasis of tranquility in one of Lisbon's prettiest neighborhoods (page 115).

✪ **VIP Executive Arts:** This streamlined four-star hotel is close to convenient transportation, shopping, and nightlife (page 115).

No. 24

For those who simply want to experience a trip on a vintage tram, tram 24, which departs from the **Camões Square** (Praça Luis de Camões) between Chiado and Bairro Alto, is a less picturesque but calmer option, without the sightseeing. This route is used by local commuters; it is a great way to see Lisbon's urban architecture and daily life, but can get busy at peak times like rush hour. It terminates in the residential parish of **Campolide.**

BAIXA
Comércio Square
(Praça do Comércio)

This vast square, with views of the Tagus River, bustles with visitors and has the statue of King José I on his horse. The impressive colonnades that frame it on three sides house several ministries, museums, shops, and restaurants. It's one of the city's main transport hubs, with many trams and buses running from here; it's also directly across from the Cais do Sodré ferry terminal. Two museums on the square are worth a visit—the **Beer Museum** and the **Lisbon Story Centre.**

Beer Museum
(Museu da Cerveja)

*Terreiro do Paço, Ala Nascente 62-65; tel.
210 987 656; www.museudacerveja.pt;
daily 11am-midnight, €5; Metro Terreiro do
Paço, Blue Line*

The Beer Museum (Museu da
Cerveja) boasts a plethora of beers
and ales from around the world, as
well as a good selection of national
beers. Inside, a fascinating museum
chronicles the history of Portuguese
beer-making and illustrates the
production process. There's also a
restaurant with a stunning modern-
vintage décor whose menu showcases fine Portuguese cuisine.
Outside, on a vast esplanade, chilled
beers are often accompanied by a
Pastel de Bacalhau cod-fish fritter,
made on-site, a traditional snack to
accompany an imperial (small draft
beer) or a Caneca (pint).

The Lisbon Story Centre

*Praça do Comércio 78; tel. 211 941 099;
www.lisboastorycentre.pt; daily 10am-8pm;
€7; Metro Terreiro do Paço, Blue Line*

The Lisbon Story Centre recounts
the key chapters of Lisbon's history
through state-of-the-art interactive
multimedia. Using an engaging
mix of intricate sets and sensory
experiences, it provides an interesting, hour-long activity suitable
for all ages and weather.

Augusta Triumphal Arch
(Arco da Rua Augusta)

*Praça do Comércio; tel. 210 998 599; www.
visitlisboa.com; daily 10am-7pm; viewing
terrace €3.50; Metro Terreiro do Paço,
Blue Line*

The formal entrance to the Baixa
neighborhood, the decorative
Augusta Triumphal Arch was built
to mark the city's resilience and
glorious rebirth following the 1755
earthquake. Historical Portuguese
figures such as explorer Vasco da
Gama and the Marquis of Pombal
adorn the gateway's six columns,
gazing over Comércio Square and
out to the river. Inside the arch, a
narrow spiral staircase made from
solid stone climbs to a viewing terrace that offers sweeping views of
the plaza.

Augusta Triumphal Arch

Archaeological Center of Rua Correeiros (Millennium BCP Foundation)
(Núcleo Arqueológico da Rua Correeiros: NARC / Fundação Millennium BCP)

*Rua dos Correeiros 15-23; tel. 211 131 070;
www.fundacaomillenniumbcp.pt/en/nucleo-
arqueologico; Mon.-Sat. 10am-5pm; free;
Metro Baixa-Chiado, Green/Blue Lines*

Overlooked by many tourists, the Archaeological Center of Rua Correeiros showcases a wealth of Roman artifacts uncovered during the construction of the bank next door. Free guided tours of Roman ruins beneath the streets of Lisbon must be booked in advance and are available in English.

Money Museum
(Museu do Dinheiro)

Largo de São Julião; tel. 213 213 240; www. museudodinheiro.pt; Wed.-Sun. 10am-6pm; free; Metro Baixa-Chiado or Terreiro do Paço, Blue Line

Part of the Bank of Portugal's premises in the heart of downtown Lisbon, this fascinating, interactive multimedia museum is probably one of Lisbon's more underrated sights. It takes visitors on a trip covering the entire history of global currency, from pre-currency civilization to payments in the modern world. In a lofty, converted 17th-century church, you can handle a real bar of gold, visit old Roman ruins in the basement, see currency from all over the world, and learn about how money is made, before popping into the on-site café.

Santa Justa Elevator
(Elevador de Santa Justa)

Rua do Ouro; tel. 214 138 679; www. carris.pt; daily 7am-11pm May-Oct., daily 7am-10pm Nov.-Apr.; round-trip €6; Metro Baixa-Chiado, Green/Blue Lines

Also called the Carmo Lift, the 19th-century neo-Gothic, wrought-iron Santa Justa Elevator is the only vertical lift in Lisbon,

connecting the Baixa area to the Bairro Alto neighborhood, saving a steep climb. Inaugurated in 1902, it is classified as a national monument. Standing at 45 m (148 ft) tall, it was designed by engineer Raoul Mesnier de Ponsard in a style similar to that of the Eiffel Tower. The lift is stunning at night when lit up and has a fabulous viewing platform at the top. Intriguingly, it can transport more people going up than coming down. It is accessed via Rua do Ouro at the bottom or Carmo Square at the top. The viewing platform (€1.50) is also accessible directly from Carmo Square, up the hill behind the lift.

Santa Justa Elevator

Rossio Square
(Praça Dom Pedro IV)

Metro Rossio, Green Line

The beating heart of Lisbon, located downtown, Rossio Square has long been one of the city's main meeting places, a lively, genteel square of Pombaline architecture lined with cafés, trees, and two grand Baroque fountains at either end. Housed in the impressive buildings framing the square are the stately **Dona Maria II National Theater (Teatro Nacional de Dona Maria II)** and the historic **Café Nicola,** which dates to the 18th century and was one of the first cafés to emerge in Lisbon. Also nearby is the ornate **Rossio train station,** which is typically Manueline in its architecture. One of the square's distinguishing features is the wavy black-and-white cobblestone paving.

Glória Funicular
(Elevador da Glória)

Calçada da Glória; www.carris.pt; Mon.-Thurs. 7:15am-11:55pm, Fri. 7:15am-12:25am, Sat. 8:45am-12:25am, Sun. and holidays 9:15am-11:55pm; round-trip €4.10; Metro Restauradores, Blue Line

The quirky Glória Funicular puts the "fun" in funicular. It has become an emblem of Lisbon, its graffiti scrawl only adding to its charm, mirroring its urban surroundings. Inaugurated in 1885, it connects the Baixa (Restauradores Square) to the São Pedro de Alcântara viewpoint in Bairro Alto via a steep track that cuts straight through a dense residential area packed with 19th-century buildings. Practical for locals, it's a treat for visitors.

CHIADO AND BAIRRO ALTO
Garrett Street
(Rua Garrett)

Named after acclaimed Portuguese poet Almeida Garrett, Garrett

Street (Rua Garrett) is the main vein traversing Chiado, a pulsing shopping street flanked by handsome cultural venues, such as the **São Carlos National Theatre, Livraria Bertrand,** believed to be one of the oldest bookstores in the world, and the century-old **A Brasileira Café,** once the meeting point of Lisbon's intellectuals and luminaries. Some smaller local shops and commerce may close on Sundays, but larger stores, particularly those in busy tourist areas, will remain open.

✪ Carmo Convent
(Convento do Carmo)

Largo do Carmo; tel. 213 460 473; www.museuarqueologicodocarmo.pt; Mon.-Sat. 10am-6pm May-Sept., Mon.-Sat. 10am-5pm Oct.-Apr.; €5; Metro Baixa-Chiado or Rossio, Green/Blue Lines

Once Lisbon's largest church, the Carmo Convent is a stark reminder of the vast devastation caused by the 1755 earthquake that razed the city and large swaths of Portugal. Originally built in 1389 by order of Nuno Álvares Pereira, an influential knight who led the Portuguese army, the church and convent sit on a hill directly opposite the São Jorge Castle. Today only its naked Gothic ruins still stand.

The convent's walls are solid, but the roof of the main nave is just a web of bare vaulted Gothic arches against the sky, a melancholy and dramatic sight. The roof is said to have crumbled onto the congregation during mass when the 1755 earthquake struck. The convent

Baixa, Chiado, Bairro Alto, and Cais do Sodré

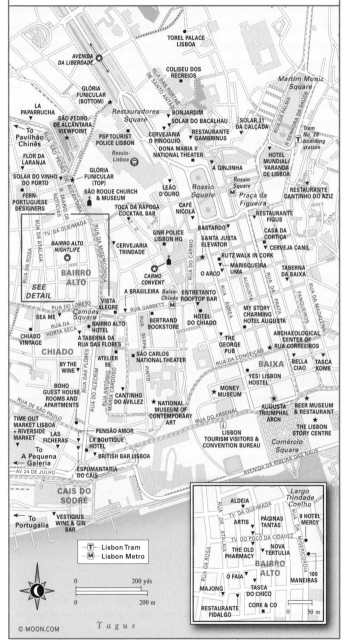

TOREL PALACE LISBOA

AVENIDA DA LIBERDADE

COLISEU DOS RECREIOS

Martim Moniz Square

GLÓRIA FUNICULAR (BOTTOM)

RUA DAS PORTAS DE SANTO ANTÃO

RUA DE SENHORA DA SAÚDE

RUA DA PALMA

LA PAPARRUCHA

To Pavilhão Chinês

SÃO PEDRO DE ALCÂNTARA VIEWPOINT

PSP TOURIST POLICE LISBON

Restauradores Square

BONJARDIM

SOLAR DO BACALHAU

SOLAR 31 DA CALÇADA

Tram No. 28 boarding station

CERVEJARIA O PINÓQUIO

RESTAURANTE GAMBRINUS

FLOR DA LARANJA

DONA MARIA II NATIONAL THEATER

HOTEL MUNDIAL / VARANDA DE LISBOA

Rossio-Lisboa

SOLAR DO VINHO DO PORTO

GLÓRIA FUNICULAR (TOP)

A GINJINHA

RUA DE SÃO PEDRO DE ALCÂNTARA

RUA DÃO DIÁRIO DE NOTÍCIAS

FERN-PORTUGUESE DESIGNERS

SÃO ROQUE CHURCH & MUSEUM

LEÃO D'OURO

Rossio Square

Rossio Square

RESTAURANTE CANTINHO DO AZIZ

TOCA DA RAPOSA COCKTAIL BAR

CAFÉ NICOLA

Praça da Figueira

TV. DA QUEIMADA

BAIRRO ALTO NIGHTLIFE

CERVEJARIA TRINDADE

GNR POLICE LISBON HQ

BASTARDO

RESTAURANTE FIGUS

RUA DA ATALAIA

SEE DETAIL

BAIRRO ALTO

RUA DA MISERICÓRDIA

SANTA JUSTA ELEVATOR

RUTZ WALK IN CORK

CASA DA CORTIÇA

CERVEJA CANIL

RUA DA ROSA

CARMO CONVENT

RUA DO CARMO

MARISQUEIRA UMA

TABERNA DA BAIXA

A BRASILEIRA

O ARCO

ENTRETANTO ROOFTOP BAR

RUA AUGUSTA

RUA DA PRATA

RUA DA MADALENA

VISTA ALEGRE

Baixa-Chiado

RUA DO LORETO

Camões Square

RUA GARRETT

HOTEL DO CHIADO

SEA ME

RUA DA

BAIRRO ALTO HOTEL

BERTRAND BOOKSTORE

MY STORY CHARMING HOTEL AUGUSTA

FANQUEIROS

CHIADO VINTAGE

HORTA SECA

A TABERNA DA RUA DAS FLORES

THE GEORGE PUB

ARCHAEOLOGICAL CENTER OF RUA CORREEIROS

CHIADO

BY THE WINE

ATELIER 55

SÃO CARLOS NATIONAL THEATER

RUA DA CONCEIÇÃO

BAIXA

BELLA CIAO

TASCA KOME

RUA DAS FLORES

RUA ANTÓNIO MARIA CARDOSO

PINTO

YES! LISBON HOSTEL

BOHO GUEST HOUSE ROOMS AND APARTMENTS

CANTINHO DO AVILLEZ

MONEY MUSEUM

RUA DE SÃO PAULO

NATIONAL MUSEUM OF CONTEMPORARY ART

AUGUSTA TRIUMPHAL ARCH

BEER MUSEUM & RESTAURANT

TIME OUT MARKET LISBOA + RIVERSIDE MARKET

PENSÃO AMOR

RUA DO ARSENAL

THE LISBON STORY CENTRE

To A Pequena Galeria

LAS FICHERAS

LX BOUTIQUE HOTEL

LISBON TOURISM VISITORS & CONVENTION BUREAU

Comércio Square

AV 24 DE JULHO

BRITISH BAR LISBOA

ESPAMANTARIA DO CAIS

AVENIDA DA RIBEIRA DAS NAUS

CAIS DO SODRÉ

To Portugália

VESTIGIUS WINE & GIN BAR

T — Lisbon Tram
M — Lisbon Metro

0   200 yds
0   200 m

© MOON.COM

Tagus

Detail (inset)

ALDEIA

Largo Trindade Coelho

TV. DA QUEIMADA

RUA DA ATALAIA

RUA DA MISERICÓRDIA

ARTIS

PÁGINAS TANTAS

9 HOTEL MERCY

RUA DA ROSA

TV. DO POÇO DA CIDADE

NOVA TERTÚLIA

THE OLD PHARMACY

BAIRRO ALTO

Ó FAIA

100 MANEIRAS

MAJONG

TASCA DO CHICO

RESTAURANTE FIDALGO

CORK & CO

0   50 m

55

was in the process of being rebuilt when religious orders were abolished in Portugal in the 1830s, leaving it half-finished. There's an eerie magic about wandering the spindly remains of the roofless site. Its former grandeur is apparent, and the many artifacts inside, such as ancient stone tools and a Peruvian mummy, are unique, but most of all, its skeletal state is a thought-provoking reminder of the twists and turns of history.

The site is also home to the Museu Arqueológico do Carmo, a museum with a collection of relics from dissolved monasteries, including sarcophagi and the grisly but well-preserved Peruvian sacrificial mummies. There are also various tombs in the archeological museum, including that of King Ferdinand I.

National Museum of Contemporary Art
(Museu Nacional de Arte Contemporânea do Chiado: MNAC)

Rua Serpa Pinto 4; tel. 213 432 148; www.museuartecontemporanea.gov.pt; Tues.-Sun. 10am-1pm and 2pm-6pm; €4.50; Metro Baixa-Chiado, Green/Blue Lines

Established by government decree in 1911, the National Museum of Contemporary Art—Museu do Chiado is housed in what was the old convent of São Francisco da Cidade. The convent was severely damaged by the 1755 Lisbon earthquake, and later by a huge fire in 1988; it was redesigned by French architect Jean-Michel Wilmotte

and re-inaugurated in 1994. It specializes in 19th- and 20th-century Portuguese contemporary art, divided into temporary exhibitions and a permanent collection displaying thematic exhibitions that span Portuguese Romantic, naturalist, modern, and contemporary art.

São Roque Church and Museum
(Igreja e Museu de São Roque)

Largo Trindade Coelho; tel. 213 235 065 / 213 235 449; http://mais.scml.pt/museu-saoroque; Tues.-Sun. 10am-6pm; church free, museum €2.50 (children free), Sun. 10am-2pm free; Metro Baixa-Chiado, Green/Blue Lines

As one of the first art museums to open in Portugal, the São Roque Museum was originally created to house an important collection of Italian art. Since its founding it has occupied a 17th-century cloister adjacent to the Church of São Roque, which had been donated to the Holy House of Mercy of Lisbon in 1768, after the expulsion of the Jesuits. Throughout the 20th century it was subject to a series of extensive refurbishments, allowing the museum to greatly expand its permanent exhibition area. Today comprising over 100 years of history, the São Roque Museum is considered one of the most beautiful and complete museums of Portuguese religious artifacts and paintings.

The church itself is also a treat to visit. Its plain exterior belies the exquisiteness of its lavish gold-leaf

Botanical Garden of Lisbon

interior and ornate embellishments. From the outside it may well be one of the city's least remarkable places of worship, but on the inside it is one of the most opulent—and said to be home to one of Europe's most expensive chapels (the fourth on the left, apparently). This church was also one of only a handful of buildings in Lisbon's westerly quarters to withstand the 1755 earthquake without major damage.

Botanical Garden of Lisbon

(Jardim Botânico da Universidade de Lisboa)

Rua da Escola Politécnica 56/58; tel. 213 921 800; www.ulisboa.pt/en/info/ gardens-0; daily 10am-5pm Oct.-Mar., daily 10am-8pm Apr.-Sept.; €5; Metro Rato, Yellow Line

Once declared the finest botanical garden in southern Europe, the Lisbon Botanical Garden is an enchanting oasis of cool and calm. Covering 4 hectares (10 acres) on the Olivete Hill, on the northern fringe of Bairro Alto, it is resplendent with rare and exotic tree and plant species, comprising flora from all over the world. Created between 1858 and 1873, it is still home to one of the largest collections of subtropical vegetation in Europe. The garden is particularly rich in tropical species from New Zealand, Australia, China, Japan, and South America, and it creates its own microclimate.

São Pedro de Alcântara Viewpoint

(Miradouro São Pedro de Alcântara)

next to the Glória Lift between Bairro Alto and the Baixa

A pretty, two-tiered garden embellishes this sprawling viewpoint.

57

The 1755 Earthquake

On the morning of Saturday, November 1, 1755, the ground shook violently in Portugal. What followed was one of the most devastating and deadliest earthquakes Europe had seen. The Great Lisbon Earthquake destroyed not only vast swathes of Lisbon but also much of Portugal, and it triggered a tsunami that tore up the Tagus River, washing out most of Lisbon's downtown area. Portugal happened to be celebrating All Saints Day on the day of the quake; widespread fires were also caused after lit candles toppled in homes and churches.

With most of its buildings destroyed or greatly damaged, the decision was made to raze Lisbon's entire downtown quarter, or what was left of it, and rebuild with an orderly, spacious, grid-like layout comprising large squares, large rectilinear avenues, and widened streets. This massive undertaking was spearheaded by Sebastião José de Carvalho e Melo, the 1st Marquis of Pombal. As a tribute, his name was lent to the rebuild that today characterizes downtown Lisbon—the Pombaline style—hence, the Baixa Pombalina. This thorough renovation saw a revolutionary anti-seismic building method, centered on the Gaiola Pombalina (Pombaline cage), a masonry building reinforced with an internal wood-lattice cage that was both sturdy and earthquake-resistant. The innovative technique was among the earliest quake-proof constructions in Europe and, when coupled with the city's neat new layout, made Lisbon one of the first truly modern cities in the world. While the handsome Pombaline buildings continue to stand firm and proud, other landmarks still bear the scars of one of Portugal's darkest days.

- **Carmo Convent:** The naked bones of the roofless Carmo Convent are a stark reminder of the extent of the devastation caused by the 1755 earthquake. Built in 1389, the once magnificent Gothic building was left ruined beyond repair.

- **Augusta Triumphal Arch:** This majestic archway was built purposely after the 1755 earthquake to signal the rebirth of Lisbon city.

- **National Museum of Contemporary Art:** Housed in the former São Francisco da Cidade convent, this complex of monastic buildings was severely damaged by the earthquake. Later, in 1988, the area was again devastated by a raging fire; the museum was completely overhauled and re-inaugurated in 1994.

- **São Roque Church:** Home to "the world's most expensive chapel," São Roque Church was one of few buildings in the westerly quarters to survive the Great Lisbon Earthquake with only minor damage. It was given to the Lisbon Holy House of Mercy to replace their church and headquarters that had been destroyed by the quake.

Located next to the Glória Lift between Bairro Alto and the Baixa, the São Pedro de Alcântara viewpoint is one of the most popular. Visitors can often be heard gasping in awe at the sweeping vistas, and telescopes are on hand. There are various ways to get to the São Pedro de Alcântara viewpoint; walking from the Baixa, on the No. 28 tram, or via the Elevador da Glória (Gloria Funicular), which connects Restauradores Square to the São Pedro de Alcântara viewpoint.

✪ AVENIDA DA LIBERDADE

Adorned with gardens and green spaces, pretty patterned cobblestone paving, and elegant water features, the area around the boulevard is a pleasant environment for locals and tourists to stroll and relax.

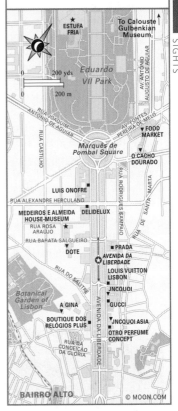

TOP EXPERIENCE

Avenida da Liberdade

The cosmopolitan boulevard is flanked by grandiose historical buildings showcasing various architectural styles, many dating back to the late 19th and early 20th centuries, built following the devastating 1755 earthquake, lending a unique and historical charm. Avenida da Liberdade is renowned for its luxury shopping boutiques and international designer brands, boasting high-end fashion stores, luxury hotels, and upscale restaurants. Throughout the year, it hosts various cultural events, festivals, and parades, such as cute Christmas markets in winter and the Popular Saints festivities in June, which adds to its lively and dynamic character.

The Avenida is well served by public transportation, including Metro stations and bus stops, making it easily accessible to both locals and tourists, and is also conveniently within walking distance of the Baixa. A walk downhill along this street is a wonderful introduction to Lisbon.

Marquês de Pombal Square
(Praça Marquês de Pombal)

The massive statue of the Marquis of Pombal towering in the middle of this busy roundabout is one of Lisbon's most recognizable landmarks. Sebastião José de Carvalho e Melo, the 1st Marquis of Pombal, was prime minister in the 18th century. His soaring statue faces the Tagus River, strategically between Eduardo VII Park and the cosmopolitan Avenida da Liberdade, the start of several main thoroughfares. Get here by taking the Metro to Marquês de Pombal station (Blue/Yellow Lines).

Eduardo VII Park
(Parque Eduardo VII)

Just behind the Marquês de Pombal Square is a sprawling, manicured garden of lush lawns and box hedges that give it a regal feel, consistent with the historical buildings surrounding it. Stand at the top of the park and enjoy magnificent views down to the Baixa and the Tagus River. Covering 26 hectares (64 acres), the park was renamed in 1902 for Britain's Edward VII, who visited Portugal that year. It is also home to the **Estufa Fria** (Cold Greenhouse; https://informacoeseservicos.lisboa.pt/en/contacts/city-directory/lisboa-greenhouse; €3.25), one of the most important gardens in the

Eduardo VII Park

Calouste Gulbenkian Museum

city center, comprising lakes, waterfalls, brooks, statues, and hundreds of different plant specimens from all over the world. It's a great place to take refuge on a hot day.

Calouste Gulbenkian Museum
(Museu Calouste Gulbenkian)

Av. de Berna 45A; tel. 217 823 000; www.gulbenkian.pt/museu; Wed.-Mon. 10am-6pm; €14 (all-inclusive); Metro São Sebastião, Blue/Red Lines

A major hub of the arts, the Calouste Gulbenkian Museum is one of Lisbon's less-celebrated treasures despite being considered by many as one of the great museums of the world. Ranging from Greco-Roman antiquity to contemporary pieces, with 18th-century French art well represented, this is the personal collection of wealthy Armenian entrepreneur and philanthropist Calouste Sarkis Gulbenkian, who spent his final years in Lisbon. Following his death in 1955, his will established his desire to create an eponymous foundation to the benefit of the community.

The museum is housed in two separate buildings—the Founder's Collection and the Modern Collection—connected by a lovely garden, and both with cafeterias. A full morning or afternoon should be set aside to see the entire collection and enjoy the grounds. The Founder's Collection showcases over 6,000 excellently presented and well-curated exotic and ancient artifacts from all over the world, while the Modern Collection celebrates works of art from the 20th century onward and is considered to be the most complete collection of modern Portuguese art in the world. The stunning works of French glass and jewelry designer René Lalique (1860-1945) are a highlight. Visiting exhibitions regularly feature works by acclaimed and emerging national and international artists and artisans, such as experimental projects by Dutch video artist Manon de Boer and renowned Portuguese artist Sarah Affonso. Art lovers could probably spend the whole day wandering this fascinating and underrated museum.

At the time of writing, the Modern Collection building—the CAM Modern Art Center—was closed for renovation, with a full reopening scheduled for late 2024.

Águas Livres Aqueduct
(Aqueduto das Águas Livres)

main entrance at the EPAL Municipal Water Museum ticket office, Calçada da Quintinha 6, Campolide neighborhood; tel. 218 100 215; www.epal.pt; Tues.-Sun. 10am-5:30pm; €3

Climb above the city to explore the formidable Águas Livres Aqueduct (Aqueduct of the Free Waters). Built between 1731 and 1799 to supply the city with water from Sintra, it is considered a remarkable example of 18th-century engineering, snaking over 58 km (36 mi) along the trajectory of an old Roman aqueduct. Despite its size, it blends into its surroundings. Visitors can walk the main portion of the platform, crossing the 1-km (0.6-mi) stretch over the Alcântara Valley, the aqueduct's highest point at 68 m (223 ft), with views of Lisbon. Guided tours (first Saturday every month, 11am) require advance booking.

Take the Portas da Benfica bus 758 (every 15 minutes; €2) from the Glória Funicular to Campolide, then walk west for 5 minutes to the aqueduct. A taxi from central Lisbon to the aqueduct costs around €8.

Medeiros e Almeida House-Museum

(Casa Museu Medeiros e Almeida)

Rua Rosa Araújo 41; tel. 213 547 892; www. casa-museumedeirosealmeida.pt; Mon.-Sat. 10am-5pm; €5; Metro Marquês de Pombal, Blue/Yellow Lines

Once a private residence, this museum is another of Lisbon's lesser-known attractions and is definitely worth a visit. Its more than two dozen rooms house a massive collection of 17th- to 20th-century artifacts, including furniture, clocks, Chinese porcelain, European paintings, silverware, and, word has it, Napoleon Bonaparte's tea

service. Set aside 1-2 hours to take in the priceless private collection, amassed by the house's former owner, businessman Antonio Medeiros e Almeida, who had an eye for fine arts and rare pieces. The grandiose manor home is replete with extraordinary artifacts that reflect a lifetime of travels and deals. The house itself is a handsome, stately mansion fit for one of the most successful Portuguese businessmen of the 20th century. Visitors will also see how upper-class homes were designed, styled, and furnished in 20th-century Lisbon.

ALFAMA

TOP EXPERIENCE

✪ São Jorge Castle
(Castelo de São Jorge)

Rua de Santa Cruz do Castelo; tel. 218 800 620; www.castelodesaojorge.pt; daily 9am-9pm Mar.-Oct., daily 9am-6pm Nov.-Feb.; €10 (+ €2.50 guided visit); tram 12 or 28 or Chão da Feira Bus, line 37

The São Jorge Castle sits on a summit high above historic Baixa. One of Lisbon's most recognizable landmarks and historically important monuments, the original fortress was built by the Visigoths in the 5th century and expanded by the Moors in the mid-11th century because of its prime defensive location. It was expanded again during Christian rule and today contains the medieval castle, ruins of the former royal palace, stunning gardens, and part of an 11th-century citadel that housed the city's elite.

The site itself is vast and impressive, hemmed in by towering ancient walls. It boasts amazing panoramic views of Lisbon, especially at sunset. The well-kept castle grounds teeming with regal peacocks are beautiful to wander; visitors can soak up the enchanting atmosphere of the garden, search for the surviving traces of Moorish influence in the design and décor, climb towers where watchmen once kept their protective sights on Lisbon, roam the ruins of the citadel's former Royal Palace, and discover the castle's many secrets, like the Door of Treason, through which elusive messengers snuck in and out.

A permanent exhibition of relics uncovered here includes objects from the 7th century BCE to the 18th century. The Black Chamber, a camera obscura, provides 360-degree views of the city through an optical system of mirrors and lenses, while an open-air viewpoint looks over the city center and the Tagus River. Wheelchair users may face some challenges due to the geographical location of the site.

Portas do Sol Viewpoint
(Miradouro Portas do Sol)
Largo Portas do Sol; open 24/7; free; tram 28

Midway between São Jorge Castle and the Sé Cathedral, this is one of Lisbon's most iconic viewpoints, a vast terrace looking over rooftops down to the Tagus River. It's also an obligatory stop for weary walkers. At the viewpoint is the cool, contemporary **Portas do Sol** (SOL Restaurant & Garden, Largo das Portas do Sol, Beco de Santa Helena; tel. 218 851 299; daily 10am-10pm), a café, restaurant, and cocktail bar all rolled into one—it's a great place to drink in the views, enhanced by a lively soundtrack of street entertainers mixed with the bustle of the city.

Lisbon Cathedral
(Sé de Lisboa)
Largo da Sé, tel. 218 866 752; www. patriarcado-lisboa.pt; daily 9am-7pm; main cathedral free; tram 28 or 12

Between the Alfama neighborhood and Castelo, Lisbon Cathedral is the oldest and most famous church in the city. Its official name is the Church of Santa Maria Maior, but it is often simply called the Sé. Construction began in 1147, and successive modifications and renovations span the centuries. Its exterior is austere, with two robust towers. Inside, a wealth of decorative features reflect different eras. The neoclassical and rococo main chapel contains the tombs of King Afonso IV and his family. You'll also see lofty Gothic vaults, sculptured Romanesque motifs, stained-glass rose windows, and a Baroque sacristy. The **Cloister** (Mon.-Sat. 10am-5pm, Sun. 2pm-5pm, extended hours until 7pm May-Sept.; €2.50) houses Roman, Arab, and medieval relics excavated during archaeological digs. The **Treasury** (Mon.-Sat. 10am-5pm; €2.50) on the second floor contains jewels

Alfama and São Vicente

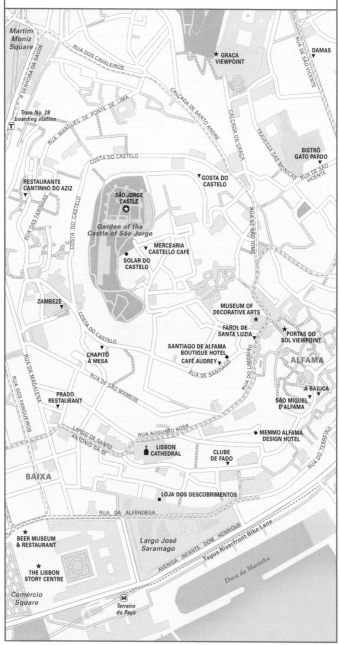

Martim Moniz Square

RUA DOS CAVALEIROS

★ GRAÇA VIEWPOINT

RUA DE SÃO VICENTE

▼ DAMAS

CALÇADA DE SANTO ANDRÉ

CALÇADA DA GRAÇA

TRAVESSA DAS MÓNICAS

R SENHORA DA SAÚDE

Tram No. 28 boarding station

RUA MARQUES DE PONTE DE LIMA

▼ BISTRÔ GATO PARDO

RUA DE SÃO VICENTE

COSTA DO CASTELO

▼ GOSTA DO CASTELO

RESTAURANTE CANTINHO DO AZIZ ▼

RUA DAS FARINHAS

COSTA DO CASTELO

SÃO JORGE CASTLE ★

RUA DE SÃO TOMÉ

Garden of the Castle of São Jorge

MERCEARIA CASTELLO CAFÉ

● SOLAR DO CASTELO

ZAMBEZE ▼

COSTA DO CASTELO

MUSEUM OF DECORATIVE ARTS ★

FAROL DE SANTA LUZIA ▼

★ PORTAS DO SOL VIEWPOINT

CHAPITÔ À MESA ▼

SANTIAGO DE ALFAMA BOUTIQUE HOTEL ▼

CAFÉ AUDREY ▼

ALFAMA

RUA DO LIMOEIRO

RUA DE SANTIAGO

A BAIUCA ▼

RUA DE SÃO MAMEDE

RUA DA MADALENA

PRADO RESTAURANT ▼

SÃO MIGUEL D'ALFAMA ▼

RUA DOS FANQUEIROS

LARGO DE SANTO ANTÓNIO DA SÉ

RUA AUGUSTO ROSA

● MEMMO ALFAMA DESIGN HOTEL

LISBON CATHEDRAL

CLUBE DE FADO ▼

RUA DO TERREIRO

BAIXA

LOJA DOS DESCOBRIMENTOS ■

RUA DA ALFÂNDEGA

BEER MUSEUM & RESTAURANT ★

Largo José Saramago

THE LISBON STORY CENTRE ★

AVENIDA INFANTE DOM HENRIQUE

Tagus Riverfront Bike Lane

Comércio Square

Doca da Marinha

Ⓜ Terreiro do Paço

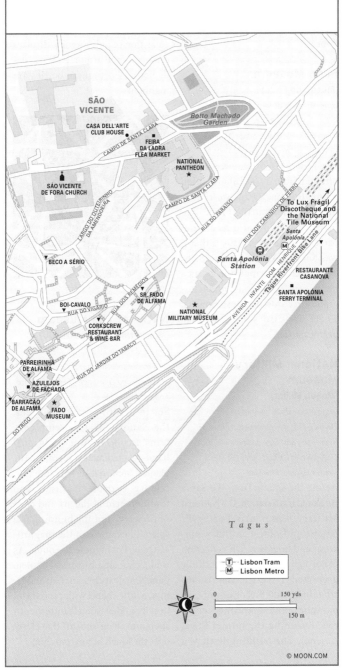

SÃO
VICENTE

Botto Machado
Garden

CASA DELL'ARTE
CLUB HOUSE

CAMPO DE SANTA CLARA

FEIRA
DA LADRA
FLEA MARKET

NATIONAL
PANTHEON
★

SÃO VICENTE
DE FORA CHURCH

LARGO DO OUTEIRINHO
DA AMENDOEIRA

CAMPO DE SANTA CLARA

RUA DO PARAÍSO

RUA DOS CAMINHOS DE FERRO

To Lux Frágil
Discotheque and
the National
Tile Museum

Santa
Apolónia

BECO A SÉRIO

Santa Apolónia
Station

Ⓜ

RESTAURANTE
CASANOVA

RUA DOS REMÉDIOS

BOI-CAVALO

SR. FADO
DE ALFAMA
★

AVENIDA INFANTE DOM HENRIQUE

Tagus Riverfront Bike Lane

SANTA APOLÓNIA
FERRY TERMINAL

RUA DO VIGÁRIO

CORKSCREW
RESTAURANT
& WINE BAR

NATIONAL
MILITARY MUSEUM
★

RUA DO JARDIM DO TABACO

PARREIRINHA
DE ALFAMA
▼

AZULEJOS
DE FACHADA
■

BARRACÃO
DE ALFAMA
▼

FADO
MUSEUM
★

DO TRIGO

Tagus

Ⓣ─ Lisbon Tram
Ⓜ─ Lisbon Metro

0   150 yds

0   150 m

© MOON.COM

from various periods. Tram 28 stops right outside the cathedral's door.

Fado Museum
(Museu do Fado)

Largo Chafariz de Dentro 1; tel. 218 823 470; www.museudofado.pt; Tues.-Sun. 10am-6pm; €5; Metro Santa Apolónia, Blue Line, buses: 728, 735, 759, 794

The Fado Museum showcases traditional fado, a soulful and often mournful musical genre that is to Portugal what the blues is to Memphis. Fado's origins are debated, but the consensus is that it was born in Alfama in the 1820s. This interactive museum hosts a permanent exhibition with photographs, records, and instruments. There are also sometimes live performances.

National Military Museum
(Museu Militar)

Largo Museu da Artilharia; tel. 218 842 453; www.exercito.pt; Tues.-Fri. 10am-5pm, Sat.-Sun. and holidays 10am-12:30pm and 1:30pm-5pm; €3; Metro Santa Apolónia, Blue Line

Across the square from the Santa Apolónia train station, the National Military Museum is Portugal's largest and oldest military museum and houses a rich collection of Portuguese militaria. Beautifully decorated, lofty, tile-clad rooms contain 26,000 pieces of military paraphernalia spanning centuries, including the former Royal Arsenal. The building itself is a striking monument, built on the site of a 16th-century foundry. A collection of old cannons, displays of wagons and armor, and frescoes depicting Portuguese battles are highlights.

tile from the National Tile Museum

National Tile Museum
(Museu Nacional do Azulejo)

Rua da Madre de Deus 4; tel. 218 100 340; www.museudoazulejo.gov.pt; Tues.-Sun. 10am-1pm and 2pm-6pm; €5; Metro Santa Apolónia, Blue Line

Set in a 16th-century convent, the National Tile Museum contains a collection of traditional hand-painted azulejo ceramic tile plaques, some dating from the 15th century. It explores the history and tradition behind the art and craft of tilework, and the building is a splendid example of the magnificence of Portuguese Baroque. As well as housing historical azulejo panels, it features ancient paintings, a little chapel with carved and heavily-gilded wood features, a gift shop, and an on-site café that closes over the lunch hour (1pm-2pm).

Museum of Decorative Arts
(Museu De Artes Decorativas Portuguesas)

Largo Portas do Sol 2; tel. 218 814 640; www.fress.pt; Wed.-Mon. 10am-5pm (guided tours 10:30am, noon, 2pm, and 3pm); €10; tram 12 or 28, bus 737

Located near the Portas do Sol viewpoint, the 17th-century Azura Palace is home to the Museum of Decorative Arts. Part of the Ricardo do Espirito Santo Silva Foundation, this wonderful museum offers a glimpse into how 18th- and 19th-century Portuguese aristocracy lived. The palace itself retains many of its original features, and it also showcases furniture and fixtures of the era. Among them are a priceless silver collection, Chinese porcelain, and ancient Flemish tapestries.

Graça Viewpoint
(Miradouro da Graça)

Calçada da Graça; open 24/7; free; tram 28

Also called the Sophia de Mello Breyner Andresen viewpoint, after Portugal's most famous poetess, this bird's-eye terrace was built in 1271 and offers dramatic sweeping vistas over Lisbon. Particularly magical at sunrise and sunset, the view of São Jorge Castle is striking. A little on-site **café** (Esplanada da Graça; tel. 218 865 341; daily 10am-2am) is a great spot for refreshments while drinking in the views. Located in front of the Graça church, this is often the

Graça viewpoint

starting point for exploring Bairro Alto.

SÃO VICENTE
National Pantheon
(Panteão Nacional)

Campo de Santa Clara; tel. 218 854 820; Tues.-Sat. 10am-6pm Apr.-Sept., Tues.-Sat. 10am-5pm Oct.-Mar., €4; Metro Santa Apolónia, Blue Line

The National Pantheon—otherwise known as the Church of Santa Engrácia—has Baroque architecture and a distinctive domed roof that can be seen from most of central Lisbon. It is on the site of the original Santa Engrácia church, which began renovations in 1681 and took more than 300 years to complete. Construction dragged on for so long that the Portuguese call any lengthy project "work of Santa Engrácia." In 1916 the church was converted into a pantheon, a process that took another 50 years. Today the building boasts a majestic nave with a polychrome marble decoration typical of Portuguese Baroque architecture. It is home to tombs of historic personalities such as writer Almeida Garrett, fado singer Amália Rodrigues, legendary soccer star Eusébio, and Portuguese presidents. The views from the front steps and the terrace around the dome are breathtaking.

São Vicente de Fora Church
(Igreja de São Vicente de Fora)

Largo de São Vicente; tel. 218 824 400; www.patriarcado-lisboa.pt, Tues.-Sun.

10am-6pm; €5; Metro Santa Apolónia, Blue Line

In its present guise, the São Vicente de Fora Church, or Monastery of São Vicente de Fora, is considered one of the finest examples of mannerist architecture in the country. Rebuilt from a 12th-century church, it dates to the 16th century and houses one of the biggest collections of Baroque glazed tiles in the world, used to clad the cloisters, stairways, and aisles. There are also two mausoleums, one belonging to the Royal House of Braganza and the other to the city's archbishops, known as the Patriarchs of Lisbon. The must-see Patriarchate's Museum showcases beautiful historical works of religious art. Enjoy fabulous views from the roof terrace.

CAIS DO SODRÉ

Cais do Sodré has recently undergone a much-needed facelift that elevated the neighborhood from seedy to swanky. Gone are the days when swashbuckling sailors sought their thrills during layovers in Lisbon and fishermen told their colorful tales in the many tackle shops that dotted the area. Nowadays the tackle shops have been converted into cool hangouts, brothels into trendy bars, and the hip **Time Out Market** is where new gastro trends are set.

Bica Lift
(Ascensor da Bica)

Calçada da Bica Pequena 1; tel. 213 613 000; Mon.-Sat. 7am-9pm, Sun. and public holidays 9am-9pm; €4.10 (round-trip, purchased on-board)

Inaugurated in 1892, this funicular connects Lisbon's downtown to the Bica and Bairro Alto neighborhoods, running every 15 minutes between Rua de São Paulo, near Cais do Sodré's Time Out Market, and Largo do Calhariz (Calhariz Square). Its route takes passengers up one of Lisbon's steepest hills, Bica de Duarte Belo Street, on what is arguably one of the city's most picturesque funicular routes, passing quaint houses and traditional commerce. The funicular's traction system was originally powered by steam engines before being electrified in 1914. It was declared a National Monument in 2002 and is one of the city's most popular tourist activities. Once up at the top, make sure to visit the **Santa Catarina viewpoint,** which offers stunning bird's-eye views of the city.

Bica Lift

Estrela Basílica

ESTRELA AND LAPA
Estrela Basílica
(Basílica da Estrela)

Praça da Estrela; tel. 213 960 915; www. patrimoniocultural.gov.pt; daily 10:30am-7:30pm; free; tram 25 or 28

The neoclassical Estrela Basílica was built in the 18th century by order of Queen Maria I, whose tomb it houses. The interior walls and flooring are clad in swaths of yellow, pink, and gray marble in stunning geometric patterns. Twin bell towers stand atop the striking facade, while the dome provides views over the city. The Estrela Basílica was the first church in the world dedicated to the Sacred Heart of Jesus.

Estrela Gardens
(Jardim da Estrela)

The exquisitely landscaped Estrela Gardens is colloquially referred to as the Central Park of Lisbon, a tranquil, lush oasis in the heart of this affluent neighborhood, bordered by the main Rua da Estrela and Avenida Ávares Cabral, with the Estrela Basílica at the bottom and a statue of explorer Pedro

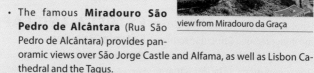

Lisbon's Best Views

Because Lisbon is laid out over seven hills, gorgeous views can be found throughout the city. Miradouros (public viewing points) offer views of the cityscape. Some are enhanced with cafés and restaurants, landscaped gardens, and even chic lounges. Best of all, they're free. Visit at sunset for a truly special experience.

view from Miradouro da Graça

- The famous **Miradouro São Pedro de Alcântara** (Rua São Pedro de Alcântara) provides panoramic views over São Jorge Castle and Alfama, as well as Lisbon Cathedral and the Tagus.

- The romantic **Miradouro da Nossa Senhora do Monte** (Largo Monte) is the highest viewpoint, offering bird's-eye views over the old quarters and castle all the way to the Tagus River.

- The **Miradouro Portas do Sol** (Largo Portas do Sol) overlooks the charismatic Alfama neighborhood.

- The **Miradouro da Graça** (Calçada da Graça) peers over São Jorge Castle.

Along with the miradouros, the **São Jorge Castle** has possibly the best views in the city. Panoramas can also be enjoyed from hotel rooftop bars, such as the **Hotel Mundial** (Praça Martim Moniz 2), where the Sunset Parties have a cult following.

Álvares Cabral at the top. Stroll past duck ponds, browse the library, and enjoy open-air concerts hosted in the wrought-iron bandstand on summer evenings.

National Museum of Ancient Art

(Museu Nacional de Arte Antiga)

Rua das Janelas Verdes; tel. 213 912 800; www.museudearteantiga.pt; Tues.-Sun. 10am-6pm; €6

A 20-minute stroll south of the Estrela Gardens is the National Museum of Ancient Art. Housed in a former 17th-century palace on one of the city's toniest streets, the opulent museum is laden with artifacts that span the 12th-19th centuries. The collection includes paintings, sculptures, textiles, and furniture. Among the most celebrated pieces are the *Panels of St. Vincent*, which depict a cross-section of 15th-century Portuguese society gathered to venerate a saint. Take the Cascais-bound train or the Santos-o-Velho bus from Cais do Sodré to Santos.

Puppet Museum
(Museu da Marioneta)

Rua da Esperança 146; tel. 213 942 810; www.museudamarioneta.pt; Tues.-Fri. 11am-5pm, Sat.-Sun. 10am-6pm; €5; tram 25 or 28

One of Lisbon's more unusual exhibited collections, the Puppet Museum is small but rather entertaining. It houses a colorful collection of marionettes from all over the world, which are odd and amusing in equal proportions. Check it out online in advance to see when live shows are on, and don't forget the obligatory puppet-selfie on your way out. Audio tour included in entry price, on request.

British Cemetery
(Cemitério dos Ingleses)

Rua de São Jorge, 6; tel. 932 101 805; Mon.-Fri. 10:30am-1pm, Sun. 11am-1pm, closed Tues. and Thurs. in Aug.; donation suggested; tram 25 or 28 (stop at Estrela Basílica)

A cemetery might not be at the top of everyone's sightseeing list, but in this case it is a must. Despite the city having a thriving British community in the 1800s, during the Inquisition, Protestants were not allowed to be buried in Catholic cemeteries. However, thanks to an agreement between English political leader Oliver Cromwell and Portugal's King João IV, a plot of land was found in 1717 for Lisbon's British citizens to be buried in—hence the name. Located just around the corner from the grand Estrela Basílica, besides providing a slice of leafy, cool tranquility away from the city's throngs, the cemetery also has lovely lush gardens surrounding the 250-plus years of history. Amid the gardens and gravestones, a raised tomb sits in tribute to novelist Henry Fielding, who died in Lisbon in 1754, although his exact final resting place remains unknown. The cemetery is also home to **St. George's Church,** a pretty pink church that has an English-speaking Anglican service (Thursday 12:30pm, Sunday 11:30am).

ALCÂNTARA
25 de Abril Bridge
(Ponte 25 de Abril)

tel. 212 947 920; www.lusoponte.pt; tolls €2.10-8.05 (northbound only)

Lisbon's iconic 25 de Abril Bridge dominates the skyline from most directions. Stand underneath it and the buzz of the vehicles whooshing above is hypnotic. Inaugurated in 1966, it was named the Salazar Bridge after statesman António de Oliveira Salazar, prior to the Carnation Revolution. Post-independence it was renamed the 25 de Abril Bridge, in tribute to the bloodless uprising that overthrew Salazar's dictatorial regime and gave Portugal independence and democracy, on April 25, 1974. Spanning 2.3 km (1.4 mi), the bright-red suspension bridge connects Lisbon to Almada, on the south bank of the Tagus River. The upper deck carries six vehicle lanes, crossed by some 150,000 cars every day, and offers the most incredible views of the city. The bottom deck is a double electrified rail track, added in 1999, that carries the Fertagus train between Lisbon and Setúbal (www.fertagus.pt; €5.35 one-way). It departs from stations including Entrecampos and Sete Rios roughly once an hour 5:30am-1am. The last train back from Setúbal leaves just after midnight. Although the bridge is closed to foot traffic and cyclists, it does open exclusively to pedestrians once a year in March for the Lisbon Half Marathon.

The bridge is also home to one of Lisbon's more recent tourist attractions, the **Pilar 7 Experience** (Avenida da Índia (N6 34); tel. 211 117 880; www.visitlisboa.com/en/places/pilar-7-bridge-experience; daily 10am-6pm; €5.50), an interactive museum that allows visitors to explore inside one of the famous bridge's pillars. Those with a head for heights can take an elevator to a 72-m-high (236-ft-high) panoramic glass viewing platform adjacent to the pillar. Vertigo-sufferers be warned—the floor is glass too. But the views are worth the shaky legs!

Christ the King
(Cristo Rei)

Alto do Pragal, Av. Cristo Rei; tel. 212 751 000 or 212 721 270; www.cristorei.pt; daily 10am-7pm; €8

25 de Abril Bridge and *Christ the King* statue

Dominating the skyline of the Tagus's south bank just across from the 25 de Abril Bridge is the *Christ the King* statue, standing with arms outstretched and epitomizing Portugal's Catholic faith. The idea to build the monument came after the Cardinal Patriarch of Lisbon visited Rio de Janeiro in 1934 and was impressed by its imposing *Christ the Redeemer* statue. Built on an isolated cliff top in the town of Almada, the statue stands 192 m (630 ft) above the Tagus River. An express elevator whizzes visitors to a viewing platform at 82 m (269 ft), which affords dazzling views over the city. At the statue's base is a chapel. The statue's interior contains a library, a large café, two halls, and another chapel. The quickest way to the statue is by taxi. Buses from downtown Lisbon stop in Almada, from where you can walk up to the monument.

BELÉM

To get to Belém from downtown Lisbon, take tram 15 (also known as 15E) from the main Comércio Square, or the Cascais train from Cais do Sodré to Cascais. Jump off when you see the Jerónimos Monastery, and walk to the sights. A taxi from downtown Lisbon costs around €14 one-way.

Belém Tower
(Torre de Belém)

Av. Brasília; tel. 213 620 034; www. torrebelem.gov.pt; daily 9:30am-6pm (ticket sales close 5pm); €6; train: Belém Station, bus 714, 727, 728, 729, 751, 113, 144, 149, tram 15, 18

Jutting into the Tagus River, magnificent Belém Tower is one of Portugal's most recognizable monuments and a UNESCO World Heritage Site, acknowledging Belém's significance as a launchpad during the Age of Discoveries. The decorative Manueline tower was originally built in the 16th century, part of a coastal defense system to guard the Tagus River mouth and the entrance to Lisbon. Today it is symbolic of one of the most significant chapters in Portugal's history. As well as protecting Lisbon, the tower also marks the spot where Portuguese explorers started and ended their journeys to the "New World."

Belém Tower

The frilly Manueline tower became a ceremonial landmark, often the last and first sight sailors had of their homeland. The sturdy little tower's ornate stonework incorporates figures related to the Age of Exploration, such as exotic animals, ropes and knots, and a statue of Our Lady of Safe Homecoming, a symbol of protection for sailors on their voyages. The navigators who set sail from Belém, in sturdy wooden caravels and nau ships built in shipyards in Lisbon and the Algarve, laid the blueprints for Portugal's colonial empire. Setting up Atlantic trade routes brought Portugal considerable wealth and established Lisbon as Europe's main trading center for spices, silk, and precious gems like pearls and diamonds. It also brought historic tragedies, namely the damage inflicted on Indigenous peoples by colonialism, and the country's role in the Atlantic slave trade.

Having also been used as a lighthouse, a customs house, and a prison, the fortification is today one of Portugal's most visited tourist sites. Its elaborate exterior belies the starkness inside: Entering the tower over an ancient drawbridge, visitors access a bulwark housing artillery, in the middle of which is a small courtyard flanked by Gothic arches. Inside the tower are the Governor's Room on the first floor, the opulent King's Hall on the second floor, the Audience Room on the third floor, and a chapel on the fourth floor. All rooms are devoid of furnishings, showcasing only the bare stonework. The floors all boast lovely balconies, connected by a narrow spiral staircase topped by a viewing terrace. It's worth the climb for views over the Tagus estuary and Belém's monuments.

National Coach Museum
(Museu Nacional dos Coches)
Av. da Índia 136; tel. 210 732 319; http:// museudoscoches.gov.pt; Tues.-Sun. 10am-6pm; €8; bus 28, 714, 727, 729, 751, tram 15

Before cars, there were horses and carriages, and Portugal has some fine examples of horse-drawn vehicles on permanent display at the National Coach Museum. From elaborately decorated Berlins that transported royalty, to children's carriages and mail buses, the various collections of 16th- to 19th-century coaches are fascinating. Located on the fringe of the **Afonso de Albuquerque Square** (Praça Afonso de Albuquerque), the museum also hosts a number of collections of other stately items, such as ceremonial clothing, instruments, tapestries, and horse tack.

✪ Jerónimos Monastery
(Mosteiro dos Jerónimos)
Praça do Império; tel. 213 620 034; www. mosteirojeronimos.gov.pt; daily 9:30am-6pm; €10, ticket including the Maritime Museum and the Archaeology Museum €12; bus 727, 728, 729, 714, 751, tram 15, suburban train to Belém

Parallel to the Tagus River, with the stately Imperial Square Gardens sprawling in front of it, the exuberant Jerónimos Monastery is Belém's breathtaking centerpiece. A prime example of ornate Manueline architecture, it is also a UNESCO World Heritage Site. Construction on the impressive landmark began in 1501 on the order of King Manuel I, who wanted to honor the memory of explorer Henry the Navigator, as well as to demonstrate his own devotion to Saint Jerome. The vast building took 100 years to complete. Its several architectural styles include Renaissance and the lavishly ornate

Spanish plateresque style. The magnificent riverside facade has a figure of Our Lady of Belém, while inside is the Latin-cross-shaped Church of Santa Maria, the final resting place of explorer Vasco da Gama and one of Portugal's greatest poets, Luís Vaz de Camões. Today the Monastery's long, regal wings house the naval museum.

Also located in the expansive wings of the Jerónimos Monastery is the **National Archaeology Museum (Museu Nacional de Arqueologia)** (€4, ticket including Jerónimos Monastery and the Maritime Museum €12), devoted to ancient Iberian art. Among its collections are ancient jewelry, busts, mosaics, and epigraphs, as well as metal artifacts, medals, and coins.

Maritime Museum
(Museu de Marinha)

Praça do Império; tel. 210 977 388; daily 10am-6pm; €7

The Maritime Museum (Museu de Marinha), also often referred to as the Navy or Naval Museum, occupies the western wing of the Jerónimos Monastery as well as a modern annex to the north. It grew from a collection started by King Luís I (1838-1889), who had a keen interest in oceanographic studies and was an accomplished navigator. It currently comprises more than 17,000 pieces and is widely regarded as one of the most important maritime museums in Europe. Exhibits include historical paintings, archaeological items, and various scale models of ships,

Jerónimos Monastery cloister

along with ancient instruments and maps, royal barges, the Fairey III *Santa Cruz* that made the first aerial crossing of the Atlantic in 1923, and the Portuguese Navy's first-ever aircraft, a flying boat. The museum also showcases Portugal's seafaring history as the pioneers of the Age of Discoveries, with the oldest exhibit—a real highlight—being a wooden figurine of the Archangel Raphael that Portuguese explorer Vasco da Gama is said to have taken with him on his expedition to India.

Monument to the Discoveries
(Padrão dos Descobrimentos)

Av. Brasília; tel. 213 031 950; www. padraodosdescobrimentos.pt; daily 10am-7pm Mar.-Sept., Tues.-Sun. 10am-6pm Oct.-Feb.; €3

A short stroll from Belém Tower along the Tagus riverside is the Monument to the Discoveries. First erected in 1940 and made permanent in 1960 to mark 500 years since Henry the Navigator's death, the monument celebrates the Age of Discoveries in the 15th and 16th centuries with statues of Henry the Navigator, Pedro Álvares Cabral, and Vasco da Gama. The Age of Discoveries, while being a significant chapter in maritime exploration that played an important role in shaping the modern world, today also raises questions about its complex ethical, social, and colonial implications. Shaped like a caravel—a small Portuguese sailing ship—the Monument to the Discoveries also houses an auditorium and a

museum with changing exhibitions and has a viewing platform on top. In the square out front is the stunning **Compass Rose,** an elaborate decorative work of paving art shaped like a compass, 50 m (164 ft) across, in black and red lioz limestone, in the center of which is a map of the world as perceived during the Age of Discoveries, surrounded by decorative figures like mermaids, stars, and leaves.

MAAT–Museum of Art, Architecture and Technology
(Museu de Arte, Arquitetura e Tecnologia)

Av. Brasília; tel. 210 028 130; www.maat. pt; Wed.-Mon. 10am-7pm; €11 (MAAT + power plant)

Inaugurated in 2016 in a contemporary building starkly contrasting with its classical peers, MAAT is one of Lisbon's newest cultural additions. It is part of a larger campus, the EDP Foundation, which spans 38,000 sq m (400,000 sq ft) and features a converted thermal power plant—the Tejo Power Station, a historical industrial structure built in 1908—along with the new MAAT building. The slinky building, by British architect Amanda Levete, has a curved design and white-tiled facade that juts out over the river like a low, gleaming spaceship. It hosts national and international exhibitions and collections of contemporary art, architecture, and technology, and is connected to the city by a footbridge. It is free to climb to the roof from outside for views over the Tagus at what has become an iconic location.

Berardo Collection Museum
(Museu Colecção Berardo)

Praça do Império; tel. 213 612 878; www. museuberardo.pt; daily 10am-7pm; €5 (Sat. free); tram 15, bus 714, 728

Lisbon's most-visited museum is indeed a must-see for modern art lovers. Comprising a vast selection of carefully curated modern and contemporary art, spanning all genres from Cubism to Pop Art, the outstanding Berardo Collection Museum is a private collection that features iconic pieces by the greats—works by Mondrian, Picasso, Duchamp, Andy Warhol, Jackson Pollock, Salvador Dalí, and Francis Bacon can all be found here—as well as emerging artists. The permanent collection occupies the entire second floor, with rotating exhibitions on the lower floor.

Cordoaria Nacional

Av. da Índia; tel. 213 637 635; www. patrimoniocultural.gov.pt; Fri. 10am-7pm, Sat.-Sun. 10am-8pm; €13-15 (prices vary weekdays and weekends); bus 727, 728, 751, 756

The Cordoaria Nacional is a former naval rope-making factory in Belém that now functions as an exhibition center. The original factory is believed to have been built on the order of the Marquis of Pombal circa 1771, being completed in 1779. Located on the main road running alongside the Tagus River, it produced sisal ropes, cables, sails, and other equipment for the Portuguese Navy and other ships. Widely revered as an outstanding example of 18th-century industrial architecture, it is now used as a space for rotating exhibitions, which have featured internationally acclaimed names such as Banksy.

Quake Museum

Rua Cais de Alfândega Velha 39; www. lisbonquake.com; Fri.-Mon. 10am-7pm, Tues.-Thurs. 2pm-7pm; from €21 (online discounts available for advance bookings)

One of Lisbon's newest and more unusual attractions, this interactive and immersive museum offers visitors the chance to experience what it would have felt like to be caught up in the 1755 earthquake, feel the power of the event and its aftereffects, and learn more about the natural disaster that reshaped Lisbon.

PARK OF NATIONS
(Parque das Nações)
Cable Cars

daily 11am-6pm, until 8pm in summer, closed in bad weather; €3.95 one-way, €5.90 round-trip

Cable cars run between the Oceanarium and the modern, 145-m (476-ft) Vasco da Gama tower, gliding over the waterfront. To get to Park of Nations from downtown Lisbon, take the Metro from Baixa-Chiado (Green/Blue Lines) to Oriente on the Red Line.

Lisbon Oceanarium
(Oceanário de Lisboa)

*Esplanada Dom Carlos I; tel. 218 917 002;
www.oceanario.pt; daily 10am-8pm (last
entry 7pm); adults €25, children 4-12 €15*

Inaugurated in 1998 for the World
Exposition, the Lisbon Oceanarium,
Europe's largest indoor aquarium, is
home to a huge assortment of ma-
rine species, from seagulls to sea
lions, sea dragons, and surgeonfish.
The star attraction is a huge tank
that houses exotic sealife, including
rays, sharks, moray eels, barracudas,
and sunfish.

Vasco da Gama Bridge
(Ponte Vasco da Gama)

*tel. 212 328 200 (office open Mon.-Fri.
8:30am-6pm); www.lusoponte.pt; tolls
€3.20-13.55 (northbound only)*

Snaking across the Tagus River to
link eastern Lisbon to the South
Bank, the Vasco da Gama Bridge
is Portugal's and Europe's longest
bridge. Measuring 17.2 km (10.7
mi), it was purpose-built for the
1998 Lisbon World Fair Exposition
(Expo '98), in the Park of Nations
area east of Lisbon city center.
Flanked by viaducts, the elegant
and sturdy cable-stayed bridge is a
feat of engineering and design. The
six-lane structure sees more than
62,000 vehicles cross it daily.

Pavilion of Knowledge–
Living Science Center
(Pavilhão do Conhecimento,
Centro Ciência Viva)

*Largo José Mariano Gago; tel. 218 917
100; www.pavconhecimento.pt; Mon.-Fri.
10am-6pm, weekends and holidays 10am-*

Park of Nations

*7pm (closed Mon. Sept.-May); €11, children
€8-9; Metro Gare do Oriente, Red Line*

Children of all ages will enjoy
spending a couple of hours at this
highly interactive and techno-
logic center dedicated to science.
It comprises a vast number of exhibitions and activities, covering
wide-ranging themes that aim to
be fun, stimulating, and educa-
tional at the same time. Located
next to the Oceanarium, it offers a
superb option for a rainy or really
hot day. Main attractions include a
suspended Skyline Bike Ride and
robotics games.

Water Gardens
(Jardins d'Água)

Ulisses boardwalk; open 24/7

Fronting the Park of Nations area

cable cars in Park of Nations

are the attractive Water Gardens, which provide leafy, cool refuge on a warm day. This peaceful oasis is a perfect complement to the neighborhood's contemporary feel and lends the built-up area some much-needed greenery. They comprise a number of pretty water features and offer splendid views over the Tagus and Vasco da Gama Bridge. The sculpted gardens hide several intriguing points of interest—such as exotic plants and trees, large wind chimes, a water volcano, and sculptures—and have plenty of seating. This is an ideal spot to sit and enjoy a book with the calming sound of running water in the background. Just behind the gardens, set back from the riverfront, is a string of restaurants and bars that form the backbone of the Park of Nations' nightlife.

Sports and Recreation

TAGUS RIVER BOAT TOURS

The opposite side of the Tagus River offers a nice view of Lisbon. Given the nation's seafaring history, a boat trip offers a uniquely appropriate vantage point to see the city.

Lisbon by Boat

tel. 933 914 740; www.lisbonbyboat.com; usual departure point: Belém Marina

Lisbon by Boat offers a variety of tours, from guided sightseeing trips to romantic sunset cruises, but all promise unforgettable views of the Portuguese capital. By motorboat

Queluz National Palace and Gardens

Palácio Nacional de Queluz e Jardins

A commuter suburb about 20 minutes northwest of Lisbon, Queluz (keh-LOOZH) is home to the **Palácio Nacional de Queluz e Jardins** (Largo Palácio de Queluz; tel. 219 237 300; www.parquesdesintra.pt; daily 9am-6pm late Oct.-late Mar., daily 9am-7pm late Mar.-late Oct., last entry 1 hour before closing time; €10, audio guide €3), a fanciful royal palace and splendid gardens, making it a historical hot spot. This is a great place to visit if you'd like to see a spectacular palace but aren't quite ready to journey as far as Sintra yet.

or by yacht, trips range 1-6 hours, starting from around €38 per person for an hour-long historical Lisbon sightseeing cruise.

Yellow Boat Tour

www.yellowbustours.com; from €20

An alternative way to explore Lisbon is on the hop-on hop-off Yellow Boat Tour. Purchase a 24-hour ticket and see main points of interest on both sides of the Tagus. There are two stops on the route, in Belém (MAAT Museum) and Terreiro do Paço. A nonstop circuit takes 1.5 hours, with a running commentary on sights in a number of languages, including English.

SEGWAY TOURS

Lisbon Segway Tours

www.lisbonsegwaytours.pt; from €45

Lisbon Segway Tours are a fun way to zip around the city and really get into its nooks and crannies. Tours visit different areas, including a riverside tour, a tour of Alfama, a city center tour, and a Belém tour. More unusual itineraries are a Lisbon by night tour, a gastronomic tour to discover the

Inside are the Corridor of Azulejos (tiles); the Throne Hall, dripping with shimmery mirrors and chandeliers; the Lantern Room, which houses the palace's biggest portrait; and the opulent Ambassadors' Hall, in which every square centimeter is gilded. Outside, visitors can wander gardens decorated with fountains and statues. **Corte em Queluz,** a 2-hour reenactment of the 18th-century life inside the palace, is staged once a month (check dates beforehand; reservations required). The €10 fee includes entrance to the palace.

HISTORY OF THE PALACE

Built in the 18th century as a summer residence, Queluz National Palace soon became a royal favorite for leisure and entertaining. Portugal's royal family lived here permanently before fleeing to Brazil in 1807 to escape French invasions. The palace's extravagance is a heady blend of Baroque, neoclassical, and rococo styles, and its French-inspired gardens draw comparisons with the Palace of Versailles.

GETTING THERE

Queluz is a 20-minute drive, 14 km (8.7 mi) north of Lisbon. Take the **N117** or the **A37** roads. A taxi will cost around €15 one-way. From Lisbon's **Oriente, Santa Apolónia** and **Rossio** stations, among others, **CP trains** (tel. 707 210 220; www.cp.pt; €1.60) run on the Sintra Line every 10 minutes during the week and every half hour on the weekend. The journey to the **Queluz-Belas** or **Monte Abraão** station takes 20-25 minutes; both are about a 1-km (0.6-mi) walk to the palace. The train ride between Queluz and **Sintra** (€2.10) also takes about 20-25 minutes.

city's foodie delights, and a 3-hour super tour that covers most of the city's main spots.

WALKING TOURS

Personalized walking tours by locals have become popular in Lisbon, allowing you to explore the city at a leisurely pace. Guided tours are available in English, and many are free. From private tours to foodie tours, pub crawls, and even sunset tours, follow a local guide who knows the city and its secrets as only a native could. Tours take place rain or shine, and their duration can range from just over 1.5 hours to the full day. On free tours, payment is in the form of tips—a suggested tip is €5-12 per person. Specialist walking-tour companies include **Discover Walks Lisbon** (www.discoverwalks.com) and **Discover Lisbon** (tel. 932 060 800; www.discoverlisbon.org).

CYCLING

Gira

tel. 211 163 060; www.gira-bicicletasdelisboa.pt; from €2

Lisbon City Hall has created an extensive shared-bicycle network and a web of cycle paths. The shared-bicycle scheme Gira comprises about 50 stations around the city, with 500 electric and standard bicycles. Conveniently located stations include spots in the Park of Nations area, Marquês de Pombal Square, and along the main Avenida da Liberdade. Download the app, buy a day pass for €2, and pedal away. Lisbon has more than 60 km (37 mi) of bicycle lanes to explore.

Lisbon Bike Tour and Outdoors

Rua Presidente Arriaga 112; tel. 912 272 300; www.lisbonbiketour.com; €39.50

Tour companies such as Lisbon Bike Tour and Outdoors have designed exciting tours—all downhill—that cover key historical areas. The classic Lisbon Bike Tour lasts around 3.5 hours and takes cyclists through the heart of downtown Lisbon and along the riverfront, finishing in Belém.

Rent-a-Fun

Rua do Jardim do Tabaco 2; www.rent-a-fun.com; from €32, children €15

Rent-a-Fun includes some uphill climbs on its tours, but its bicycles are electric. It specializes in the Seven Hills tour. Standard bike tours take 3 hours. Rent-a-Fun also rents out electric, regular, and folding bicycles (daily 9am-6pm; from €39/day), including a helmet and lock.

SPECTATOR SPORTS
Soccer (Football)
Luz Stadium (Estádio da Luz)

Av. Eusébio da Silva Ferreira; tel. 217 219 500; www.slbenfica.pt; Metro Colégio-Militar/Luz or Alto-dos-Moinhos, Blue Line

The 64,642-seat Luz Stadium (Estádio da Luz), the Stadium of Light, is the home of soccer team Benfica, one of the country's Big Three (along with cross-city rivals Sporting and northern team Porto). Architecturally impressive, its wavy roof of steel arches is designed to feel light and transparent. At the stadium there is a store, a museum, and 20-minute guided tours (daily 10am-6pm; €12.50, with museum €17.50). Game tickets start around €30.

José Alvalade Stadium (Estádio José Alvalade)

Rua Professor Fernando da Fonseca; tel. 217 516 164; www.sporting.pt; Metro Campo Grande, Green Line

A short distance from Luz Stadium is José Alvalade Stadium (Estádio José Alvalade), or Lions' Stadium, home to the soccer team Sporting, "the lions." Predominantly green to echo its home team's colors, the stadium was designed by architect Tomás Taveira in a mall complex with a 12-screen movie theater, a health club, and a soccer museum. There are four guided tours daily of the stadium and museum (from €14). Game tickets start at €30.

Arts and Entertainment

OPERA

São Carlos National Theater (Teatro Nacional de São Carlos)

Rua Serpa Pinto 9; tel. 213 253 000; https://tnsc.bol.pt; Metro Baixa-Chiado, Green/Blue Lines

Portugal's national opera house, the São Carlos National Theater, was inaugurated on June 30, 1793, built in the Chiado neighborhood by order of Queen Maria I to replace the Tejo Opera House in Comercio Square, which was destroyed by the 1755 earthquake. Inspired by Italy's grandiose La Scala theater in Milan and the San Carlo Theater in Naples, it is still today the only Portuguese theater that produces and showcases opera and choral and symphonic music. Classified a National Monument, the beautiful neoclassical building with ornate rococo touches has long been a centerpiece of the country's cultural scene.

CONCERT AND DANCE VENUES

Coliseu dos Recreios

Rua Portas de Santo Antão 96; tel. 213 240 580; www.coliseulisboa.com

Inaugurated in 1890, the famed Coliseu dos Recreios, located just north of the Baixa neighborhood, regularly welcomes international productions, traditionally from the realm of ballet, theater, and opera, as well as pop stars, circus troupes, and comedians. Architecturally, the Coliseu was ahead of its time with cutting-edge ironwork, seen in its spectacular German-made iron dome and iron roof.

Calouste Gulbenkian Foundation

Av. de Berna 45A; tel. 217 823 461; www. gulbenkian.pt

One of Lisbon's newer cultural venues, the Calouste Gulbenkian Foundation (Fundação Calouste Gulbenkian) has offerings beyond the world of art and exhibitions, with jazz, choral, and orchestral concerts, sometimes held in the lovely gardens.

Altice Arena

Rossio dos Olivais; tel. 218 918 409; http:// arena.altice.pt

Huge Altice Arena, formerly known as the Meo Arena, is a futuristic-looking multipurpose venue on the Park of Nations riverside, hosting the biggest concerts and events, including in recent years U2, Beyoncé, Ariana Grande, Justin Bieber, Cirque du Soleil, and the 2018 Eurovision Song Contest.

Bela Vista Park

Av. Almirante Gago Coutinho/Rua José Régio

A sprawling green space wedged between downtown Lisbon and the Expo area, Bela Vista Park hosts some of Lisbon's biggest musical events, such as the biennial Rock in Rio Lisboa. Covering around 85 hectares (200 acres), lovely lawns lined with leafy trees make this a nice spot for a stroll or a picnic any time of year.

THEATER

Dona Maria II
National Theater
(Teatro Nacional Dona Maria II)
Praça Dom Pedro IV; tel. 213 250 800;
www.tndm.pt

Dona Maria II National Theater

Prestigious Dona Maria II National Theater (Teatro Nacional Dona Maria II) is a national jewel and cultural heavyweight on noble Rossio Square. Built between 1842 and 1846 in neoclassical style, it celebrates the performing arts with a full agenda of plays, shows, and concerts.

FESTIVALS
AND EVENTS

Lisbon loves to party, and these annual events draw crowds. The Santo António festival is without a doubt Lisbon's main event, the biggest traditional religious celebration in the country. Lisbon hosts an array of summer music festivals and fairs, and concerts by international artists throughout the year, mostly at Altice Arena in the Park of Nations.

Spring
Carnival
(Carnaval)
throughout Lisbon; mid-Feb.-early Mar.

Portugal goes into party mode for Carnival, and Lisbon has a succession of colorful floats and costumed dancers shimmying through the city's main avenues in a cloud of colorful confetti and streamers to the energetic rhythms of hot South American and popular Portuguese folk music, regardless of the weather. Carnival typically falls around mid-February or early March and lasts a number of days, during which concerts, masquerade balls, and street events are also held.

Summer
Santo António and
June Festivities
throughout Lisbon; June

Dedicated to Saint Anthony, the city's patron, Santo António is Portugal's biggest traditional religious festival. Celebrations are staged throughout the capital for the whole month of June, reaching their peak on June 12, with jubilant parades and processions into the night. On June 13 the time-honored Casamentos de Santo António (Santo António weddings) are held. Established in 1958, these are a mass wedding of a dozen of the city's cash-strapped couples, selected from hundreds of applicants. The entire ceremony, from the bridal outfits to the honeymoon, is funded by city hall and other sponsors. Over these two days, the city parties to pay homage to "matchmaker" Saint Anthony, from the afternoon through the early morning.

During Santo António, Lisbon is at its prettiest. Every garden and square is decked out with colorful trimmings and lights. Food and drink stalls, tables, and chairs are set up with small stages for local artists to perform traditional folk songs. Grilled sardines, sangria, and traditional caldo verde (potato and kale) soup are served from stalls to fuel the merriment. The neighborhoods of Alfama and Bica are the most popular for Santo António. Each neighborhood also designs a float and takes part in a grand procession along the city's main avenues in the pinnacle of the celebrations to decide which neighborhood wins. Santo António shouldn't be missed if you're in Portugal in June.

Shopping

Lisbon has a sophisticated shopping scene, from upscale stores along stylish Avenida da Liberdade to smaller boutiques and craft shops in the neighborhoods surrounding Baixa. It also has shopping centers galore and plenty of open-air markets.

Baixa itself, between Rossio Square and the riverside plazas and smaller boulevards, is the heart of commerce in Lisbon, where mainstream chain stores adjoin traditional grocery stores, boutiques, and souvenir shops. The two main shopping streets in the Baixa are **Rua da Prata** and **Rua Augusta,** parallel to each other from the main Comércio Square up to Rossio. However, for more unique souvenirs, you may want to venture further afield to neighborhoods like Alfama, Chiado, and Bairro Alto.

CHIADO AND BAIRRO ALTO
Arts and Crafts
Atelier 55
Rua António Maria Cardoso, 70-74;
tel. 213 474 192;
www.atelier55.blogspot.com;
Mon.-Sat. 11am-7pm

A trove of authentic Portuguese arts and crafts, Atelier 55 brims with handmade ceramics, embroidery, and paintings from local artists.

Vista Alegre
Largo do Chiado 20-23; tel. 213 461 401;
https://vistaalegre.com/pt; daily 10am-8pm

A short walk from the Carmo Convent, Vista Alegre is one of the highest-held names in Portuguese porcelain and crystal-ware, established in 1824. The pieces aren't cheap, but they are heirlooms.

Chiado Vintage

Rua Chagas 17; tel. 926 257 740; www.facebook.com/p/Chiado-Vintage-100057744180004; Mon.-Sat. noon-7pm

Snap up vintage treasures at Chiado Vintage, a trove of unique furniture, decorative items, and art from bygone eras.

Books

Bertrand Bookstore (Livraria Bertrand)

Rua Garrett 73-75; tel. 210 305 590; www. bertrand.pt; daily 9am-10pm; Metro Baixa-Chiado, Green/Blue Lines

Distinguished by Guinness World Records as the oldest working bookshop in the world, the Bertrand Bookstore in Chiado is housed in a beautiful old building clad in traditional blue and white azulejo tiles. Open since the mid-1730s, this wonderful bookshop has several rooms packed with literature from some of Portugal's greatest authors—including José Saramago, Eça de Queiroz, Almada Negreiros, Alexandre Herculano, and Sophia de Mello Breyner—as well as a cozy café where visitors are encouraged to "try before you buy" (the books, not the cakes or coffee!).

Cork

Cork & Co

Rua das Salgadeiras 10; tel. 216 090 231; www.corkandcompany.pt; Mon.-Sat. 11am-8pm, Sun. 5pm-8pm

Everything at Cork & Co, from hats to shoes and all accessories, is made from natural cork. Sustainable, vegan, and cruelty-free, products range from trinkets like bracelets and coasters, which make fabulous souvenirs and are light in the luggage, to backpacks, briefcases, and bowls.

Rutz Walk in Cork

Rua dos Sapateiros 181; tel. 212 477 039; www.rutz.pt; daily noon-8pm

Rutz Walk in Cork is a Portuguese brand specializing in shoes, bags, accessories, and gifts made from cork. Eco-vegan shoes are a standout product.

Casa da Cortiça

Rua de Santa Justa 25; tel. 218 862 378; Mon.-Sat. 9:30am-7pm

Located near the Santa Justa Elevator, Casa da Cortiça (Cork House) houses the best quality cork products, from bags and wallets to home décor.

Clothing

FERN - Portuguese Designers

Rua da Rosa 197; tel. 213 470 208; www. fernandapereira.net; Mon.-Fri. 10:30am-7pm, Sat. 2:30pm-7pm

FERN carries unique and individual items of clothing by arty Portuguese fashion designer Fernanda Pereira.

AVENIDA DA LIBERDADE

Lisbon's most famous avenue, and priciest real estate, Avenida da Liberdade has serious shopping. At 90 m (295 ft) wide and more than 1 km (0.6 mi) long, this fancy street—the busiest in

Lisbon's Best Souvenirs: Cork and Azulejos

cork souvenirs

Two of Portugal's most distinctive products are cork goods and beautiful azulejo tiles and ceramics.

CORK

Once used to create only bottle stoppers for prestigious champagnes, today Portuguese cork has become fashionable for shoes, handbags, jewelry, and even clothing. **Bairro Alto** is the place to go cork-hunting, and **downtown Baixa-Chiado** brims with local arts and crafts.

Where to buy:

- Cork & Co (page 86)

- Rutz Walk in Cork (page 86)

- Casa de Cortiça (page 86)

AZULEJO

Azulejo hand-painted tile plaques adorn walls throughout the city. Many smaller-size replicas of plaques and tiles are now produced as souvenirs. **Alfama** is the place to head for azulejos, with shops offering miniature versions of these ceramic squares.

Where to buy:

- Loja dos Descobrimentos (page 88)

- Azulejos de Fachada (page 89)

Portugal—has fashion's biggest players, including **Louis Vuitton Lisbon** (Av. da Liberdade 190; tel. 213 584 320; www.eu.louisvuitton.com; Mon.-Thurs. 10am-7:30pm, Fri.-Sat. 10am-8pm), **Prada** (Av. da Liberdade 206; tel. 213 199 490; Mon.-Sat. 10am-7:30pm), and **Gucci** (Av. da Liberdade 180; tel. 213 528 401; www.gucci.com; Mon.-Sat. 10am-7:30pm).

With exquisitely patterned cobblestone walkways and magnificent period architecture lining the stately boulevard, enhanced by cool, leafy gardens, it's often compared to Paris's Champs-Élysées. Most buildings along the avenue date from the 19th century, built after the devastating 1755 earthquake that razed most of Lisbon.

Food and Wine
DeliDelux
Rua Alexandre Herculano 15A; tel. 213 141 474; www.delidelux.pt; Mon.-Fri. 8am-11pm, Sat.-Sun. 9am-11pm

Just off the Avenida da Liberdade at Rua Alexandre Herculano is the stylish DeliDelux, stocked with beautifully packaged gourmet products like wine, olive oil, and canned fish, which make great gifts.

Clothing and Accessories
Luís Onofre
Av. da Liberdade 247; tel. 211 313 629; www.luisonofre.com; Mon.-Sat. 10am-7:30pm

Women's shoe designer Luís Onofre built his brand on generations of family shoemaking history;

the shoes are manufactured at a state-of-the art workshop in northern Portugal.

Boutique dos Relógios Plus
Av. da Liberdade 129; tel. 210 730 530; https://boutiquedosrelogios.pt; Mon.-Sat. 10am-7pm

Home to some of Lisbon's most expensive luxury wrist-pieces (the guards at the door might give it away), Boutique dos Relógios Plus sells high-end, handmade timepieces by renowned international names such as Breitling, Bvlgari, Cartier, Montblanc, and Rolex, as well as from brands such as Balmain, Calvin Klein, Omega, Seiko, Swatch, and Tissot.

Perfumes
Otro Perfume Concept
Galerias Tivoli Forum, D, Loja 6, Av. da Liberdade 180; tel. 213 421 472; www.otroperfume.com; Mon.-Sat. 10am-8pm

This high-end luxury boutique sells exclusive and unique perfumes handpicked from around the globe for the national market.

ALFAMA
Tiles and Ceramics
Loja dos Descobrimentos
Rua dos Bacalhoeiros 14B; tel. 218 865 563; www.loja-descobrimentos.com; daily 9am-7pm

Loja dos Descobrimentos is a shop and workshop selling brightly colored hand-painted tiles and ceramics in styles from all over Portugal. Meet the artisans in the atelier and watch as they work on tiles, or paint your own.

Azulejos de Fachada

Beco do Mexias 1; tel. 966 176 953;
www.azulejosdefachada.com; Mon.-Fri.
10:30am-12:30pm and 2pm-5:30pm

Another top place for authentic hand-painted tiles and ceramics with a bright modern twist, Azulejos de Fachada will also take custom orders and ship overseas.

SÃO VICENTE
Market
Feira da Ladra Flea Market

Tues. and Sat. 9am-6pm

Dating to the 12th century, the São Vicente Feira da Ladra Flea Market, which literally translates as "Thieves' Fair," is a chance to experience the sights and sounds of old-time Lisbon. With an eclectic mix of antiques and second-hand family heirlooms, vendors tout everything from jewels to junk. The vast market starts by the São Vicente Archway, near a stop for tram 28, and fills the streets around the Campo de Santa Clara

Feira da Ladra Flea Market

square. While some of the traders have properly laid-out stalls, others simply pile their wares onto blankets on the ground.

CAIS DO SODRÉ
Arts and Crafts
A Pequena Galeria
(The Little Art Gallery)

Avenida 24 de Julho 4C; tel. 213 950 356;
www.apequenagaleria.com; Wed.-Sat.
5pm-7:30pm; free; Metro Cais do Sodré,
Blue Line

The Little Art Gallery is a collective project that occupies a snug space right on the riverside, aimed at exhibiting, informing about, and selling art. In the same vein as The Little Galleries of the Photo-Secession—later known as the 291 Art Gallery—in New York, this funky gathering place mainly focuses on photography.

ALCÂNTARA
Arts and Crafts
LX Factory

Rua Rodrigues de Faria 103; tel. 213 143
399; www.lxfactory.com; daily 9am-
10:30pm; free; tram 15

Less factory, more arty-hive, this historical industrial complex comprises more than 200 restaurants, shops, businesses, and offices under one roof. Converted from an old fabric-production plant spanning 23,000 square m (248,000 square ft), today LX Factory is a hive of cool creativity and a rising tourist attraction. The LX Factory's first floor is entirely dedicated to an ethical market. There is also a food court, and open-plan workspaces allow visitors to see artisans in action. Enjoy the laid-back hipster vibe and grab a drink on one of the terraces overlooking the iconic 25 de Abril Bridge. Live music performances and other events are also staged on occasion—check the website.

Food

Lisbon's food scene is a crossroads of traditional and contemporary, offering everything from street food and vegan restaurants to gourmet market stalls and Michelin-star restaurants. One thing that sets Lisbon apart from other European capitals is value for money.

BAIXA

Bustling Baixa is a hub of restaurants, cafés, and bars, plenty of them arranged around the main Comércio Square, promising people-watching and alfresco dining.

Portuguese

Restaurante Bastardo

Rua da Betesga 3; tel. 213 240 993; www. restaurantebastardo.com; daily noon-11pm; €25

Located in the International Design Hotel overlooking gorgeous Rossio Square, bohemian Restaurante Bastardo serves up classic Portuguese cuisine with an international twist, like codfish with kombu seaweed, along with fabulous cocktails. Have there ever been so many different types of chairs under one roof?

Taberna da Baixa

Rua dos Fanqueiros 161-163; tel. 218 870 290 or 919 847 419; www.facebook.com/ tabernadabaixa; Sun.-Fri. noon-3pm and 6:30pm-10:30pm, Sat. 6pm-10pm; €15

This little gem is the perfect place to sample Lisbon's flavors. With a cozy, rustic-chic feel, the small restaurant showcases regional produce in the likes of shared cold platters paired with handpicked wines, and its signature dish, slow-cooked black pig cheeks in red wine.

Beer Museum & Restaurant (Museu da Cerveja)

Terreiro do Paço, East Wing 62-65; tel. 210 987 656; www.museudacerveja.pt; d aily noon-midnight; €20

Located in Comércio Square, fashionable Museu da Cerveja showcases the finest mainstream and craft beers produced in Portugal. A range of snacks and meals includes famous codfish cakes that complement the brews.

Restaurante Figus

Praça da Figueira 16; tel. 218 872 194; www.tablegroup.pt; daily 7:30am-midnight, €20

Elegant and sophisticated Restaurante Figus is in the

Beautique Hotel Figueira in Praça da Figueira (Figueira Square) downtown. It has a varied à la carte menu and a refined selection of wines. Favorites include a chourciço and morcela sausage platter, steak in Portuguese sauce, gourmet burgers, fish, and pasta dishes. Don't miss the fig cheesecake for dessert.

Restaurante Gambrinus

Rua das Portas de Santo Antão 23; tel. 213 421 466; www.restaurante-gambrinus. business.site; daily noon-midnight; €20-40

Established in 1936, acclaimed Restaurante Gambrinus has a dedicated following for its tapas and seafood, served in a classic setting with polished dark wood and crisp white tablecloths.

Restaurante Cervejaria O Pinóquio

Praça dos Restauradores 79; tel. 213 465 106; www.restaurantepinoquio.pt; daily noon-midnight; €25

The home cooking at Restaurante Cervejaria O Pinóquio is a legendary variety of quality tapas and entrées, specializing in excellent steak and seafood. The decor is clean and modern, using national materials such as marble and ceramics, but the outdoor terraces are charming. Although it's always busy, service is fast.

Varanda de Lisboa Restaurant

Praça Martim Moniz 2; tel. 218 842 000; www.hotel-mundial.pt; daily 12:30pm-3pm and 7:30pm-10:30pm; €25

The name of Varanda de Lisboa

Beer Museum & Restaurant

Restaurant (the veranda of Lisbon) refers to the panoramic views of the Baixa from its location at the top of the Mundial Hotel. It prepares accomplished dishes to match, like flambéed meats and cataplanas (seafood stews). Lunchtimes feature Suggestion of the Day traditional Portuguese dishes, while evenings are contemporary Portuguese specialties á la carte.

Prado Restaurant

Travessa das Pedras Negras 2; tel. 210 534 649; www.pradorestaurante.com; Wed.-Sat. noon-3:30pm and 7pm-11pm, Sun. noon-5pm; €30

Prado takes clean, fresh flavors of the farm and the sea and magics them into contemporary dishes for the table. Housed in a lofty, bright former factory dressed with plenty of greenery, the menu is a celebration of seasonal Portuguese produce, a farm-to-fork concept concocted into dishes such as black pork tenderloin with quinces and chocolate peppers and Barrosã beef sirloin steak and lettuce salad. Wines are organic. Reservations are compulsory for groups of more than six.

Café

✪ Café Nicola

Praça Dom Pedro IV 24-25; tel. 213 460 579; daily 7am-midnight; €8

With a prime position on posh Rossio Square, the landmark Café Nicola epitomizes European coffee culture with its art deco interior,

excellent coffees, and top-notch breakfasts. It was a favorite of poet Manuel du Bocage, who is memorialized in a statue out front. The celebrated café is excellent for people-watching, but prices are steeper than the average café.

Seafood

Solar 31 da Calçada

Calçada Garcia 31; tel. 218 863 374; www.solar31.com; Mon.-Sat. 11am-11pm; €15

With simple and quaint decor that blends into its local neighborhood, Solar 31 da Calçada serves traditional Portuguese food with a focus on fresh fish and shellfish. Choose from a fantastic selection of starters and wines.

✪ Solar do Bacalhau

Rua do Jardim do Regedor 30; tel. 214 016 718; www.solardobacalhau.com; daily 11:30am-midnight; €20

Cod is king at charming Solar do Bacalhau, one of the best spots to enjoy the Portuguese specialty bacalhau. It also serves other meat and fish dishes in a setting with natural stone walls and elegantly laid tables.

Leão d'Ouro

Rua 1 de Dezembro 105; tel. 213 426 195; www.facebook.com/leaodeourorossio; daily noon-11pm; €20

At Leão d'Ouro, dark wood and traditional tiled walls provide an almost medieval complement to rich fish and shellfish dishes such as oven-baked cod.

Appetizers Aren't Free

As soon as you sit down at any table in Lisbon, waiters will almost immediately bring you an array of mouthwatering appetizers, such as a fresh bread basket, butter and pâtés, fritters, and olives and cheeses. Beware—these are not a complimentary welcome gift; the tab is totting up from the moment you butter that bread. Anything you don't want, don't be afraid to politely decline or send back. Always be clear on prices beforehand, as some cheeses and sausages can be pricy, and make sure you pay only for what you eat.

Marisqueira Uma

Rua dos Sapateiros 177; tel. 962 379 399; https://umamarisqueira.com; daily 11am-10:30pm; €20

This small and simple seafood joint is famous for its specialty, seafood rice—a rich, flavor-packed steel rice pot teeming with shrimp, crayfish, crab, and mussels.

International
O Arco

Rua dos Sapateiros 161; tel. 213 463 280; Thurs.-Tues. noon-3pm and 7pm-10:30pm; €15

Hidden on a backstreet, bright, eclectically decorated O Arco serves up a selection of tasty Mediterranean favorites, from spicy chicken curry to flavorful prawn dishes.

Restaurante Cantinho do Aziz

Rua de São Lourenço 5; tel. 218 876 472; www.cantinhodoaziz.com; daily noon-11pm; €15

At popular, family-run Restaurante Cantinho do Aziz, savor exotic flavors from Mozambique in fare such as samosas, crab curry, and traditional Yuca Malaku and Yuca Miamba curries. The atmosphere is relaxed. Sit inside or on the long outdoor street terrace.

Tasca Kome

Rua da Madalena 57; tel. 211 340 117; www.kome-lisboa.com; Tues.-Thurs. noon-2:30pm and 7pm-10pm; Fri. noon-3pm and 7pm-10pm, Sat. 12:30pm-3pm and 7pm-10pm; €15

Established by powerhouse Japanese chef Yuko Yamamoto, whose Lisbon supper clubs were sell-out events, Tasca Kome is a Japanese tavern in the heart of the Baixa. Serving authentic Japanese fare, staples on the menu include miso soup, sushi and sashimi, plus house specials such as fried octopus balls, salmon zuke-don, and parmesan cheesecake.

CHIADO AND BAIRRO ALTO

Bohemian Bairro Alto might be better known for its nightlife, but it doesn't disappoint when it comes to restaurants, with a rainbow of international flavors.

Local Specialties

Ask anyone what Lisbon's most typical dishes are, and here's some of what you will hear:

ginjinha cherry liqueur

- **Salted codfish (bacalhau),** for which the Portuguese claim to have a different recipe for each day of the year

- The ubiquitous **pastel de nata custard tart,** the national pastry; Pastéis de Belém bakery has its own recipe, which it calls pastel de Belém

- **Seafood** features heavily on menus throughout the city, with other popular dishes including caldeirada (fish stew), shellfish, and octopus creations

- **Bite-size snacks** like codfish pasty (pastéis de bacalhau), green bean fritters (peixinhos da horta), and codfish fritters (pataniscas de bacalhau) are also popular, available at most restaurants and snack bars, to be washed down with a cold beer

- Try a **ginjinha cherry liqueur** at its home, the historic A Ginjinha bar in the Baixa's São Domingos Square

Portuguese
Cantinho Lusitano
Rua dos Prazeres 52; tel. 218 065 185; Tues.-Sat. 7pm-11pm; €7
Located on the doorstep of Bairro Alto in the upscale Prince Real area, small and simple Cantinho Lusitano is a family-run joint serving up a colorful assortment of Portuguese tapas. The restaurant also serves as a café and wine bar.

A Taberna da Rua das Flores
Rua das Flores 103; tel. 213 479 418; Mon.-Sat. noon-4pm and 6pm-11:30pm; €15

This long, narrow, typically Portuguese eatery, located in an old greengrocer's store, retains original vintage features such as its door and floor tiles. The cozy tavern is popular among locals and tourists alike, serving traditional tapas of yesteryear with a contemporary twist.

Restaurante Fidalgo
Rua da Barroca 27; tel. 213 422 900; www.restaurantefidalgo.com; Tues.-Sat. 5pm-midnight; €20
A traditional, family-run

Portuguese restaurant founded in 1972, Fidalgo serves good old-fashioned Portuguese food at reasonable prices. All the classics—rabbit stew, fresh fish, octopus, and codfish dishes—are on the menu, along with homemade desserts and an excellent selection of national wines that line the walls of the cozy eatery.

Cantinho do Avillez

Rua Duques de Bragança 7; tel. 211 992 369; www.cantinhodoavillez.pt; daily 12:30pm-3pm and 7pm-midnight; €40

Cantinho do Avillez is part of a chain of restaurants run by Michelin-star awarded chef José Avillez. Informal but upmarket, it serves accomplished Portuguese cuisine.

Specialty

100 Maneiras

Rua do Teixeira; tel. 910 918 181; www.100maneiras.com; daily 7pm-1am; €140

Owned by Bosnian celebrity chef Ljubomir Stanisic, one Michelin-starred little 100 Maneiras serves creative set-course tasting menus based on fresh seasonal produce and flavors heavily inspired by Stanisic's Bosnian roots. The restaurant is divided into three distinct dining areas: The Glass Room, The Dining Table, and The Back Room. Reservations are recommended.

Café

A Brasileira

Rua Garrett 122; tel. 213 469 541; www.abrasileira.pt; daily 8am-midnight; €5

The century-old A Brasileira café is one of the oldest and most famous cafés in Lisbon. The emblematic venue has an air of antique grandeur, with its art deco chandeliers, wooden booths, mirrored walls, and checkerboard floors. It is a time-honored meeting place for Lisbon's coffee-lovers and has a fascinating history, having once been frequented by the city's intellectuals, artists, writers, and free thinkers. A regular, allegedly, was famous Portuguese poet Fernando Pessoa, and a bronze statue of him sits permanently outside the busy café in tribute. Today it is a must-see tourist attraction, but the coffee is still as popular as it was when A Brazileira opened in the 19th century.

A Brasileira

Seafood
Sea Me
*Rua do Loreto 21; tel. 213 461 564; www.
peixariamoderna.com; Mon.-Fri. 12:30pm-
3:30pm and 7pm-midnight, Sat.-Sun.
12:30pm-midnight; €28*

Modern, informal Sea Me pays homage to Lisbon's fishmongers with seafood purchased from the counter to be cooked in the kitchen, in a fusion of Japanese and Portuguese cuisines.

Aldeia
*Travessa da Queimada 32; tel. 213 420
401; https://restaurantealdeiadobairroalto.
eatbu.com; Mon.-Sat. 1pm-2am; €30*

With a focus on traditional national cuisine, this beautiful old-world Portuguese restaurant is a real find for those wanting to sample genuine flavors of Portugal. Aldeia specializes in seafood, although excellent meats and tasty tapas are also on the menu.

International
Flor da Laranja
*Rua da Rosa 206; tel. 213 422 996; Tues.-
Sat. 7pm-11pm; €14*

At welcoming and intimate Flor de Laranja, authentic Moroccan food is handmade by the Morocco-born chef, who is also the owner and the waiter. Reservations are required.

Bella Ciao
*Rua da Costa 10; tel. 210 935 708; www.
bellaciao.pt; Tues.-Sat. noon-3pm and 7pm-
11pm, Sun. noon-3:30pm; €15*

Quintessential Italian trattoria with the traditional red-and-white-checkered tablecloths and

starched white napkins. Italian chef Marcello Di Salvatore brings genuine flavors of Italia to the heart of Lisbon, with homemade classics including spaghetti carbonara, risotto ai funghi, and tiramisu.

La Paparrucha
*Rua Dom Pedro V 18-20; tel. 213 425 333;
www.lapaparrucha.com; Mon.-Fri. noon-
11:30pm, Sat.-Sun. 12:30pm-11:30pm; €25*

Modern meets rustic and meat rules at La Paparrucha, a firm favorite among locals. Almost everything is cooked on an authentic Argentinean grill.

Brewery
✪ Cervejaria Trindade
*Rua Nova da Trindade 20C; tel. 213 423
506; www.cervejariatrindade.pt; Sun.-
Thurs. noon-midnight, Fri.-Sat. noon-1am;
€30*

One of Portugal's oldest and most beautiful breweries, bright and bold Cervejaria Trindade dates from the mid-1800s, when it was the choice for writers, poets, and politicians. Its huge medieval banquet rooms can accommodate groups of up to 200. National and international beers are accompanied by a different dish of the day, as well as typical Portuguese fish and meat dishes like steak in beer sauce.

AVENIDA DA LIBERDADE
Lisbon's chic Avenida da Liberdade caters to every taste and budget, from cheap and cheerful "grill"

restaurants (churrasqueiras) to the latest in haute cuisine and gastronomic trends.

Portuguese
Bonjardim
Travessa de Santo Antão 11; tel. 213 424 389; daily noon-midnight; €12

Nestled on a tranquil side-street, pretty and plain Bonjardim has been favored by locals since the 1950s. It's the place to go for finger-licking, succulent "piri-piri" chargrilled chicken, a Portuguese staple, served with chips and salad.

A Gina
Parque Mayer; tel. 213 420 296; daily noon-4pm and 7pm-2am; €20

This unpretentious little eatery just off the main Avenida serves wholesome, unfussy, authentic Portuguese food at fair prices. Homey inside with a pretty alfresco patio, A Gina serves mains such as grilled fish and seafood, succulent meats, and plenty of fresh vegetables and salad; it's very popular with the locals.

Dote
Rua Barata Salgueiro 37A; tel. 216 027 858; www.dote.pt; daily noon-1am; €12

Boasting a stylish modern brewery concept, popular Dote oozes designer cool. Its menu bridges signature dishes of Lisbon and Porto as well as international favorites. This is where you can enjoy sticky ribs with slaw, a typical Porto francesinha, or traditional Portuguese cod fish and steak dishes, washed down with a selection of great Portuguese beers, in the heart of the capital.

Fine Dining
JNcQUOI
Avenida da Liberdade 182-184; tel. 219 369 900 (Tivoli Forum) or 210 513 000 (Asia-Avenida); www.jncquoi.com; daily noon-midnight; €50

Lisbon's main Avenida da Liberdade is lined with trendy hangouts and fashionable places to frequent, but none perhaps as talked about as the JNcQUOIs. Situated practically side-by-side, the flagship JNcQUOI is located in the upmarket Tivoli Forum building. Expect contemporary Portuguese cuisine with an international twist and fabulous interior decor (mind the dinosaur skeleton in the middle of the room). Its Asian-influenced younger sibling **JNcQUOI Asia** (Avenida da Liberdade 144) is a short stroll down the road, on the same side of the Avenida. Not to be outdone, it also has a (dragon) skeleton—on the ceiling. Reservations are highly recommended for both.

Market
Food Market
Av. Fontes Pereira de Melo 8A; tel. 210 199 258; Mon.-Fri. 8am-10pm; from €5

Just off the Marquês do Pombal roundabout (northeast), Food Market covers breakfast, brunch, lunch, and dinner. The eclectic food hall's stalls tout everything from oysters to éclairs, grilled chicken to smoked fish, to eat in or take out.

Seafood
O Cacho Dourado

Rua Eça de Queiroz 5; tel. 213 543 671; Mon.-Fri. noon-11:30pm; €15

Specializing in authentic Portuguese fish and seafood dishes, O Cacho Dourado is off the tourist track but always busy with regulars. If you visit on a Friday, try the famous codfish dish that has been served on Fridays only for nearly half a century.

ALFAMA

As a hilly neighborhood, it's fortunate that Alfama has a vast range of traditional and contemporary eateries dotting its atmospheric streets, for explorers to enjoy a little rest and some refueling.

Portuguese
CorkScrew Restaurant & Wine Bar

Rua dos Remédios 95; tel. 969 563 664; www.facebook.com/corkcrew; Thurs.-Sat. noon-2am, Sun.-Wed. 1pm-midnight; €15

CorkScrew Restaurant & Wine Bar is a hidden gem. It serves great Portuguese tapas of cheeses, cured meats, and fish preserves, accompanied by a huge variety of fantastic Portuguese wines, many by the glass.

✪ Chapitô à Mesa

Costa do Castelo 7; tel. 218 875 077; www.chapito.org; Mon.-Sat. noon-6pm and 7pm-1:30am, Sun. 7pm-1:30am; €25

Part of a famous circus arts school, Chapitô à Mesa offers fun, flamboyant cuisine alongside gorgeous views of Lisbon. Choose the snack

bar, an alfresco grill terrace, or the elegant restaurant. Menu favorites include grilled shrimp with tropical fruit, and pork cheeks with clams and sautéed potatoes.

Gosta do Castelo

Costa do Castelo 138; tel. 218 870 743; daily 8:30am-11:30pm; €25

The traditional tiled facade enhances the cozy chic-vintage interior of Gosta do Castelo, which serves a lovely array of unusual takes on national staples, with a nice selection of wines. Try the Portuguese cheese platter with mango chutney. Entrées include duck magret with apple in port wine. Gosta do Castelo also has a brunch menu and a snack menu.

Barracão de Alfama

Rua de São Pedro 16; tel. 218 866 359; Mon.-Tues. and Thurs.-Fri. 7pm-10:30pm, Sat. and Sun. 12:30pm-3pm and 7pm-10:30pm; €15

Located in lower Alfama on a quiet little square surrounded by bustling alleyways, small and smart Barracão de Alfama serves up authentic Portuguese cuisine—including quality homecooked fish and meat dishes—off the tourist trail at down-to-earth prices.

Cafés
Mercearia Castello Café

Rua das Flores de Santa Cruz 2; tel. 218 876 111; daily 10am-8pm; €8

Tradition meets cool at Mercearia Castello Café, a funky little eatery and grocery store. Its wood-clad interior harks back to the old days, and its location at the top of the hill near the castle is second to none. The fresh homemade fare includes quiches, crêpes, and sandwiches made from quality regional products—it hits the spot after climbing to the castle.

Café Audrey

Rua Santiago 14; tel. 213 941 616; daily 7:30am-11pm; €12

Adjacent to the main entrance of the São Jorge Castle, Café Audrey is not just a café—it's a café, grill, and bistro bar. An eccentric little place with an eclectic menu, it serves breakfast, lunch, and dinner dishes ranging from eggs Benedict to Goan curry. Meals are divided into four separate menus available throughout the day: Breakfast Menu, All Day Menu, Afternoon Tea Menu, and Evening Bistro Menu.

Seafood
Farol de Santa Luzia

Largo de Santa Luzia 5; tel. 218 863 884; Mon.-Sat. 6pm-11pm; €18

Rustic Farol de Santa Luzia is set in an 18th-century building directly opposite the Santa Luzia viewpoint, near São Jorge Castle. Menu favorites include octopus salad, shellfish açorda (a soupy bread dish), and pork cataplana with shrimp, clams, and chouriça sausage.

International
Restaurante Casanova

Av. Infante Dom Henrique Loja 7; tel. 218 877 532; www.pizzeriacasanova.pt; daily 12:30pm-midnight; €10

Adjacent to the Santa Apolónia cruise passenger terminal, canteen-style Restaurante Casanova has a privileged riverside location with long tables conducive to sharing authentic Italian food. Wood-oven-fired pizzas are the specialty.

Zambeze

Calçada Marquês de Tancos, Edifício EMEL, Mercado Chão do Loureiro; tel. 218 877 056 or 925 200 631; www. zambezerestaurante.pt; daily 10am-11pm; €40

Situated in the heart of Alfama, Zambeze is housed in a restored historical marketplace. The clean and minimalistic interior accentuates the intriguing fusion of Euro-African flavors. An alfresco terrace boasts fantastic views over downtown Lisbon and the Tagus River. You can order a set menu of the chef's favorites for €19.50.

Experimental
Boi-Cavalo

Rua do Vigário 70 B; tel. 938 752 355; www.boi-cavalo.pt; Wed.-Sun. 7pm-1am; €40

Housed in an old butcher's shop, Boi-Cavalo (which translates literally as "Ox-Horse") is indeed a place of experimental fusions. It is where inventive dishes inspired by the local communities shape an ever-changing menu. Tasting menus change regularly, in accordance to the availability of seasonal ingredients, although the overriding focus is on quality national cuisine. Wine pairing available.

SÃO VICENTE

One of the city's oldest and more traditional areas, São Vicente has a more grown-up attitude that is reflected in its restaurants, which offer classic Portuguese and Mediterranean fare and cozy bistro-type eateries.

Café
Bistro Gato Pardo

Rua de São Vicente 10; tel. 218 873 647; Fri.-Tues. 4:30pm-11:30pm; €15

With its exposed stone wall and brick floor, hidden hole-in-the-wall Bistro Gato Pardo is inviting for a snack, coffee, or a cozy meal. Tasty lamb, risotto with fish, and shrimp dishes are favorites.

Seafood
✪ Cervejaria Ramiro

Av. Almirante Reis 1-H; tel. 969 839 472; www.cervejariaramiro.pt; Tues.-Sun. noon-midnight; €20

Established in 1956, authentic beer house Cervejaria Ramiro is a famed institution featured on many travel programs. Expect long queues outside the restaurant. The rainbow of seafood includes prawns al guilho. The prego no pão is a steak sandwich with a cult following, which many eat at the end of meals in lieu of dessert. Wash it down with a chilled beer.

International
Damas

Rua da Voz do Operário 60; tel. 964 964 416; Tues.-Thurs. 12:30pm-1am, Fri. 12:30pm-4am, Sat. 1pm-4am, Sun. 7:30pm-midnight; €10

At no-frills hipster hangout Damas, craft beers and excellent food accompany live music. The menu is scribbled on the tile-clad wall and changes daily. Dishes from across the Mediterranean include smoked lamb, almond tagine with falafel, and seitan meatballs. On weekends, DJ sets and live concerts are held in a small back room.

Beco a Sério

Calçada de São Vicente 42; tel. 218 872 805; www.facebook.com/becoaserio; daily 7pm-11pm; €20

A selective menu packed with simple, clean flavors is what Beco a Sério is all about. Choices are limited, but the menu includes tapas, vegetarian, salads, children's menu, vegan, gluten-free, and fish and meat entrées, with homemade starters and desserts. Quality Portuguese dining, this is a small, family-friendly restaurant located up a quaint alley.

CAIS DO SODRÉ

This waterfront wharf has shed its former seedy image and is now a cool place to eat, drink, and be merry. It's also the location of hip **Pink Street,** which makes it a convenient spot to spend an evening.

Portuguese
Espumantaria do Cais

Rua Nova do Carvalho 39; tel. 210 522 474; www.grupochamp.pt; daily 7pm-4am; €20

Located on Cais do Sodré's famous Pink Street, swanky and minimalistic Espumantaria do

Cais is a marble-clad quayside tapas and Champagne bar. Pop open a bottle of bubbly, order a sharing platter like the popular cheeseboard or salmon tacos, and have a wonderful evening with some fizz.

Vestigius Wine & Gin Bar
Cais do Sodré 8; tel. 938 660 822; www. vestigius.pt; daily noon-10pm; €20

Set in a lofty quayside warehouse, shabby-chic Vestigius Wine & Gin Bar has huge windows and a terrace overlooking the water. A team of young chefs shape innovative flavors into bite-size tapas with Portuguese and Angolan influences. Dishes include calamari with aioli sauce, beef carpaccio, and beef osso buco.

Market
✪ Time Out Market Lisboa + Riverside Market
(Mercado TimeOut + Mercado da Ribeira)
Avenida 24 de Julho 49; tel. 210 607 403; daily 10am-midnight; free; Metro Cais do Sodré, Blue Line

After its concession was taken over by the team behind the Lisbon edition of *Time Out* magazine, this landmark market hall—the historical Mercado da Ribeira, or Riverside Market, formerly one of Europe's most renowned markets—is today among the city's coolest hangouts. Despite being more than 100 years old (it first opened in the 1890s), this market is livelier than ever, with a huge, often chaotic food court that boasts

Time Out Market Lisboa

a vast variety of gourmet stalls showcasing innovative and traditional Portuguese fare. The two-dozen-plus stands are allocated to chefs and restaurants handpicked by *Time Out*'s food writers. The eastern portion of the building still houses the traditional fruit and veg market, which also sells fresh fish, flowers, bread, and souvenirs. It operates 6am-2pm and offers early risers a glimpse of genuine Lisbon market trading. Live music adds to the ambience.

Seafood
Portugália - Cais do Sodré
Rua da Cintura do Porto de Lisboa 1; tel. 938 477 521; www.portugalia.pt; daily noon-midnight; €25

Famed for its steak in Portugália sauce, chain restaurant Portugália, on Cais do Sodré, offers lovely views over the docks and a vast range of fresh fish and seafood dishes that are perfect for a meal by the river.

International
Las Ficheras
Rua dos Remolares 34; tel. 213 470 553; www.lasficheras.com; Sun.-Thurs. noon-1am, Fri.-Sat. noon-3am; €20

Hip and happening Las Ficheras provides five-star Mexican food with great cocktails in a warm, welcoming setting.

ESTRELA AND LAPA

Estrela's culinary scene follows the same feel as the neighborhood: refined and upscale with a pinch of cool.

Portuguese
Churrascaria o Lavrador
Calçada da Estrela 193; tel. 213 961 807; Tues.-Sun. 11:30am-3:30pm and 6:30pm-10pm; €15

A proper local's favorite and aptly called "Farmer's Grill," this modest restaurant serves fresh meat and fish straight off the grill, with hearty helpings of potatoes and salad.

Restaurante XL
Calçada da Estrela 57; tel. 213 956 118; daily 6:30pm-1am; €30

Facing Parliament, chic XL attracts a well-heeled crowd with a fusion of international haute cuisine and old-fashioned Portuguese home cooking. Specialties include soufflés, steaks, and "the best cheeseburger on the planet."

Market
Mercado de Campo de Ourique
Rua Coelho da Rocha 104; tel. 211 323 701; www.facebook.com/mercadodecampoeourique; daily 10am-11pm (until midnight Sat.); €10-20

Lisboetas love to meet at trendy Mercado de Campo de Ourique, a neighborhood gastro market with a buzzing food court that feels both traditional and contemporary. Explore the many different stalls and choose what takes your fancy.

Fine Dining
Loco
Rua Navegantes 53; tel. 213 951 861; www.loco.pt; Tues.-Sat. 7pm-11pm; €160

Each meal at ultra-swanky Loco is a masterpiece. With two different tasting menus, this culinary experience is twice as nice, complemented by little-known Portuguese wines.

BELÉM
Portuguese
Prova - Enoteca

Rua Duarte Pacheco Pereira 9E; tel. 215 819 080; www.facebook.com/ ProvaEnoteca; Tues.-Thurs. 11am-3pm and 6pm-10pm; €10

As the name of this trendy deli and wine bar indicates (it loosely translates as "try"), the aim here is to sample excellent local produce with a good wine. Plates of cured cold meats and cheeses, salads, veg platters, and fish tapas are all there for the taking, to be paired with a careful selection of great Portuguese wines.

Feitoria

Altis Belém Hotel & Spa, Doca do Bom Sucesso; tel. 210 400 200; www. restaurantefeitoria.com; Tues.- Sat. 7pm-11pm; €150 (excludes drinks)

Enjoying on a prime position overlooking the Tagus River, Feitoria is a swish, cool, Michelin-star-awarded eatery renowned for its contemporary take on Portuguese classics. Located in the Altis Belém Hotel & Spa, the creative signature set menus are an exciting culinary journey for a special occasion.

O Prado

Rua da Junqueira 472; tel. 213 642 412; www.oprado.pt; Tues.-Sat. 9am-midnight, Sun. 9am-5pm; €15

Located just behind the National Coach Museum, O Prado is your typical little no-frills neighborhood eatery. Popular among locals, it serves simple and tasty traditional Portuguese food, like grilled meats and fish stews, in healthy doses at affordable prices. Dishes of the day vary, and seafood specialties are great for snacking with a cool drink.

Bakery
✪ Pastéis de Belém

Rua Belém 84-92; tel. 213 637 423; www. pasteisdebelem.pt; daily 8am-10pm; €5

No visit to Lisbon is complete without a taste of the humble, iconic pastel de nata custard tart. It can be found throughout Portugal, but Belém is its birthplace. Pastéis de Belém started making the delectable tarts in 1837, following a secret recipe from the Jerónimos Monastery. The buttery pastry contains a creamy, eggy filling, slightly caramelized top, and a sprinkling of cinnamon. Other fresh-baked sweet and savory treats can be enjoyed in the large seating area, which is always packed full.

PARK OF NATIONS

The modern Park of Nations is home to eateries offering a kaleidoscope of cuisines, most located along the riverfront.

Seafood
Restaurante D'Bacalhau

Rua da Pimenta 45; tel. 218 941 296 or 932 323 009; www.restaurantebacalhau.com; daily noon-4pm and 7pm-11pm; €20

As its name indicates, bright Restaurante D'Bacalhau specializes

Pastel de Belém vs. Pastel de Nata

It might look like Portugal's omnipresent pastel de nata (custard tart), it might even taste like the ubiquitous pastel de nata, but the pastel de Belém is a tart in its own right.

pastel de Belém

HISTORY

While the pastel de nata is found throughout Portugal, the pastel de Belém is local to Belém. History has it that the pastel de Belém's secret recipe emerged in the 19th century from the Jerónimos Monastery.

In 1834, when all the monasteries and convents of Portugal were forced to close, the workers decided to start selling the sweet treats to make a living, in the same spot where the **Pastéis de Belém** bakery is today. The bakery was officially inaugurated in 1837.

TRYING PASTEL DE BELÉM TODAY

Reputedly, to this day the tarts are handmade following the same ancient original recipe that came from the Jerónimos Monastery. This recipe is a closely guarded secret, known only by a handful of master bakers at the Belém bakery, which has become one of the area's top tourist attractions.

There's an old saying that states going to Belém without trying a pastel de Belém is like going to Rome without seeing the Pope, and judging by the queues that form outside the bakery every day, there might be some truth in it.

---

in codfish dishes from across the country, including a platter of four of the most traditional bacalhau concoctions; you can also enjoy a classic fish pasty.

International
Brasserie de l'Entrecôte
Alameda dos Oceanos 43A; tel. 218 962 220; www.brasserieentrecote.pt; Sun.-Thurs. noon-11:30pm, Fri.-Sat. noon-midnght; €24

Next to Lisbon Casino, on the

main Park of Nations Avenue, classy, contemporary Brasserie de l'Entrecôte is a French-inspired steakhouse specializing in delicious ribs and succulent cuts.

Fine Dining
Fifty Seconds
Cais das Naus, Torre Vasco da Gama; tel. 211 525 380; www.fiftysecondsexperience. com; Wed.-Fri. 7pm-10pm; €205

Located on the top floor of the Vasco da Gama Tower, Fifty

Seconds is spearheaded by Spaniard Martín Berasategui, a multi-Michelin-star-awarded chef. An extraordinary culinary experience with mind-blowing 360-degree views over the Tagus, Fifty Seconds takes its name from the time it takes to climb the 120 m (393 ft) to the restaurant in the elevator. Pricy, but an absolutely unique experience. Taster menus start from around €205.

Bars and Nightlife

Bohemian and cosmopolitan in equal measures, Lisbon's nightlife has a different vibe in each part of the city, from the giddy Bairro Alto and atmospheric Alfama to the funky Pink Street in Cais do Sodré and the trendy Park of Nations.

BAIXA

In comparison to other parts of Lisbon, and with the exception of peak seasons like summer and Christmas, nightlife in the Baixa is rather tame. It's more about having a quiet drink at the end of the day than a big night out.

Bars and Pubs
A Ginjinha
Largo São Domingos 8; tel. 218 145 374; daily 9am-10pm
Home to Portugal's award-winning ginjinha cherry liqueur, A Ginjinha is a historical hole-in-the-wall serving tiny glasses of the sweet drink over its sticky slab of marble bartop. Ginjinha is served as a shot, with a cherry in the glass if you ask. Soft drinks and beer are also available. This place is standing room only and crowded.

Hotel Mundial Rooftop Bar & Lounge
Praça Martim Moniz 2; tel. 218 842 000; www.hotel-mundial.pt; daily 3:30pm-11pm
The swanky terrace of Hotel Mundial Rooftop Bar & Lounge has stunning views. During the warmer months, it is a fashionable in-crowd hangout, popular for sunset parties. The views over Lisbon's downtown are worth a visit, but drinks are pricy, and the terrace can get crowded.

A Ginjinha

The George Pub

Rua do Crucifixo 58-66; tel. 960 301 718;
www.facebook.com/thegeorgepublisbon;
Mon.-Fri. 5pm-1am, Sat.-Sun. noon-1am

A good old-fashioned British pub in the heart of downtown Lisbon, The George is the kind of place where everyone knows your name (especially if you're an expat regular) and also has a following for its famous eggs Benedict. Comfy couches and gleaming wooden surfaces lend original pub charm to this top spot for a refreshing pint and live sports.

Cerveja Canil

Rua dos Douradores 133; tel. 218 873 321;
www.cervejacanil.com; daily noon-2am
(opens 3pm Mon.)

A beer-lover's heaven. In this warm and welcoming watering hole with attentive service, you can enjoy over 30 craft beers on tap and over 100 bottled beers, washed down to rock music, accompanied by tasty snacks like Portuguese sausage balls and codfish croquets.

✪ CHIADO AND BAIRRO ALTO

A quaint and traditional part of Lisbon that is sleepy during the day, bohemian Bairro Alto comes to life at night. The cobbled streets are packed with people and cool nightspots, ranging from chic wine bars to historical fado houses and renowned jazz clubs.

Bars and Pubs
Entretanto Rooftop Bar

Rua Nova do Almada 114; tel. 213 256 100;
www.hoteldochiado.pt; daily 11am-10pm

Perched on top of the Hotel do Chiado, Entretanto Rooftop Bar is a fab spot to enjoy a sundowner with bird's-eye views of the Baixa. It's small, so space can be limited.

Toca da Raposa Cocktail Bar

Rua da Condessa 45; tel. 968 759 192;
www.facebook.com/Tocadaraposabar;
Tues.-Sun. 6pm-2am

An ode to the art of mixology, stylish Toca da Raposa (the fox den) is a cocktail-lover's paradise. Only fresh Portuguese ingredients are used to make the drinks, served on the solid marble bar.

Nova Tertulia

Rua do Diário de Notícias 60; tel. 918 505 655; daily 6pm-2am

This popular meeting point in the heart of Bairro Alto is the place to be for shots and beers galore.

Majong

Rua da Atalaia 3; tel. 915 214 803; Mon.-Fri. 6pm-2am, Sat.-Sun. 6pm-3am

One of Bairro Alto's best-known bars, Majong is a favorite among the younger arty crowd, with a cool boho-chic interior, quirky decor, and a huge choice of cocktails.

Park Terrace

Calçada do Combro 58;
tel. 215 914 011;
Mon.-Sat. 4pm-2am

One of the best watering terraces in Lisbon, Park is the place to go for a sundowner, with regular live music and fantastic views of the 25 de Abril Bridge.

Pavilhão Chinês

Rua Dom Pedro V 89; tel. 213 424 729; daily 6pm-2am

Take a trip back in time at Pavilhão Chinês, a sumptuously upholstered tearoom with a web of nooks and crannies spread over five rooms. The walls and cabinets of this popular hangout, converted from a grocery store, are filled with a vast private collection of shiny treasures and relics: mugs, plates, books, and ancient maps. Besides more than 40 different types of tea, the Pavilhão Chinês (Chinese pavilion) also serves wine, beers, cocktails, and liquors.

Wine Bars
The Old Pharmacy

Rua do Diário de Notícias 73; tel. 920 230 989; daily 5:30pm-midnight

The Old Pharmacy is a quirky bar that offers a wide selection of wines by the glass or bottle. Wine bottles now fill the cabinets that were once stocked with medicines. Dim lighting and wine-barrel tables add to the allure.

Artis

Rua do Diário de Notícias 95; tel. 213 424 795; Sun. and Tues.-Thurs. 5:30pm-2am, Fri.-Sat. 5:30pm-3am

Iberian-rustic Artis is the ideal place for long conversations over wine, cheese, and tapas.

Solar do Vinho do Porto

Rua São Pedro de Alcântara 45; tel. 213 475 707; Mon.-Fri. 11am-midnight, Sat. 3pm-midnight; glasses from €2

Directly opposite the romantic São Pedro de Alcântara viewpoint and housed in an 18th-century palace, Solar do Vinho do Porto is run by the Port Wine Institute. It showcases more than 300 different types of port, many of which can be sampled by the glass, including rarer vintages that date as far back as 1937.

By the Wine

Rua das Flores 41-43; tel. 213 420 319; daily 6pm-midnight; glasses from €6

In the heart of the Chiado neighborhood, By the Wine is stylish with high stools and barrel tables. It boasts an extensive selection of well-known Portuguese wines—the entire range from one of Portugal's leading producers—plus some foreign offerings, that can be tried by the glass.

Jazz Clubs
Páginas Tantas

Rua do Diário de Notícias 85; tel. 966 249 005; daily 9pm-2am

Partake in some foot-tapping at Páginas Tantas, a popular jazz bar with live music. The instrument-themed decor and portraits of jazz greats give the club a colorful, contemporary vibe. Rising and established musicians jam live nightly on a little stage in the corner.

TOP EXPERIENCE

Fado
✪ O Faia

Rua da Barroca 54-56; tel. 213 426 742; www.ofaia.com; Mon.-Sat. 7:30pm-1am; minimum €65

Founded in 1947, O Faia is a famed

Wines of Portugal

Portugal has deservedly earned itself a spot among Europe's top producers of quality wines, alongside the likes of France, Spain, and Italy. While it creates a vast range of excellent reds and whites—even most of Portugal's table wines are perfectly drinkable—it is also producer of a number of unique, indigenous wines and spirits.

- **Vinho verde:** The so-called Green wine, which originated in the Minho region, is a slightly fizzy, fruity, crisp young wine that is actually a pale yellow in color, as opposed to green.

- **Port wine:** Exclusive to the Porto region, this sweet, warming fortified wine has a history as long and fascinating as Portugal's. Available in several varieties—ruby, tawny, white, and pink among them—no visit to Porto is complete without a tour of a port wine cellar in neighboring Vila Nova de Gaia.

- **Madeira wine:** A fortified wine from the subtropical island of Madeira, Madeira wine is baked to a thick, sweet consistency, giving it a distinct texture and flavor. It was hugely fashionable in 18th- and early-19th-century Europe and is today synonymous with Madeira Island.

- **Mateus Rosé:** Portugal is also the producer of one of the most famous rosé wines in the world—the acclaimed Mateus Rosé.

- **Ginjinha:** Though not a wine, this cherry liqueur has been enjoyed in Portugal for over a century. Made from the morello cherry, it is one of Lisbon most traditional tipples, served with or without a cherry, sometimes chilled, with a squeeze of fresh lemon, or in little chocolate cups.

Among Portugal's main wine-producing regions are the **Douro Valley** (northern Portugal), **Dão** (central Portugal), the **Alentejo** (lower central Portugal), Lisbon, Tejo, and **Setúbal,** just south of Lisbon. Bairro Alto boasts some of Lisbon's best wine bars, such as the **Old Pharmacy, Artis,** and **Solar do Vinho do Porto.** Lisbon's wine bar scene has flourished in recent years and boasts a sophisticated selection of arty, elegant, and cozy bars that showcase the entire spectrum of national wines—from the most popular to the least-known. These will often be sold by the glass and accompanied by typical tapas, while some bars will even offer wine tastings. Lisbon's wine bars are popular spots for socializing and part of a thriving cultural scene that is enjoying a growing following and interest.

fado house with a cult following; it hosts nightly shows and has a restaurant that serves traditional Portuguese cuisine with a contemporary twist.

Tasca do Chico

Rua do Diario de Noticias 39; tel. 961 339 696; daily 7pm-2am; €15

Unlike other fado venues, Tasca do Chico is more of a fado bar than a restaurant. Dim lighting in this tiny tavern enhances the atmospheric experience. Drinks and typical Portuguese tapas, such as plates of cured meats, are served. There is no minimum consumption fee, but it's cash only.

CAIS DO SODRÉ

Created through a clever urban renewal program, the Pink Street project has taken a part of town that once was a red-light district and turned it into one of the hippest hangouts in Lisbon, with varying ambience along a short, colorful stretch.

Bars and Pubs
Lounge

Rua Moeda 1; tel. 214 032 712; daily 10pm-4am

Expect a packed dance floor at this cozy cocktail bar, where the lineup of live music is the main draw—ranging from bands beginning the night to DJs finishing in the small wee hours.

British Bar Lisboa

Rua Bernadino Costa 52; tel. 213 422 367; daily noon-4am

A time-honored institution dating back to the 1920s, British Bar Lisbon is a warm and friendly haven serving great beers from around the world to a rock 'n' roll soundtrack.

Pensão Amor

Rua do Alecrim 19; tel. 213 143 399; www.pensaoamor.pt; Sun.-Wed. 2pm-3am, Thurs.-Sat. 2pm-4am

A former inn that once rented rooms to sailors and ladies of the night, Pensão Amor is now a lively and bohemian hangout.

ALFAMA

Enjoy dinner and a show with spellbinding fado. Restaurants are intimate and offer traditional Portuguese dining. Many fado houses have a minimum fee that covers dinner and the show. It is customary for spectators to be silent while melodic fado is being sung, out of respect for the fadista (singer) and the accompanying musicians. With livelier songs, however, guests and even the staff join in. Reservations are strongly recommended.

Fado
Sr. Fado de Alfama

Rua dos Remédios 176; tel. 218 874 298 or 963 179 419; www.sr-fado.com; Wed.-Mon. 11am-midnight; €48

Family-run Sr. Fado de Alfama belongs to fadista Ana Marina and is a cultural mainstay, with good traditional Portuguese food and a healthy dose of fado. Guests are welcomed

An Evening of Fado

Enjoy dinner and a show with spell-binding fado. This moving, soulful genre of music can be traced back to Lisbon in the early 19th century, often associated with darkened backstreet taverns where singers, the fadistas, accompanied by musicians with traditional Portuguese instruments like guitars and violas, would entertain crowds with melodic tales of longing and daily hardships of the era, with songs ranging from mournful and melancholic to upbeat and jovial. Some of Portugal's biggest musical stars were fado singers, who, like the great Amália Rodrigues, the Queen of Fado, became revered personalities.

fado venue in Alfama

As fado gained popularity as a tourist attraction, it became mainstream for shows to be preceded by a set-price dinner. Most fado restaurants are cozy and offer traditional Portuguese dining; many fado houses have a minimum fee that covers dinner and the show. It is customary for spectators to be silent while melodic fado is being sung, out of respect for the fadista and the accompanying musicians. With livelier songs, however, guests and even the staff join in. Reservations are strongly recommended. It's not customary to tip the musicians, nor is it a requirement, but if you feel you would like to show your appreciation, then tip them directly.

In Lisbon, the best neighborhoods to see fado are Alfama and Bairro Alto; Alfama is widely believed to be the birthplace of fado, but Bairro Alto is popular for its maze of streets with intimate little fado restaurants and characterful bars.

into the small, cozy restaurant with a friendly greeting. Typical rustic dishes include fish and seafood cataplana, as well as meat and vegetarian options and traditional desserts. The fixed-price menu also includes a carafe of wine. There are only nine tables in this quaint little eatery, so be sure you make your reservation.

São Miguel d'Alfama

Largo de São Miguel; tel. 968 554 422; www.saomigueldalfama.com; Tues.-Sun. 7pm-midnight; €25

Intimate, arabesque-styled São Miguel d'Alfama is famous for its fado and traditional Portuguese food. Inside, the restaurant has a warm, homely feel, like someone's dimly lit front room, with authentic flagstone flooring, brick arches, and rustic Portuguese paraphernalia adorning the walls. The select set menu comprises a handful of meat, fish, or vegetarian choices, all traditional dishes, such as Portuguese-style pork and codfish with cream, rounded off with typical sweets.

Clube de Fado

Rua de São João Praça 86-94; tel. 218 852 704; www.clube-de-fado.com; daily 7:30pm-1am; €40

In the heart of Alfama, behind an unremarkable exterior, famous Clube de Fado serves excellent Portuguese cuisine to the sound of the Portuguese guitar accompanying the fadista. It has a warm, romantic, and almost mystic atmosphere.

A Baiuca

Rua São Miguel 20; tel. 218 867 284; Thurs.-Mon. 8pm-midnight; €25 minimum pp includes dinner, drinks, and dessert

An authentic, classic fado dinner haunt, tiny tavern A Baiuca serves tasty home-cooked Portuguese fare on long tables where patrons sit snugly together. The convivial atmosphere is conducive to a great evening enjoying the magic of fado and new friends.

Parreirinha de Alfama

Beco do Espírito Santo 1; tel. 218 868 209; www.parreirinhadealfama.com; Tues.-Sun. 8pm-1am; €50 minimum consumption pp

Small and atmospheric, Parreirinha is one of Lisbon's oldest and most popular fado haunts. A legendary restaurant inextricably intertwined with fado, it was established in 1939 and is owned by acclaimed fado singer Argentina Santos. Some of Portugal's most famous fado singers have graced the stage of Parreirinha over the years, including the great Amália Rodrigues. Its food is equally renowned, based on typical Portuguese flavors. Mains include monkish rice and roast kid. Fado is sung nightly.

ALCÂNTARA

Situated directly beneath the 25 de Abril Bridge, the **Santo Amaro Docks,** or Docas, have long been one of Lisbon's most popular nightlife spots. A long row of old port warehouses belonging to Lisbon Docks were renovated in 1995 and are enjoying a second lease on life as cool bars, restaurants, and clubs catering to a multitude of tastes—from Italian restaurants to Irish pubs and African-beat nightclubs—flanked by sports courts and street food to enjoy at sunrise. It overlooks a smart recreational marina, and the constant hum of traffic crossing the bridge overhead adds to the atmosphere. Take tram 15 or a train from Cais do Sodré to get there, getting off at Alcântara-Mar. Trains run every 20 minutes.

Bars and Pubs
Quimera Pub

Rua Prior do Crato 6; tel. 917 070 021; www.quimerabrewpub.com; Wed.-Sun. 5pm-late

Fancy sipping a beer inside a cool

300-year-old tunnel? Then this is the place to go! This newly coined brewpub couples great music with great beer, specializing in craft beers—home-brewed and from national microbreweries—as well as the traditional pub grub.

BELÉM
Bars and Pubs
Bar 38° 41'

Avenida Brasília BP; tel. 210 400 210; www.altishotels.com; daily 11am-midnight

Sit and watch the world sail by at this trendy dockside lounge-bar with guest DJs Thursday through Sunday in summer.

Casual Lounge Café

Rua Bartolomeu Dias 148b; tel. 213 019 024; www.facebook.com/casuallounge; Mon.-Sat. 1pm-2am

Chill out with a cocktail, coffee, or glass of wine at this laid-back, arty lounge.

PARK OF NATIONS

Enjoy dinner and a drink in style in this funky new part of town.

Bars and Pubs
Irish & Co.

Rua Pimenta 57; tel. 218 940 558; https://irishco.pt; noon-2am daily

For authentic Irish warmth and good craic, head to the traditional pub Irish & Co., where you'll find a friendly ambience with live music. With its vast open front on the riverside and a pub menu, it's a great place to spend a convivial few hours.

Shisha Tea Food

Alameda dos Oceanos 44301M; tel. 930 679 030; www.instagram.com/shisha_teafood; daily 4:30pm-2am

Shisha Tea Food is a funky Middle Eastern-inspired hookah bar and lounge with a warm Moroccan vibe and exotic shisha (water pipes) and great drinks, including teas and cocktails, and an alfresco esplanade.

Clubs
LuxFrágil Discotheque

Av. Infante Don Henrique, Warehouse; tel. 218 820 890; www.luxfragil.com; Thurs.-Sat. 11pm-6am; cover €10-20

Co-owned by actor John Malkovich, Lux Discotheque is one of Lisbon's most exuberant nightspots, renowned throughout Europe as the place to go to see and be seen. On two different levels, it regularly puts on live acts and DJs. Upstairs the music is mainstream, while the groove on the bottom floor is left to the resident or guest DJ. Outside is a huge terrace where you can watch the sun come up over the Tagus River.

Accommodations

Lisbon is awash with cool and interesting places to stay, from historical townhouses to converted palaces. The Baixa area is central and convenient. Lodging is generally pricy, but there are quality budget hostels and guesthouses.

BAIXA
Under €100
✪ Yes! Lisbon Hostel
Rua de São Julião 148; tel. 213 427 171; www.yeshostels.com; €32 dorm, €140 d with shared bath

Yes! Lisbon Hostel has it all: an excellent location, good service, and budget-friendly prices. Custom-made bunks ensure a good night's sleep, and reception is happy to provide tips on how to get the most out of your stay.

€100-200
✪ Hotel Mundial
Praça Martim Moniz 2; tel. 218 842 000; www.hotel-mundial.pt; €150-200 d

Despite its plain exterior, four-star Hotel Mundial is an institution because its rooftop has a great view. Decor is tasteful, beds are comfortable, and the location is second to none. It is a short walk from Rua do Comércio.

€200-300
My Story Charming Hotel Augusta
Rua de São Nicolau; tel. 211 147 899; www.mystoryhotels.com; €200 d

In an excellent spot just a short walk from Rossio Square and São Jorge Castle, the location here is second to none. Housed in a typical building on the main Augusta Street, the hotel is compact but rooms are quiet, clean, and comfortable.

Over €300
Torel Palace Lisboa
Rua Câmara Pestana 23; tel. 218 290 810; www.torelboutiques.com; €470 d

Located high on a hill set back from the Avenida da Liberdade with stunning views over the Baixa, luxury boutique Torel Palace Lisboa occupies two handsome Pombaline buildings packed with authentic character. It also has a leafy pool terrace, an on-site fine-dining restaurant, and an excellent location to get to downtown Lisbon's main attractions.

CHIADO AND BAIRRO ALTO
€100-200
9 Hotel Mercy
Rua da Misericórdia 78; tel. 212 481 480; www.9-hotel-mercy-lisbon.pt; €130-200 d

Trendy little 9 Hotel Mercy offers contemporary class, a bohemian vibe, and panoramic views from its stylish rooftop bar.

Hotel do Chiado
Rua Nova do Almada 114; tel. 213 256 100; www.hoteldochiado.pt; €170-250 d

The charming Hotel do Chiado is housed in historical former

warehouses that were renovated by leading Portuguese architect Siza Vieira following the catastrophic 1988 neighborhood fire. It is famed for stunning city views from its seventh-floor rooftop terrace and its afternoon tea.

Over €300
✪ Bairro Alto Hotel
Praça Luis de Camões 2; tel. 213 408 288; www.bairroaltohotel.com; €400-500 d

Wedged between bohemian Bairro Alto and trendy Chiado, the five-star Bairro Alto Hotel enjoys a dominant position on the main square and has handsome 18th-century architecture. Within walking distance of shops, restaurants, and bars, the 55 rooms include twins, doubles, and suites.

ALFAMA
€100-200
✪ Solar do Castelo
Rua das Cozinhas 2; tel. 218 806 050; www.solardocastelo.com; €160-250 d

Small, romantic Solar do Castelo is the only hotel within the walls of the São Jorge Castle. Converted from an 18th-century mansion, this eco-retreat with medieval and contemporary style even has specially commissioned furniture to enhance its uniqueness.

€200-300
✪ Memmo Alfama Design Hotel
Travessa Merceeiras 27; tel. 210 495 660; www.memmoalfama.com; €200-300 d

Cool and contemporary Memmo

Alfama Design Hotel is a 44-room urban retreat with a reputation for its chic, clean design, which blends well with the historical Alfama neighborhood.

Santiago de Alfama Boutique Hotel
Rua de Santiago 10 a 14; tel. 213 941 616; www.santiagodealfama.com; €200-300 d

A former 15th-century palace has been reborn as cosmopolitan Santiago de Alfama Boutique Hotel, which oozes authenticity from its tiled floors to its prime location in Alfama. It's one of Europe's most outstanding urban hotels.

SÃO VICENTE
€200-300
Casa dell'Arte Club House
Campo de Santa Clara 125; tel. 968 851 513; www.casadellartelisbon.com; €200-300 d

Housed in an elegant 19th-century building with a typical azulejo facade, this upscale guesthouse overlooks the National Pantheon and combines traditional features with touches of glamour.

CAIS DO SODRÉ
€100-200
LX Boutique Hotel
Rua do Alecrim 12; tel. 213 474 394; www.lxboutiquehotel.com; €100-200 d

Overlooking the Tagus River, the decadently decorated LX Boutique Hotel is an atmospheric 19th-century hotel conveniently at the nexus of Chiado, Baixa, and Cais do Sodré.

Boho Guest House Rooms and Apartments

Travessa do Alecrim 3; tel. 932 648 200; €75-110 d

A stone's throw from the Cais do Sodré train and Metro stations, Boho Guest House gives guests access to modern and spotlessly clean individual rooms, with shared kitchen and bathroom facilities, as well as Wi-Fi.

ESTRELA AND LAPA
€100-200
As Janelas Verdes Lisbon Hotel

Rua das Janelas Verdes 47; tel. 213 968 143; www.asjanelasverdes.com; €150-250 d

A night at the plush 18th-century As Janelas Verdes Lisbon Hotel feels like staying in someone's very grand home, with stunning views from the rooftop terrace.

Hotel da Estrela

Rua Saraiva de Carvalho 35; tel. 211 900 100; www.hoteldaestrela.com; €100-200 d

Occupying an old school building, the 19th-century Paraty Palace, the small Hotel da Estrela blends contemporary with quirky.

BELÉM
€100-200
✪ Hotel Palácio do Governador

Rua Bartolomeu Dias 117; tel. 212 467 800; www.palaciogovernador.com; €150-250 d

Poised and polished five-star Hotel Palácio do Governador occupies the 16th-century Governor's Palace, carefully conserving its original features. With 60 rooms and two pools, it is a whitewashed and manicured oasis of tranquility in one of Lisbon's prettiest neighborhoods.

€200-300
Pestana Palace Hotel

Rua Jau 54; tel. 213 615 600; www.pestana. com; €200-300 d

Feel like royalty with a stay at five-star Pestana Palace Hotel, in an exquisite 19th-century palace with gorgeous gardens.

Over €300
Altis Belém Hotel & Spa

Doca do Bom Sucesso; tel. 210 400 200; www.altishotels.com; €350-450 d

Along the river, the contemporary Altis Belém Hotel & Spa has a modern design inspired by the Age of Discoveries, with nautical themes in all of its 50 rooms, which include five suites.

PARK OF NATIONS
€100-200
✪ VIP Executive Arts

Av. Dom João II 47; tel. 210 020 400; www. viphotels.com; €100-200 d

The stylish and streamlined four-star VIP Executive Arts is within walking distance of the Oriente transport hub, the Vasco da Gama shopping center, the Altice Arena, and riverside nightlife.

Information and Services

VISITOR INFORMATION

"Ask Me" tourist information desks can be found throughout Lisbon, at the airport, and major bus and train stations and monuments. Most are open daily about 9am-6pm. Also available are the main **Lisbon Tourism Visitors and Convention Bureau** (Rua do Arsenal 21; tel. 210 312 700; www.visitlisboa.com; Mon.-Fri. 9:30am-7pm) and the national tourist board, **Turismo de Portugal** (Rua Ivone Silva, Lote 6; tel. 211 140 200; www.visitportugal.com, www.turismodeportugal.pt; Mon.-Fri. 9am-1pm and 2:30pm-5:30pm; Metro: Campo Pequeno, in the northern part of the city).

EMBASSIES

- **United States:** Av. das Forças Armadas 133C; tel. 217 273 300; https://pt.usembassy.gov; Mon.-Fri. 8am-5pm; Metro: Jardim Zoologico (Zoo)/Sete Rios

- **Canada:** Av. da Liberdade 196; tel. 213 164 600; www.canadainternational.gc.ca; Mon.-Fri. 8:30am-12:30pm and 1pm-5:15pm; Metro: Avenida

- **United Kingdom:** Rua de São Bernardo 33; tel. 213 924 000; www.gov.uk; Mon., Wed., and Fri. 9:30am-2pm; Metro: Rato

- **Australia:** Av. da Liberdade 200; tel. 213 101 500; www.portugal.

embassy.gov.au; Mon.-Fri. 10am-4pm; Metro: Avenida

MONEY

In Lisbon, most hotels, currency exchanges, travel agencies, some banks, and even some shops have currency exchange facilities, or use your debit card to make a withdrawal from an ATM (multibanco), which can be found throughout the city. The currency exchange company **Unicâmbio** (www.unicambio.pt) has more than 80 offices around the country, including the airports at Lisbon, Faro, and Madeira, the Rossio train station in central Lisbon, the Cais do Sodré station in Baixa, and El Corte Inglês shopping mall (Av. António Augusto de Aguiar 31).

There is a centrally-located **CTT Post Office** just off the main Praça do Comércio Square (Praça do Município 6; tel. 210 471 616; Mon.-Fri. 9am-6pm).

HEALTH AND EMERGENCIES

- **European free emergency number:** 112

- **GNR Police Lisbon headquarters:** Largo do Carmo 27; tel. 213 217 000; www.gnr.pt

- **PSP Metropolitan Police Lisbon headquarters:** Av. Moscavide 88; tel. 217 654 242; www.psp.pt

- **PSP Tourist Police Lisbon:**

Praça dos Restauradores, Palácio Foz; tel. 213 421 623

- **INEM medical emergency:** Rua Almirante Barroso 36; tel. 213 508 100; www.inem.pt

- **Lisbon Fire Brigade:** Av. Dom Carlos I, tel. 218 171 411; www.cm-lisboa.pt

- **CUF Private Hospital:** Travessa do Castro 3; tel. 213 926 100; www.saudecuf.pt

- **24-Hour pharmacy:** Farmácia Largo do Rato, Av. Alvares Cabral 1; tel. 213 863 044; www.farmaciasdeservico.net

Getting There and Around

GETTING THERE
Air
Getting To and From the Airport

Lisbon's airport is 7 km (4.3 mi) north of the city center. The **Metro** runs directly from the airport to Lisbon; the Red Line runs from just outside the airport's main entrance and connects with the Green Line at Alameda station, which runs to the Baixa and Cais do Sodré riverfront, and ends on the Blue Line, at the São Sebastião station. A journey to downtown Lisbon (€1.80) requires one transfer and takes 20 minutes. Municipal bus company **Carris** (www.carris.pt; €1.85 one-way) runs five bus routes between Lisbon Airport and the city center. **Taxis** can be found outside the arrivals terminal; a trip to Lisbon city center should cost up to €15. Alternately, call an **Uber** (www.uber.com) ride.

Bus

The two main bus terminals in Lisbon are Sete Rios, a Rede Expressos' hub, and the modern

Gare do Oriente, closest to the airport.

The two main bus terminals in Lisbon are **Sete Rios** (Rua Professor Lima Basto 133, opposite Lisbon Zoo; tel. 707 223 344; ticket office daily 7am-11:30pm; Metro Jardim Zoológico, Blue Line), a Rede Expressos' hub, and the modern **Gare do Oriente** (Av. Dom João II, Park of Nations; tel. 218 956 972; Metro Oriente, Red Line), closest to the airport.

Train

Trains run to Lisbon from most major towns across the country, and train travel can be a cheap and scenic option.

The four main railway stations in Lisbon are **Entrecampos** (Rua Dr. Eduardo Neves), **Oriente** (Av. Dom João II), **Sete Rios** (Rua Professor Lima Bastos), and **Santa Apolónia** (Av. Infante Dom Henrique). The Alfa-Pendular runs from Oriente, Santa Apolónia, and Entrecampos.

Car

Two main motorways connect

Lisbon to the country's extremities: the **A1** to the north (Porto) and the **A2** to the south (Algarve). The **A6** is the main motorway from the east. From outside Portugal, you'll cross the entire country from any border point to get to Lisbon. The scenery makes up for any potholes or wrong turns you might endure.

There are two crossings to Lisbon from the south over the Tagus River: the **25 de Abril Bridge,** to the western end of the city, or the newer **Vasco da Gama Bridge**—the longest in Europe—to the Park of Nations area. Both provide stunning views of the city on approach.

Cruise Ship

There are two main cruise hubs: **Alcântara** (Alcântara Docks, Port of Lisbon; tel. 213 611 000; www.portodelisboa.pt), west of the main downtown area (Baixa) and **Santa Apolónia** (Avenida Infante Dom Henrique Warehouse B, Shop 8; tel. 213 611 000; www.portodelisboa.pt), east of the Baixa. Taxis will be readily available from both hubs. A **hop-on hop-off bus** is always a good option to see the essential sights in a short time.

GETTING AROUND

Getting around Lisbon can be cheap and easy on public transport, or expensive if you opt for novelty transport like the city's tuk-tuks.

Lisboa Card

The Lisboa Card (www.lisboacard.org), Lisbon's official tourist pass, includes unlimited travel on public buses, trams, the Metro, elevators, and funiculars as well as travel on CP train lines to Sintra and Cascais; free access to 26 museums, monuments, and UNESCO World Heritage Sites; and deals and discounts on tours, shopping, and nightlife. The cost is €22 for a 24-hour card, €37 for a 48-hour card, and €46 for a 72-hour card. Children's cards are half price. These cards can be purchased online, for which a voucher is given that can be exchanged at main tourist points such as the Lisboa Welcome Center, Foz Palace, and Lisbon Airport.

Public Transit

Single trips on buses, trams, ferryboats, and the Metro generally cost €1.80-3, and the rechargeable **Viva Viagem/navegante card** can be bought at most newsagents and kiosks, stations, and terminals for €0.50. A **24-hour public transport pass** can be loaded onto the card; it costs €6.80 and covers all forms of local public transport (buses, trams, and Metro). Add ferryboat trips to Cacilhas to the 24-hour pass and it costs €9.80, or €10.80 including trains to nearby Sintra and Cascais. Some public transport timetables can vary depending on the season, with hours extended later in summer.

Bus

The capital has an efficient bus service, **Carris** (www.carris.pt), which also manages the city's tram system. It provides good coverage of the city, as well as service to neighboring towns and suburbs, and is inexpensive, with most trips under €2. Most buses run 6am-9pm daily, with the busiest lines running until midnight. Tickets can be purchased from the driver (cash only) or at main transport hubs. Buying tickets from the driver is more expensive than using the Viva Viagem/navegante card.

Tram

Carris (www.carris.pt) operates a network of historical trams and funiculars, a unique way to get into the city's backstreets. Five tram routes carry 60 trams, most of which are vintage vehicles. The star of the show is the famous **tram 28,** which circumnavigates Lisbon's historical neighborhoods Bairro Alto, Alfama, Baixa, and Chiado. A downside is that it is plagued by petty thieves, so stay alert. Trams and funiculars generally operate 6am-11pm daily. Tickets can be purchased onboard from the driver, although this is more expensive than using the Viva Viagem/navegante card.

Metro

The **Metro** (www.metrolisboa. pt) has four main lines—Green, Yellow, Red, and Blue—and is simple to navigate, covering the city's important points. Trains run regularly and reliably. It is divided into two zones: central Lisbon and the outskirts. All main

the famous tram 28

tourist attractions are within zone 1, the wider city center. Single trips cost €1.80. A 24-hour pass that also covers funiculars, trams, and buses costs €6.80. The Metro runs 6:30am-1am daily. All Metro stations have ticket vending machines and manned stations. The most useful lines for tourists are the **Blue** and **Green** Lines, which run through the main downtown area, and the **Red** Line, which connects to Park of Nations and the airport.

Ferry

Commuter ferries chug continuously across the Tagus River between Lisbon and Setúbal, operated by **Transtejo & Soflusa** (tel. 808 203 050; www.transtejo.pt), generally 5am or 6am to 1am daily, although crossings are more frequent on weekdays. Boats get busy during rush hours (before 9am and after 4:30pm weekdays) and depart from three terminals along Lisbon's riverside: Terreiro do Paço, Cais do Sodré, and Belém. The five stops on the Setúbal side are Montijo, Barreiro, Seixal, Cacilhas, and Porto Brandão-Trafaria. The Cais do Sodré-Cacilhas crossing is the busiest.

Commuter ferries are much cheaper than tourist boats, with single trips under €3. A charged Viva Viagem/navegante public transport card can be used to pay for tickets. Crossings provide awesome views of Lisbon's iconic 25 de Abril Bridge and of the city.

Taxi and Ride-Share

Taxis in Portugal are plentiful and easy to spot: beige or black with a minty green roof. Each is identified with a number, usually under the driver's side mirror. There are lots of taxi stands throughout the city at train and bus stations, central plazas, and near shopping malls. Hotel reception desks will call a taxi for you, or simply hail one on the street. The main taxi firms in Lisbon are **Taxis Lisboa** (tel. 218 119 000; www.taxislisboa.com), **Cooptaxis** (tel. 217 932 756; www.cooptaxis.pt), and **Teletaxis** (tel. 218 111 100; www.teletaxis.pt).

Uber cars are also now popular and widely available in Lisbon, giving taxi drivers a run for their money.

Tuk-Tuk

A novel way of exploring Lisbon is to jump on a tuk-tuk. These nifty little vehicles have taken the city by storm in recent years; it's rare to turn a street corner without hearing or seeing one of the colorful three-wheelers buzzing along. They have the advantage of fitting on streets and lanes where cars can't go, and they're cute and comfortable—but they are more expensive than public transport or taxis. Tuk-tuk operators include **Tuk Tuk Lisboa** (www.tuk-tuk-lisboa.pt), **City Tuk** (www.citytuk.pt), **Eco Tuk Tours** (www.ecotuktours.com), and **Tuga Tours Tuk Tuk** (www.tugatours.pt). Expect to pay €55-80 per person for an hour's tour of the sights.

Car

Getting around Lisbon without a car is easy and convenient thanks to the comprehensive public transport network.

Driving in Lisbon can be fast, furious, and overwhelming. Main arteries such as the Segunda Circular ring road, which bypasses the airport, can become gridlocked during rush hour; signage is hit-and-miss (although it's slowly improving), and there are one-way roads to contend with. Lisbon's historical areas are a web of narrow, steep streets that can be daunting to drive, and finding parking, particularly in the busy city center, can be challenging. Most public parking spaces, including car parks, entail a hefty fee.

If you do rent a car to drive in Lisbon, check whether your hotel has private parking (which will entail additional cost), or find an underground car park that offers lower-cost "holiday fees," such as the one in Marquês de Pombal Square.

Hop-On Hop-Off Bus

Lisbon has various companies operating modern hop-on hop-off buses, which are an excellent way to see everything the city has to offer, in a relatively short amount of time. An audio guide is available onboard in various languages to provide an explanation of the city's history and main monuments—although the quality and sound of the narrative can be poor. Due to their—and Lisbon's—popularity, there can be long queues for the buses. A good tip is to first stay onboard for the entire circuit, and then get off at what interests you the second time around. There are three main companies operating hop-on hop-off tours; tickets start from around €20 for 24 hour-tickets on basic routes:

- **Yellow Bus – Carristur:** www.yellowbustours.com

- **Cityrama Gray Line:** www.cityrama.pt

- **City Sightseeing:** www.city-sightseeing.com

The Portuguese Riviera

The coastal area to the west of Lisbon is often referred to as the Portuguese Riviera, because it includes the popular towns of Estoril and Cascais, as well as the Boca do Inferno and the windswept Cabo da Roca, Europe's most westerly point. The Marginal Road, also known as the N6, is a popular scenic drive from Lisbon along the coast, and one of Portugal's most iconic routes. A very picturesque drive, the N6 passes countless interesting sights en route, including museums and forts, gorgeous beaches, and parks.

Highlights

⭐ **Estoril-Cascais Boardwalk:** Spanning 3 km (2 mi), this scenic ocean-front boardwalk is one of the nicest ways to take in the sights, sounds, and smells of Lisbon's most famous coastal retreats (page 128).

⭐ **Boca do Inferno:** The unique shape of this cavernous chasm and the formidable force of the waves that carved it give it its dramatic name, Hell's Mouth (page 136).

⭐ **Cabo da Roca:** Make sure to take a photo when you stand on the windy cliffs of Cabo da Roca—mainland Europe's most western point (page 137).

The Marginal starts at Lisbon's Cais do Sodré docks and ends in Cascais, which at a leisurely drive takes between 45 minutes and 1 hour, depending on traffic. However, the road is generally busy; it is widely used by commuters and tourists, even more so on weekends when the locals head out of the city for a change of pace. As one of the main thoroughfares to the nearest beaches, it can become pretty congested in summer. Luckily, it's possible and very easy to take the train to most of the Portuguese Riviera's prettiest spots and avoid the traffic if needed.

ORIENTATION

Estoril and **Cascais** are located west of Lisbon; Estoril is approximately 25 km (16 mi) west, and Cascais a little further along, about 35 km (22 mi). The beautiful coastal retreats are popular among Lisbon locals and holidaymakers looking for an antithesis to the hustle and bustle of the capital. Many Lisboetas drive to Cascais and Estoril for a coffee and a stroll on Sundays, and flock to their **beaches** in summer.

One of the main attractions is the 3 km (2 mi) **seafront promenade** that runs between Estoril and Cascais. Other popular draws

---

Previous: Cascais; **above:** Cascais beachfront; Cabo da Roca.

123

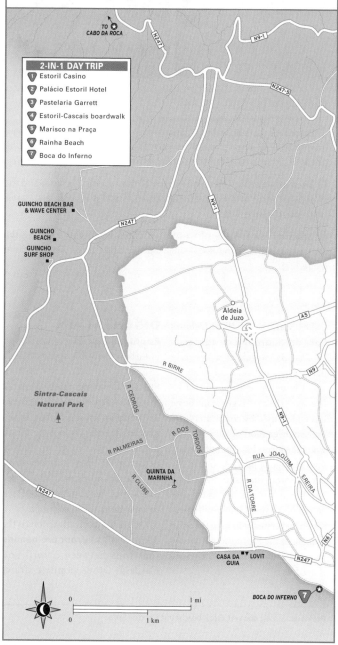

The Portuguese Riviera

2-IN-1 DAY TRIP
1. Estoril Casino
2. Palácio Estoril Hotel
3. Pastelaria Garrett
4. Estoril-Cascais boardwalk
5. Marisco na Praça
6. Rainha Beach
7. Boca do Inferno

TO CABO DA ROCA

N247

N9-1

N247-5

N9-1

GUINCHO BEACH BAR & WAVE CENTER

GUINCHO BEACH

GUINCHO SURF SHOP

N247

Aldeia de Juzo

A5

N9

Sintra-Cascais Natural Park

R BIRRE

R CEDROS

R DOS TORDOS

R PALMEIRAS

R CLUBE

QUINTA DA MARINHA

RUA JOAQUIM EREIRA

R DA TORRE

N9-1

CASA DA GUIA

LOVIT

N247

N6

BOCA DO INFERNO

0   1 mi
0   1 km

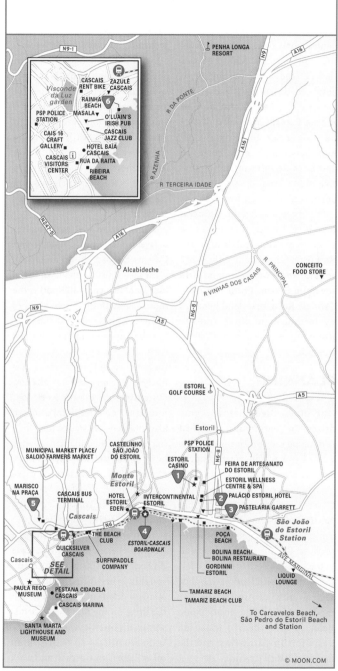

PENHA LONGA RESORT

Visconde da Luz garden

CASCAIS RENT BIKE

ZAZULÉ CASCAIS

RAINHA BEACH

MASALA

6

PSP POLICE STATION

O'LUAIN'S IRISH PUB

CAIS 16 CRAFT GALLERY

CASCAIS JAZZ CLUB

CASCAIS VISITORS CENTER

HOTEL BAÍA CASCAIS

RUA DA RAITA

RIBEIRA BEACH

R DA PONTE

R AZENHA

R TERCEIRA IDADE

Alcabideche

R PRINCIPAL

CONCEITO FOOD STORE

R VINHAS DOS CASAIS

ESTORIL GOLF COURSE

Estoril

MUNICIPAL MARKET PLACE/ SALOIO FARMERS MARKET

CASTELINHO SÃO JOÃO DO ESTORIL

PSP POLICE STATION

ESTORIL CASINO

1

FEIRA DE ARTESANATO DO ESTORIL

MARISCO NA PRAÇA

5

CASCAIS BUS TERMINAL

Monte Estoril

ESTORIL WELLNESS CENTRE & SPA

PALÁCIO ESTORIL HOTEL

2

HOTEL ESTORIL EDEN

INTERCONTINENTAL ESTORIL

PASTELARIA GARRETT

3

São João do Estoril

Cascais

THE BEACH CLUB

QUICKSILVER CASCAIS

ESTORIL-CASCAIS BOARDWALK

4

POÇA BEACH

São João do Estoril Station

Cascais

SEE DETAIL

SURFNPADDLE COMPANY

BOLINA BEACH/ BOLINA RESTAURANT

GORDINNI ESTORIL

PAULA REGO MUSEUM

PESTANA CIDADELA CASCAIS

LIQUID LOUNGE

CASCAIS MARINA

TAMARIZ BEACH

AVE MARGINAL

SANTA MARTA LIGHTHOUSE AND MUSEUM

TAMARIZ BEACH CLUB

To Carcavelos Beach, São Pedro do Estoril Beach and Station

© MOON.COM

include **Tamariz beach** (right in front of **Estoril train station**); the natural pools along the promenade; the many majestic manor houses that dot the main thoroughfares between Estoril and Cascais, including the **Castelinho de São João e Estoril,** a spooky, castle-like house said to be one of the most haunted places in Portugal; and **Boca do Inferno,** an impressive rock formation a short walk northwest of Cascais town center.

Windswept and wild, **Guincho Beach,** a surfing hotspot, is a 15-minute (7 km/4 mi) drive northwest from Cascais, along the **N247 coastal road** or the inland **Rua Joaquim Ereira.** From Guincho, **Cabo da Roca,** mainland Europe's westernmost point, is another 15-minute drive north, continuing along the N247.

PLANNING YOUR TIME

One of Portugal's most scenic drives, the Marginal coastal road runs along the northern side of the Tagus River, west to where it opens into the Atlantic. The road stretches loosely between the chic town of Cascais and downtown Lisbon, passing ever-changing scenery, through charming neighborhoods such as Belém, Carcavelos, and Estoril. It takes drivers on a leisurely cruise past landmark sights, such as the 25 de Abril Bridge, the modern MAAT museum, iconic Belém Tower, the São Julião da Barra fort in Carcavelos, and the majestic Estoril Casino.

Allocate **a full day** to explore **Estoril** and **Cascais.** Due to their proximity to Lisbon, and to each other, it is possible to do both in one day—though Estoril is a popular holiday resort, making it perfect for an overnight stay. From Estoril, you can enjoy a leisurely stroll to nearby Cascais, while Cascais is the better day-trip option if you had to choose just one. Getting to these cities from Lisbon is easy and takes just under an hour by either car or train.

There are several main routes between Lisbon and Estoril and Cascais; by road, the **A5** motorway is the fastest (tolls apply), while the **Marginal (N6 coastal) Road** is the most scenic. Both options can become congested due to the high number of commuters who use them. The Marginal Road is worth the patience and perseverance. It is likely most congested at peak commute times during the week (before 9am and after 5pm) and can also be busy on weekends when the weather is good, as Lisboetas head out of town to the beaches. However, an early-morning drive or late-night cruise of the Marginal offers a certain romantic quality, and should be less congested.

By **train,** the **Cascais Line** has frequent services between **Cais do Sodré** and Cascais, which run roughly every 30-40 minutes. A one-way ticket costs €2.40. Though the drive on the Marginal Road is scenic, it's often easier to take the train from Cais do Sodré; jump off at Estoril (or Cascais) and walk the **boardwalk** between the two. Trains typically run back to Lisbon until 1:30am. At the time of writing, part of the train service, between Algés and Cais do Sodré, was replaced by buses 10:30pm-1:30am.

Both towns are interesting to explore, but it's recommended to spend a couple of hours in Estoril first, in the morning, and to head to Cascais for lunch. Cascais has more to do and see and is a lovely place for a light meal and a spot of people-watching. If you have time to spend the night in the area, Estoril has a romantic vibe, perfect for a seafront sunset or dinner and a show in the **casino,** while Cascais has a lively town center filled with family-friendly restaurants and bars.

Itinerary Idea

2-IN-1 DAY TRIP

1 Take the train (or drive) from Lisbon to Estoril. From Estoril train station walk north, toward the extravagant **Estoril Casino** and its pretty gardens. Have a wander in the gardens and admire the fountains. There is parking available around the casino if you're driving.

2 Opposite the gardens to the east is the famous **Palácio Estoril Hotel,** a luxurious 1930s hotel once a popular haunt of spies and high society; head over and have a look inside, and feel the glamour and intrigue.

3 Indulge in a coffee and a fresh-baked sweet treat at the famous **Pastelaria Garrett,** just down the road from Palácio Estoril.

4 Make your way west to the **Estoril-Cascais boardwalk** and take the 25-minute walk along the seafront promenade to Cascais. Weather permitting, have a dip in the sea en route, or stop in one of the promenade's many restaurants for a cool drink. If you drove, you'll want to take your car.

5 Enjoy the freshest seafood lunch at **Marisco na Praça** in Cascais and explore the city's chic boutiques.

6 Lounge the afternoon away on **Rainha Beach,** a short walk from town center.

7 Later in the afternoon, burn off all the good food by taking a walk up to the **Boca do Inferno** rock formation (about 20-40 minutes), before taking the train (or driving) back to Lisbon.

Estoril

. . . .

Glitzy Estoril is a stylish seaside resort and home to the largest casino in Europe. Beaches are long and spacious, with a series of rocky outcrops and piers; calm, clean water; and a laid-back, romantic ambience. It is a popular escape for families and couples on weekends. Estoril is spread over a lengthy stretch of coastline fronted by a glorious promenade and a string of cosmopolitan restaurants and bars and dotted with intriguing historical properties and lush green spaces.

Estoril's heyday was in the mid-1900s, when it was a playground for the Portuguese aristocracy and European high society. During World War II, the resort's reputation as a hangout for spies gave it a sense of intrigue. This is where Ian Fleming wrote the first part of *Casino Royale*, which launched the James Bond series. Mainstream tourism has stripped Estoril of a little of its elitism, but it is still one of the most glamorous beach destinations in Portugal.

A 3-km (2-mi) promenade connects Estoril and Cascais, and the views along the way are fantastic, with a long stretch of golden sand along a string of historical properties, restaurants, bars, and cafés. The promenade offers a safe alternative to the short drive and is well illuminated at night.

SIGHTS
Estoril Casino

Av. Dr. Stanley Ho; tel. 214 667 700; www. casino-estoril.pt; daily 3pm-3am

The largest in Europe, Estoril Casino is in the heart of Estoril, separated from the coast by sprawling, manicured gardens that slope gently upward toward the glitzy casino building. During World War II, the casino was a convergence point for spies and dispossessed royals. Its colorful history also provided inspiration for Ian Fleming's James Bond 007 novel *Casino Royale*. With nightly entertainment and myriad slot machines, Estoril Casino is the ultimate place for dinner and a show. As well as the main games area, it has restaurants, bars, nightclubs, and a theater.

✪ Estoril-Cascais Boardwalk

The Estoril-Cascais boardwalk (Paredão) is a pleasant 3-km (2-mi) promenade that hems the beachfront between the two towns. Trimmed by bars and restaurants on one side and stunning beach views and the ocean on the other, it is popular among exercise-loving locals who take advantage of its smooth, flat surface to jog and power-walk and use some of the open-air exercise equipment. The promenade is bookended by

viewpoint along the Estoril-Cascais boardwalk

two train stations: the São João do Estoril (a quieter, residential neighborhood adjacent to Estoril) station at the eastern end and the Cascais terminus at the western end. Along the route are interesting historical buildings, unusual-looking mansions, and some of the finest beaches in the region. The entire stretch is dotted with restaurants and cafés, which are perfect spots for a sunset meal, cocktail, or an ice cream, with sweeping sea views. If the weather is warm, make sure to stop at the sea pool in front of a huge futuristic-looking H-shaped tower, just before Cascais, for a refreshing dip. The boardwalk is particularly wonderful on a balmy summer's evening and can get pretty heavy with foot traffic on weekends.

Castelinho São João do Estoril

EN6, São João do Estoril seafront

Watch out for this quizzical cliff-top property, also known as the Little Castle, located along the main Marginal Road just before Estoril. Though not open to visitors, it's reputedly one of the most haunted places in Portugal, and it has an austere, Gothic-like exterior that plays up its spooky reputation. Local legend has it that a childlike ghost holding a doll has been spotted roaming the grounds and cliff tops in front of the property. Urban stories say this is the ghost of a blind girl who fell from the cliffs to her death. With its patterned turrets and oversized pointy battlements, the property is incredibly theatrical and worth a photo.

It is located on the seafront in the small town of São João do Estoril, just before Estoril proper.

SPORTS AND RECREATION

Beaches

Tamariz Beach

(Praia do Tamariz)

Avenida Marginal, directly in front of Estoril train station; no parking; open 24/7; lifeguards on duty during beach season, roughly May-Oct.

A medieval castle overlooks family-friendly Tamariz Beach (Praia do Tamariz), long, wide, calm, and clean but crowded in summer. Facilities include sun beds and umbrellas, lifeguards, public restrooms, and reasonably priced restaurants and bars. Adjacent to the beach is a saltwater pool, great for swimming when the waves get rough.

Poça Beach (São João do Estoril Beach)

(Praia da Poça/Praia de São João do Estoril)

Avenida Marginal, São João do Estoril; limited parking in vicinity; open 24/7; lifeguards on duty during beach season, roughly May-Oct.

Poça Beach (also known as São João do Estoril Beach) in São João do Estoril is a small, sandy beach smattered with rocky patches, along the back of which runs a pretty promenade lined with beach bars and cafés. It is delimited by

Tamariz Beach

two large cliffs, on top of which stand a couple of old fortresses: Forte Velho, also known as Forte da Poça, at the one end, and the Forte de São Teodósio da Cadaveira at the other. This beach is located halfway between the São João do Estoril and the main Estoril train stations, so it's easily accessible by public transport and by car.

São Pedro do Estoril Beach
(Praia de São Pedro do Estoril)
Avenida Marginal, São Pedro do Estoril; open 24/7; lifeguards on duty during beach season, roughly May-Oct.

Conveniently located a short walk from the São Pedro do Estoril train station, this wide wedge of golden sand is not as big as some of its neighbors, but it is just as popular. It appeals to an array of visitors: The choppy surf attracts surfers, while the low tidepools are loved by families. Nestled between beautiful ravines, São Pedro do Estoril Beach is particularly popular among body-boarders and very busy in summer.

Carcavelos Beach
(Praia de Carcavelos)
Avenida Marginal, 15-minute drive from Lisbon along Marginal Road; good parking; open 24/7; lifeguards on duty during beach season, roughly May-Oct.

Carcavelos Beach is a sprawling, popular beach, with plenty of parking on the doorstep, though it does fill up fast in the warmer months. A quick 20-minute train ride from Lisbon's Cais do Sodré station, exiting in Carcavelos, it is one of the largest beaches in the Lisbon region, with 1.5 km (0.9 mi) of soft, golden sands. Carcavelos Beach has excellent facilities, including plenty of sun beds and umbrellas, surf and sports equipment rentals, and restaurants. Carcavelos's array of sport and surf facilities attracts a young, active crowd, as well as families, thanks to its clean, safe waters. The waves are moderately sized for most of the year, except late autumn and winter, when the swells grow and the surf becomes rougher, making it popular among more experienced surfers. At the eastern end of the beach is the imposing São Julião da Barra fort, the largest and most impressive military defense complex in the Vauban style remaining in Portugal.

Golf
Estoril Golf Course
Av. República; tel. 214 648 000; www.clubegolfestoril.com; from €50

Acclaimed 18-hole, par 69 Estoril Golf Course is nestled in the woods above the beach. It was designed by Jean Gassiat and Mackenzie Ross and opened in 1929.

Spas
Estoril Wellness Center & Spa
Rua Particular Hotel Palácio; tel. 214 658 600; www.estorilwellnesscenter.pt; daily 7:30am-9pm

The Estoril Wellness Center & Spa harnesses the natural properties of the local springs for soothing treatments, including whirlpools and massages.

Surfing

Carcavelos Beach, São Pedro do Estoril Beach, and Bolina Beach are all popular with surfers of all capabilities, from learners to pros.

SurfnPaddle Company

Praia da Duquesa; tel. 933 258 114; www. surfnpaddle.com; daily 9am-7pm (may vary in winter)

In Estoril proper, the SurfnPaddle Company offers a variety of surf lessons, stand-up paddleboarding (SUP) classes, organized SUP and surf group parties, and gear rentals.

SHOPPING

Feira de Artesanato do Estoril

Av. Amaral; tel. 214 677 019 or 912 590 249; weekdays 6pm-midnight, weekends 5pm-midnight, June-early Sept.

A nightly summer handicraft fair called FIARTIL, Feira de Artesanato do Estoril, is held behind the Estoril Casino, featuring about 300 artisans working on their wares, plus food stands. The traditional Portuguese entertainment starts at around 9pm nightly.

FOOD

✪ Pastelaria Garrett

Av. Nice 54; tel. 214 680 365 or 914 873 155; daily 7:30am-11pm; €5

Open since 1934, celebrated bakery and cake shop Pastelaria Garrett was once frequented by royalty and remains a popular haunt for Portuguese celebrities. Its displays are crammed with colorful sweet treats. It's busiest at lunchtime, and in December queues for traditional Christmas cakes spill into the street.

Gordinni Estoril

Av. Marginal 7191; tel. 214 672 205; Tues-Sun. noon-3:30pm and 7pm-11:30pm; €15

In the heart of Estoril with views over the bay, cozy Gordinni Estoril has a huge menu of freshly baked pizzas and pastas and is famous for its sangria and caipirinha cocktails.

Bolina Restaurant

Rua Olivenca 151; tel. 214 687 821; www. bolina.fish; Wed.-Mon. noon-11pm; €20

With a prime position on the boardwalk, long-established Bolina Restaurant, founded in 1973, specializes in simple grilled fish, seafood, and meats—and sunset views.

NIGHTLIFE AND ENTERTAINMENT

Tamariz Beach Club

Av. Marginal 7669; tel. 963 833 006; Wed.-Sun. 11:30pm-4:30am

Fashionable Tamariz Beach Club is a popular place to be seen with a cocktail in hand. It has great views over the coast and gets lively after the sun goes down.

Liquid Lounge

Av. Marginal 5579; tel. 914 097 418; www. facebook.com/liquidlounge.pt; Wed.-Mon. 4pm-11pm

Make sure to bring the camera because Liquid Lounge is the ultimate sundowner spot. Located on the Marginal Road just before reaching Estoril, right on the waterfront, the only thing better than the cocktails are the panoramic sunset views. The lounge has a live DJ on weekends.

ACCOMMODATIONS

€100-200

Hotel Estoril Eden

Av. de Saboia 209, Monte Estoril; tel. 214 667 600; www.hotelestorileden.pt; €188 d

A 200-m (220-yd) walk from the beach, four-star Hotel Estoril Eden once hosted grand parties but is now a firm family favorite with 162 rooms. Most of its verandas offer nice views.

Over €300

✪ Palácio Estoril Hotel

Rua Particular and Av. Biarritz; tel. 214 648 000; www.palacioestorilhotel.com; €300 d

Built in 1930, the storied Palácio Estoril Hotel was the refuge of choice for royalty fleeing World War II. Frequented by artists, writers, and spies, it later served as a set for the James Bond movie *On Her Majesty's Secret Service*. The hotel still retains many of its original features, decor, and beautiful gardens.

Palácio Estoril Hotel

Intercontinental Estoril

Av. Marginal 8023; tel. 218 291 100; www. estorilintercontinental.com; €410 d

The imposing modern, glass-fronted Intercontinental Estoril stands out from the coastal landscape. All rooms have floor-to-ceiling sliding doors and private balconies, making the most of the views from its prime position midway between Estoril and Cascais.

INFORMATION AND SERVICES

- **PSP police station:** just behind Estoril Casino; tel. 214 646 700; www.psp.pt
- **Main post office:** Rua 9 de Abril 371; tel. 214 649 977

GETTING THERE AND AROUND

A lovely and safe 3-km (2-mi) seafront promenade connects Estoril to Cascais, providing an enjoyable walk between the two. The town of Estoril is easily covered on foot.

Car

Estoril is a 25-km (16-mi) drive west of Lisbon. The easiest and fastest route (20 minutes) is the **A5** motorway, which has tolls. The scenic **Marginal coastal road (N6)** is toll-free but takes a little longer (about 45 minutes) and gets busy at commuter rush hours and on weekends. There are several car parks in Estoril, as well as parking along streets, mostly paid. Main spots include car parks by the beach and casino.

Train

The train is the quickest, easiest, and most straightforward way of traveling between Lisbon, Estoril, and Cascais. **CP trains** (tel. 707 210 220; www.cp.pt) run about every half hour from **Lisbon's Cais do Sodré station** 36 minutes along the coast to the **São João do Estoril Station** (€2.40 one way) and continue to Cascais. Trains are less frequent after dark. There are four stations in Estoril: **São Pedro do Estoril, São João do Estoril, Estoril** (for the town, the casino, and Tamariz Beach), and **Monte Estoril** (halfway between Estoril and Cascais).

Bus

There is no direct bus route from Lisbon to Estoril. Most buses from Lisbon will be operated by **Carris Metropolitana** (tel. 210 418 800; www.carrismetropolitana.pt) and travel to the area's main hub, Cascais, from where a local Mobi Cascais bus runs to Estoril. Some bus lines from Lisbon might pass through Estoril en route to Cascais.

Municipal transport company **Mobi Cascais** (tel. 800 203 186; https://mobi.cascais.pt) operates over 40 different routes, extensively covering the entire Estoril-Cascais region, including between Estoril and Cascais (lines M07 and M12), although the route takes a long way round. Day tickets usually cost around €2 one-way, bought on board.

Cascais

Perched on the western tip of the coastline, cosmopolitan little Cascais (kash-KAIZH), with its picturesque bay and elegant marina, is one of Lisbon's wealthiest suburbs. King Luís I of Portugal made the seaside hamlet his summer home in the 1870s, and it has been a magnet for the rich and famous ever since. Despite hosting some of the most exclusive resorts in the country, Cascais maintains the charm of a fishing village.

On weekends, city dwellers drive the scenic Marginal coast road from Lisbon to Cascais to enjoy people-watching in its cafés and bars. Just north of town is windswept Guincho Beach, popular among surfers. A beachside promenade connects to nearby Estoril, perfect for an after-lunch or evening stroll.

SIGHTS
Santa Marta Lighthouse and Museum
(Farol Museu de Santa Marta)

Praceta Farol; tel. 214 815 383; www. cascais.pt; Tues.-Sun. 10am-1pm and 2pm-6pm (closes 5pm Sat.-Sun.); €5

Built in 1868, the distinctive

Cascais's Best Views

Cabo da Roca

The Cascais coastline has some of the most dramatic and inspiring scenery in the country, from romantic twinkling lights, sea, and stars, to awe-inducing waves and cliffs.

- **Estoril-Cascais Boardwalk:** Join the locals for some power-walking or enjoy a romantic stroll as you take in the scenery of the stunning Estoril-Cascais coastline and beaches that stretch out along the boardwalk. This is a particularly lovely walk at dusk or dawn (page 128).

- **Boca do Inferno:** Admire the enormity of the coast and the vastness of the Atlantic from this uniquely shaped rock formation (page 136).

- **Guincho Beach:** The rugged dunes and rolling waves of wind-battered Guincho give this stretch of coast a formidable landscape, perfect for an invigorating stroll (page 138).

- **Cabo da Roca:** Who doesn't love the novelty of being able to say they have stood on the westernmost point of mainland Europe? And the coastal and ocean views are just as dramatic (page 137).

blue-and-white-striped Santa Marta lighthouse peers over Cascais Marina. Located to the south of Cascais center, it is a beacon for sailors around the bay. The quadrangular tower stands 8 m (26 ft) tall and houses an interesting little museum in a neighboring building dedicated to lighthouse history. The views over Cascais from the top of the tower are fantastic, but it can be climbed only on Wednesdays.

Paula Rego Museum
(Casa das Histórias Paula Rego)

Avenida da República 300; tel. 214 826 970; www.casadashistoriaspaularego.com; Tues.-Sun. 10am-6pm; €5

An intriguing building dedicated to one of Portugal's most famous and divisive current artists, the Paula Rego Museum was designed by acclaimed Portuguese architect Eduardo Souto de Moura at the artist's personal request. Paula Rego is a Portuguese-born visual artist best known for her thought-provoking storybook-based paintings and prints, whose descriptions range from disturbing to brilliant. Inaugurated in 2009, the ochre-red, pyramid-like building sits in stark contrast with its azure, palm-tree-lined, Riviera-like surroundings.

Consisting of four wings, comprising permanent collections and temporary exhibitions, it also has an auditorium, a café, and a gift shop; the collection includes 15 paintings by Rego's late husband, Victor Willing.

✪ Boca do Inferno

1.5 km (1 mi) west of Cascais town

The dramatically named Boca do Inferno (Hell's Mouth) is a striking rock formation carved by relentless tides. After the ceaseless pounding caused the original cave to give way, it left behind an intriguing rock formation in the shape of a grotto and a large archway. Stunning coastal views can be enjoyed from the paths up and down the cliff. In summer, when

Boca do Inferno

⭐ Cabo da Roca

Cabo da Roca lighthouse

For invigorating sea air, stand on mainland Europe's most westerly point at Cabo da Roca, flanked by gigantic granite boulders and dramatic vertical cliffs that drop 100 m (328 ft) to the Atlantic. A solitary rock monument marks the spot with a crucifix and an engraved quote from Portugal's greatest poet, Luís de Camões, who declared in his epic *Os Lusíadas* that this is where "land ends and sea begins." A short walk away, Portugal's first purpose-built **lighthouse** has a **gift shop** that offers certificates confirming that visitors set foot on the western edge of Europe. Pack a jacket; this promontory is blustery and cold.

GETTING THERE AND AROUND

By **car**, Cabo da Roca is 40 km (25 mi) west of **Lisbon,** 15 km (9.3 mi) north of **Cascais.** The drive takes around 25 minutes following the **N247** road.

Lisbon **bus** company Carris Metropolitana (tel. 210 418 800; www. carrismetropolitana.pt) has a direct service (1624) which runs roughly hourly from **Cascais** to Cabo da Roca. The journey takes just over half an hour and costs about €4 one-way. Tickets can be bought from the driver.

the seas are calmer, the translucent turquoise water laps gently around the formation's base. In winter, huge waves lash the rock and cliffs—at times the spray from the crashing waves can dwarf the cliffs themselves. It's about 1.5 km (1 mi) west of Cascais town, roughly a half-hour stroll along the coast. A scattering of cafés and market stalls selling souvenirs and gifts can be found here. You'll probably need around an hour to walk around the site, admire the views and the waves crashing against the cliffs, take a few photos, and enjoy

Guincho Beach

Guincho Beach

Seven km (4.3 mi) northwest of Cascais, rugged and windswept Guin-cho Beach (Praia do Guincho) is unbridled, with vast coastal dunes that make the landscape almost desolate. At 800 m (0.5 mi) long, Guincho faces straight out into the Atlantic, meaning waves and winds can be powerful and the water is significantly cooler than elsewhere along the Estoril-Cascais coast. The untamed beach is a popular location for in-ternational surfing competitions, plus there are a handful of surf rental outfits and excellent seafood restaurants on hand. It falls within Sintra-Cascais Natural Park, and Guincho's beautiful white sand dunes sit in

a coffee or an ice cream from one of the nearby cafés.

There are a number of routes to walk from Cascais town center to Boca do Inferno, which all gener-ally take 20-40 minutes (depending on the pace). The most enjoyable is perhaps along the mostly flat **Avenida Rei Humberto II de Itália,** a seaside route that offers delight-ful ocean views as you walk past Cascais marina and lighthouse. You can also **bike** along the cycle path there, or take a cab.

Casa da Guia
(Guia House)

Avenida Nossa Senhora do Cabo 101; tel. 214 843 215; http://casadaguiacascais. com; 10am-7pm Oct.-Apr; 10am-8pm May-Sept.; free

A 30-minute walk from Cascais town center, this 19th-century manor house is surrounded by 2 hectares (5 acres) of lovely gardens. Within the walls of the historical mansion are arts and crafts stalls, novelty shops, cafés and restaurants, and glorious ocean views, which stark contrast with the deep green carpet that covers the rolling hills of the Sintra mountain range.

For those who are planning to spend a morning, afternoon, or even a full day here, the beach has good facilities, including public showers and toilets, beach bars, restaurants, and surf shops. There is plenty of beach-side parking, and a mostly flat cycle path runs 10 km (6 mi) between Cascais and Guincho.

SURFING LESSONS AND RENTALS

Guincho Surf Shop (Praia do Guincho Estalagem Muchaxo; tel. 214 850 286; www.guinchosurfshop.com; daily 9am-6pm), right on the beach, provides everything from lessons to equipment rentals.

Situated just 50 m (55 yds) from the beach, the **Guincho Beach Bar & Wave Center** (tel. 214 647 013 or 918 500 041; www.bardoguincho.pt/en/wave-center; daily 9am-late) covers a multitude of needs. It offers lockers, board and equipment rentals, a surf school, a shop that stocks equipment and beachwear, and changing rooms with hot showers.

GETTING THERE AND AROUND

By **car,** Guincho is a 15-minute drive northwest from Cascais, following the Rua Joaquim Ereira road or the N247 coastal road.

Arrive by **bus** on the municipal MobiCascais network (tel. 800 203 186; https://mobi.cascais.pt). Lines M05, M15, and M43 run between Cascais (from the main terminal) and Guincho at least once an hour. Tickets cost about €2.

Alternately, rent a **bicycle** in Cascais from a shop such as the **Cascais Rent Bike** (Rua da Palmeira 39A; tel. 935 292 193; www.rentbike.pt; daily 9am-9pm) to ride the scenic 5-km (3-mi) cycle path from Cascais to Guincho.

altogether makes it worth spending an hour or two in Casa da Guia. There is limited parking on the road outside the mansion, which runs between Cascais and Guincho.

TOP EXPERIENCE

BEACHES

Ribeira Beach

(Praia da Ribeira)

Passeio de Dom Luis I

Cascais's main beach, Praia da Ribeira, also often referred to as Praia dos Pescadores (Fishermen's Beach), is a charming little chunk of sand directly in front of the main town center. Overlooking Cascais's marina and docks, the beach can get pretty crowded in summer and on weekends, but there are plenty of parking lots in the vicinity. The water is very calm and cool, and the beach is just a short walk from the Cascais train station.

Rainha Beach
(Praia da Rainha)
Beco da Praia da Rainha
Just before Cascais's main Ribeira Beach, heading west from Estoril to Cascais, is Rainha Beach, a small, clean, bay-like beach with crystal-line waters and soft sands studded with rock formations. Sun beds and umbrellas are available to the pub-lic to rent for around €20 per day. The beach is a 50-m (150-ft) walk to Cascais high street.

SPORTS AND RECREATION
Sailing
Cascais Marina
Casa de São Bernardo; tel. 214 824 800; www.marinacascais.com
With a capacity for several hundred vessels, Cascais Marina regularly hosts sailing competitions and in-ternational events. It's also home to elegant restaurants and boutiques.

Surfing
The number one spot in this area for all types of surfing is rugged, windswept **Guincho Beach** (page 138), a short drive from Cascais on Portugal's west coast.

Quicksilver Cascais
Rua Frederico Arouca; tel. 966 250 339; www.quiksilver.pt; daily 10am-7pm
A short walk from Estoril to Cascais, the Quicksilver Cascais store over-looks Cascais's Ribeira beach. It stocks clothing for men, women, and children, as well as sports items and surf gear and equipment.

Cycling
The **MobiCascais sustainable public mobility network** (https://mobi.cascais.pt/servicos/bike-sharing) operates an eco-friendly bicycle- and scooter-sharing system with a dozen stations and five main kiosks in Cascais, one of which is by the train station. Traditional or electric bikes or scooters can be rented, all year round, usable 7am-8pm, with prices starting from €2 per hour.

Cascais Rent Bike
Rua da Palmeira 39A; tel. 935 292 193; www.rentbike.pt; daily 9am-9pm; rentals from €15
Cascais Rent Bike offers city bikes for a relaxing ride on the cycle path. Mountain bikes (from €50) are also available. All rentals include a hel-met and bike lock.

Ciclovia do Guincho
Enjoy one of Cascais's most pop-ular bike rides, a 10-km (6-mi) round-trip along a flat and smooth purpose-made cycle path between Cascais and the stunning surfing beach of Praia de Guincho. It's an enjoyable half-day activity, taking in dramatic coastline, cliffs, beau-tiful beaches, and numerous inter-esting sights such as the **Boca do Inferno** and **Casa da Guia.** Stop at Guincho Beach for a fresh seafood lunch at the swanky beach-shack-chic **Porto Santa Maria Restaurant** (Estrada do Guincho; tel. 214 879 450; www.portosantamaria.com; daily noon-11pm; €60).

Golf

Penha Longa Resort

Estrada da Lagoa Azul Sintra Linhó; tel. 219 249 031; www.penhalonga.com/en/golf; €50-91 depending on season

The Penha Longa resort is home to one of Europe's top 30 golf courses, the 18-hole Atlantic Championship course with rolling greens, world-class facilities, and the Sintra Mountains as a backdrop.

Quinta da Marinha

Rua do Clube; tel. 214 860 100; www. quintadamarinha.com; from €87

Quinta da Marinha is the site of an 18-hole, par 71 course designed by Robert Trent Jones, with a different challenge on every hole and amazing views over the mountains and the Atlantic.

SHOPPING

The lovely pedestrian street **Rua da Raita** is Cascais's main shopping street. It's a pleasant, pedestrianized, cobbled street with a distinctive black and white wavy pattern, lined with European fashion boutiques and the obligatory tourist souvenir shops.

Markets

Every Saturday and Sunday, **antiques and handicrafts fairs** are held in the **Visconde da Luz garden** in the heart of the town center and at nearby **Casa da Guia** (Av. Nossa Senhora do Cabo 101; tel. 214 843 215) in a 19th-century mansion on the road from Cascais to Guincho Beach, a 2-km (1.3-mi) walk west of town that takes about 30 minutes.

Visconde da Luz Garden Antique Fair

Visconde da Luz Garden, Av. dos Combatentes da Grande Guerra; Wed. only 9am-8pm

Soak up the sights, sounds, and smells of yesteryear at this bustling antique market brimming with interesting paraphernalia and collectors' items, from silverware to books and vinyl records.

Saloio Farmers Market/ Municipal Market Place

Rua Padre Moisés da Silva 29, Municipal Market Place; tel. 214 825 000; Wed. and Sat. 6:30am-2pm

Get your fill of tasty fresh produce or pack for a picnic at the Saloio Famers Market, which showcases the best regional delicacies, like cured meats and cheeses.

Zazulê Cascais

Avenida Valbom 28B; tel. 915 075 507; https://zazuletiles.com; daily 10am-8pm

Have a happy holiday snap or your favorite photo printed onto a traditional Portuguese azulejo tile for a unique and personalized memento.

Cais 16 Craft Gallery

Rua Afonso Sanches 16; tel. 214 833 141; www.facebook.com/cais16.craftgallery; daily 10am-10pm

A great little shop to pick up a made-in-Portugal souvenir, Cais 16 Craft Gallery is packed with typical handmade arts and crafts of all sorts and sizes to take home, from quirky ceramics to cork and wood items, fragrances, and tinned preserves.

Saloio Farmers Market/Municipal Market Place

FOOD

Masala

Rua Frederico Arouca 288; tel. 214 865 334; www.restaurantemasala.pt; daily 11:30am-midnight; €15

Time-honored Indian restaurant Masala is a little jewel with vibrant decor to match the food. Long popular among the locals, the extensive menu features authentic Indian staples and specialties, served in a cozy and exotic ambience.

✪ Marisco na Praça

Rua Padre Moisés da Silva 34; tel. 214 822 130; daily noon-midnight; €20

Don't miss the Marisco na Praça for old-fashioned seafood. In the town center, in a busy market, this no-frills marisqueira is both market stall and eatery, offering fresh catch. Have the seafood cooked here and served at the table.

LOVit

Av. Nossa Senhora do Cabo 101, Guincho; tel. 214 862 230; www.restaurantelovit. com; daily 12:30pm-11pm; €25

Trendy sushi restaurant LOVit has visually stunning delicacies served overlooking the sea from the Casa da Guia cliffs, a short stroll west of Cascais center.

Conceito Food Store

Rua Pequena; tel. 218 085 281; www. conceitofoodstore.pt; Tues.-Sat. 7:30pm-11pm; set tasting menus from €64

Traditional Portuguese cuisine is given a modern overhaul at Conceito Food Store, an in-demand restaurant on the outskirts of town with minimalist decor. Products from local suppliers are transformed into contemporary masterpieces. Taster menus add to the gastronomic experience.

BARS AND NIGHTLIFE

Cascais Jazz Club

Largo Cidade da Vitória 36; tel. 962 773 470; www.facebook.com/cascaisjazzclub; Wed.-Sun. 8:30pm-2am

This surprisingly agreeable little jazz house has live jazz and blues sessions every night from Wednesday to Sunday to get those feet tapping.

O'Luain's Irish Pub

Rua da Palmeira 4; tel. 214 861 627; www.facebook.com/oluainscascais; Mon.-Tues. 4pm-1am, Wed.-Sun. noon-4pm

There's always good craic at this typical Irish pub in the heart of old town Cascais, just back from the main beach. With live music on Fridays, Saturdays, and Sundays, it's a popular hangout among expats and holidaymakers.

The Beach Club

Alameda Duquesa de Palmela 29a; tel. 913 272 605; Beach Club daily 10am-8pm, Cocktail Bar Wed.-Mon. 7pm-midnight

A popular hangout by the sea, The Beach Club is located on the boardwalk, just coming in to Cascais, on Duquesa Beach. It's a scenic spot for a refreshing drink after a pleasant walk along the boardwalk, or for a nice lunch or dinner.

Crow's Bar

Tv. da Misericórdia 1; 967 093 023; www.facebook.com/crowsbarcascais; daily 4pm-1:30am

Small with a cozy pub feel, Crow's Bar is a favorite meeting spot for groups of friends, visitors, and locals to enjoy a beer or cocktail to the sound of good old-fashioned rock. The bar also screens all major international sports matches.

ACCOMMODATIONS
Over €300

✪ Hotel Baía Cascais

Av. Marginal; tel. 214 831 033; www.hotelbaia.com; €230 d

In the heart of Cascais, on the beachfront, the large three-star Hotel Baía Cascais offers a first-rate location at accessible prices. Ideal for families or groups, it has 113 rooms, 66 of which have sea-view verandas.

Pestana Cidadela Cascais

Av. Dom Carlos I, tel. 214 814 300; www.pestana.com; €250-350 d

Luxury hotel Pestana Cidadela Cascais, converted from a 16th-century fortress, is perched on an elevated citadel wall overlooking Cascais Marina. Its exterior is centuries old, but inside, the petite five-star hotel is chic and contemporary. A short walk into Cascais town center, it offers complimentary breakfast and round-the-clock room service.

INFORMATION AND SERVICES

- **PSP police station:** Rua Afonso Sanches 26; tel. 214 814 060; www.psp.pt

- **Cascais Visitors Center:** Praça 5 de Outubro; tel. 215 870 256 or 912 034 214; daily 10am-2pm and 3pm-7pm

- **Main post office:** Av. Ultramar 2; tel. 214 827 281

GETTING THERE AND AROUND

Once you arrive, compact Cascais itself is easily covered on foot.

Car

Cascais is 35 km (22 mi) west of Lisbon's city center. The two main routes are the **A5** motorway, which has tolls, or the more scenic but often much busier **Marginal coastal road (N6),** which runs parallel to the A5, passing pine-tree countryside, luxury villas, and old forts. On a good day, both routes take 30 minutes. With traffic, the Marginal can crawl, but the scenery is lovely. It's busiest at rush hour on weekdays and on weekends in good weather.

Train

During the day, **CP trains** (tel. 707 210 220; www.cp.pt) run approximately every 30 minutes from the **Cais do Sodré** station in Lisbon along the coast to Cascais (€2.40 one way). The journey takes approximately 40 minutes. Trains are less frequent after dark but still run until around 1:30am. The **train station** in Cascais is on Largo da Estação, a 10-minute stroll east of the town center.

The CP train on the Lisbon-Cascais line runs frequently and is the quickest way to travel between Cascais and **Estoril's** seafront station. The journey takes just 3 minutes, and a one-way ticket (€1.45) can be bought at the station from machines or the ticket office. Cascais is also a pleasant 3-km (2-mi) walk west from Estoril along a lovely flat seafront promenade with lots to see—tidepools, cafés and bars, and quirky old houses.

Bus

Lisbon bus company **Carris Metropolitana** (tel. 210 418 800; www.carrismetropolitana.pt) operates services (1625 and 1623) from Lisbon to Cascais, but might require a change of bus en route. These buses run roughly every 20 minutes from Oriente station and cost about €3.

Once in Cascais, the best way to get around by bus is using the local bus service operated by municipal transport company **Mobi Cascais** (tel. 800 203 186; https://mobi.cascais.pt). Mobi Cascais operates over 40 different routes, extensively covering the entire municipality, including to destinations such as Estoril and Guincho. Buy your tickets on board. Day tickets usually cost around €2 one-way.

Sintra

If Sintra had to be summed up in just one word, it would be "magical"—a whimsical resort nestled amidst the beautiful, hilly landscape of the Sintra Mountains. Inland from windy Cabo da Roca and Guincho Beach, this fairytale forest town has a misty microclimate all its own, cooled by the Atlantic breeze that comes rolling up the plains from the coast, made fragrant by the umbrella pine trees that cover the hills. This cooler climate made Sintra a popular spot for summer residences for Europe's aristocrats

Highlights

⭐ **Pena Palace:** The Disney-like Pena Palace, high on a hill overlooking Sintra, is one of Portugal's most recognizable and popular attractions (page 150).

⭐ **Moorish Castle:** The ruins of sturdy Moorish Castle hark back to the stronghold's former glory days and offer breathtaking views over Sintra and beyond (page 152).

⭐ **Regaleira Estate:** With its grand Gothic facade, gargoyles, mystic gardens, and secret passages, the Regaleira Estate is eerie and enthralling in equal measure (page 153).

and wealthy artists, whose flamboyant mansions were inspired by the Romanticism of the era. Sintra's most famous attraction, the hilltop Pena Palace, is straight out of a Disney movie, while the town center's multihued historical mansions are swaddled by lush greenery. It's a little hub of theatrical extravagance. Other fascinating sights include the Gothic Sintra National Palace and the spooky Quinta da Regaleira (Regaleira Estate).

ORIENTATION

Most of Sintra's major sights are within walking distance of the historical town center, though one or two entail steep-ish climbs:

walking from the town center to Pena Palace is quite a distance and recommended only for avid hikers.

Sintra National Palace is in the heart of Sintra's historical center; as such, it is also often referred to as the Town Palace. **Pena Palace,** the **Regaleira Estate,** and the **Moorish Castle** are all located in the hills west of the town center.

Quinta da Regaleira is the closest and easiest attraction to reach on foot from the town center, a 15-minute walk up a couple of small hills. Both Pena Palace and the Moorish Castle take around 50 minutes to reach on foot, up challenging climbs. The route to Pena Palace involves a particularly steep

Previous: Regaleira Estate; **above:** Pena Palace; Moorish Castle.

hill, so taking the **434 tourist bus** from the **train station** or town center to visit these two sights is recommended. The train station is located just outside the town center on its northeastern fringe, about 3 km (2 mi) from Pena Palace.

Another tourist bus—the **435**—connects Sintra train station to the **Regaleira Estate** (a short walk from Sintra center), and **Monserrate Palace,** among others.

Most of the shops and restaurants in Sintra are clustered in the town center.

PLANNING YOUR TIME

Packed with elaborate mansions, grand monuments, and quirky attractions—and often much cooler than the rest of Lisbon (pack a windbreaker, just in case!)—Sintra is a wonderful place that offers so many amazing vistas and experiences that it should definitely be top of the agenda when visiting Lisbon.

Deservedly popular, Sintra sadly has become victim of its own soaring popularity, and the town can often be packed with tourists and traffic, especially in peak season (July and August), which means long queues, especially for its most popular attractions (purchasing tickets online ahead of your trip can be one way to shorten the queuing process) and a lack of parking. Driving here is not recommended, even more so because public transport from Lisbon is cheap and easy. At least **a full day** should be allocated to really enjoy the essence of

Sintra and see its top attractions, but there's enough to see and do here to justify spending a night, if you have the time. An **overnight stay** will allow you to visit the most popular monuments outside the usual day-tripper hours, such as first thing in the morning, when it might be quieter and the queues shorter. You will also have time to see some of Sintra's lesser-known attractions. It's worth noting that last entries to most of Sintra's monuments will be an hour or half an hour before the announced closing time. Tickets to its most popular attraction, Pena Palace, must be reserved in advance with a date and entry time.

Sintra is located some 25 km (15.5 mi) west of Lisbon; **trains** run regularly from Lisbon, with the journey taking just under an hour. Trains generally run roughly every half hour 5:30am-10:30pm, less frequently on weekends. Last trains back are typically 10pm-11:30pm depending on which station in Lisbon.

From Sintra train station or the town center, the local **Scotturb bus** (www.scotturb.com) runs a circular route of the main spots in and around the historical center (the 434 Pena Circuit), which includes Pena Palace, Moorish Castle, the town center, and the station. There will also be plenty of **taxis** waiting outside the station. Scotturb also operates the 435 Villa Express 4 Palaces circuit, which stops at other monuments such as Monserrate Palace and Quinta da Regaleira.

Sintra's main sights—the **National Palace, Pena Palace, Moorish Castle,** and **Quinta da Regaleira**—are all within walking distance (some much closer to the town center than others), but you'd be hard-pressed to see them all in a day, at least not at a leisurely pace. Key to squeezing as much out of Sintra in a day trip as possible is booking tickets in advance and doing plenty of pre-planning. Staying the night allows you to go slightly further afield, for example to the **Montserrate Historic Park and Palace.**

Alternatively, consider a guided private or small group tour combining Sintra's monuments and historical center, led by a knowledgeable local guide, such as those run by go2lisbon tours (https://go2lisbon.pt).

Enjoy lunch at one of the many charming little restaurants that can be found in the town center, but be aware: as with the monuments, they can be quite busy, especially during summer.

Itinerary Idea

ESSENTIAL SINTRA

Leave Lisbon for Sintra as early as possible. Trains from **Rossio** or **Oriente** run roughly 6am-midnight. This itinerary can easily accommodate an **overnight** visit: Do everything up to the National Palace on Day 1, saving the Regaleira Estate for the next day and adding a stop at **Monserrate Palace.**

1 Take the 434 bus from outside Sintra train station straight to **Pena Palace,** getting there as early as possible. Allow at least a few hours to see the palace, including its magnificent gardens.

2 Walk the 200 m (220 yds) from the palace to the **Moorish Castle;** allocate another hour to explore this sturdy fortress nestled in the hills.

3 Take the 434 bus back down to the historical center for a spot of lunch at **Café Saudade.**

4 After lunch, head to **Sintra National Palace** in the historical center.

5 Time (and legs and energy) allowing, round off your day by strolling up to the **Regaleira Estate.** Alternatively, save your legs and catch the 454 bus to the estate.

Sintra

ESSENTIAL SINTRA

1. Pena Palace
2. Moorish Castle
3. Café Saudade
4. Sintra National Palace
5. Regaleira Estate
6. Nau Palatina
7. Quinta da Regaleira and Monserrate Palace

© MOON.COM

6 Finish your day in Sintra with Mediterranean and Portuguese tapas at **Nau Palatina** before returning to Lisbon by train.

7 If staying overnight, catch the 435 bus from Sintra town center or station and visit the other attractions, such as **Quinta da Regaleira** and **Monserrate Palace.**

Sights

SINTRA NATIONAL PALACE

(Palácio Nacional de Sintra)

Largo Rainha Dona Amélia; tel. 219 237 300; www.parquesdesintra.pt; daily 9:30am-7pm late Mar.-late Oct., daily 9:30am-6pm late Oct.-late Mar.; €10

In the town center, Sintra National Palace, with its two distinctive conical chimneys, was the residence of Portugal's royal families in the 15th-19th centuries and today is the first stop for many visitors. Its white Gothic exterior, with some Manueline features, is minimalist, a counterpoint to the extravagance of the fanciful Pena Palace on the hilltop. The wow factor of the detailed interior makes up for the exterior. A bird motif is evident in the Magpie Room and the Swan Room, with its octagonal paneled ceiling. The rudimentary Moorish kitchen is topped with huge twin cones. Most splendid is the 16th-century Coats of Arms room, where the paneled ceiling contains the coats of arms of 72 aristocratic families. Reservations and online discounts are available via the website.

TOP EXPERIENCE

✪ PENA PALACE

(Palácio Nacional da Pena)

Estrada da Pena; tel. 219 237 300; www.parquesdesintra.pt; daily 9:30am-8pm; €14; bus 434

Portugal's finest example of 19th-century Romantic architecture, perched on a rocky peak often shrouded in clouds, the colorful, whimsical Pena Palace wouldn't look out of place in any fantastical movie. Its roots stretch back to the 12th century, when a chapel was, according to history, built at the site following an apparition of the Virgin Mary and, centuries later, housed a monastery. But it was in 1838 that its current format was commissioned by the young German-born King Ferdinand II to serve as a summer residence for the Royal family. Built on the site of the abandoned 16th-century monastery, the project was entrusted to amateur architect Wilhelm Ludwig von Eschwege. The imitation medieval fortress that resulted includes a jumble of watchtowers, turrets, terraces, a tunnel, and even a drawbridge. Its uniqueness saw Pena Palace classified a National Monument in 1910 and a UNESCO World Heritage Site in 1995.

On a clear day, the bold pink, gray, and ocher can be seen on top of its craggy green throne for miles. The interior is just as eccentric and mishmashed, with stuccos, trompe-l'oeil murals, and azulejo plaques. Note the exquisite carved chairs and vaulted ceiling in the Royal Dining Room, the rich upholstery in the Noble Room, and the orchestra of brass pots and pans in the kitchen. The Queen's Terrace and a clock tower offer sweeping views over the Sintra mountain range. There are many interesting details to be spotted throughout a visit, like the gargoyles that peer down from many of the decorative cornerstones. A particularly menacing half-man half-fish gargoyle glares down from an elaborate gateway over a tunnel that opens on to the Terrace of the Triton. The stained-glass window in the Great Hall is another highlight.

Tickets to visit the palace must be booked in advance for a specific date and time, but you still should expect long queuing times at the palace. Reservations and online discounts are available via the website. The 434 bus stops right outside Pena Palace, and there is a paid (optional when booking tickets) shuttle bus service that runs regularly inside the palace grounds to take visitors from the entrance to the palace itself, which is otherwise quite a long climb through the gardens.

Due to the sheer volume of visitors to Pena Palace, large groups are channeled through in one long continuous line, in their respective times slots, so don't expect to be able to wander freely and see the rooms at leisure.

The surrounding Pena Park offers a more tranquil escape; around 200 hectares (500 acres) of lush, romantic, and exotic greenery, labyrinth-like pathways, and gentle streams that provide a cool refuge on a hot day.

Pena Palace

Sintra's Best Views

Moorish Castle

- **Pena Palace:** Perched atop a steep hill on the outskirts of Sintra town, the vividly colorful Pena Palace offers a plethora of viewpoints, from all angles and fronts, giving bird's-eye views of the surrounding landscape (page 150).

- **Moorish Castle:** Magnificent panoramic views of Sintra can be enjoyed from the battlements of the Moorish Castle, which stands on a craggy hill high above Sintra town, swaddled by dense forest (page 152).

✪ MOORISH CASTLE

(Castelo de Mouros)

Estrada da Pena, Parque de Monserrate; tel. 219 237 300; www.parquesdesintra. pt; daily 9:30am-8pm late Mar.-late Oct., daily 9:30am-7pm late Oct.-late Mar.; €8; bus 434

Surrounded by dense forest, the crumbling old Moorish Castle provides excellent views from its towering stone walls and extensive ramparts. Built in the 9th century during Moorish occupation, the castle fell into disrepair after the Christian reconquests but was later restored in the 19th century by Ferdinand II, who incorporated it into the vast gardens surrounding the Pena Palace. As one of Portugal's most recognizable landmarks, the hilltop Pena Palace is a feast of architectural geniality, one of the most remarkable examples of 19th century Romanticist castles in the country, as well as one of its most unique and theatrical tourist attractions. A series of ornately decorated rooms, fanciful details, and stunning views await those who make their way to this fairy-tale palace.

Initiation Well at Regaleira Estate

✪ REGALEIRA ESTATE

(Quinta da Regaleira)

Rua Barbosa do Bocage 5; tel. 219 106 650; www.regaleira.pt; daily 9:30am-5pm; €11; bus 435

The sprawling Regaleira Estate, near the town center, is a spooky Gothic palace awash with gargoyles and spiky pinnacles and topped with a striking octagonal tower. Inside, a warren of hallways and stairways lead to rooms spread over five floors. The lush surroundings have hidden passages and secret spots with lakes, grottoes, wells, and fountains. The estate once belonged to the Viscountess of Regaleira, who was from a wealthy merchant family in Porto. The current building was completed in 1910. Inside, make sure to see the Initiation Well, a deep hollow carved into the ground like an upside-down tower, with a spiraling stone staircase that, according to folklore, connects to the rest of the estate by secret passages. Descending the well leads to a pink compass at the bottom and feeds off into underground tunnels that open out to a pretty waterfall and grottoes. The original purpose of the Well is unknown, though the theories are varied and mystical.

The 435 bus from Sintra center or station runs to Quinta da Regaleira, but it's an easy and enjoyable 15-20-minute walk. Expect long queues both outside the Quinta to get in and inside to see its main highlights, especially the Initiation Well—but it is worth the wait. Inside the Well, there's a no-stopping policy as you descend, to keep the long line moving, but there's time enough to take a few photos.

MONSERRATE HISTORIC PARK AND PALACE

(Parque e Palácio de Monserrate)

Rua Visconde de Monserrate; tel. 219 237 300; www.parquesdesintra.pt; park daily 9:30am-8pm late Mar.-late Oct., daily 9:30am-7pm late Oct.-late Mar., palace daily 9:30am-7pm late Mar.-late Oct., daily 9:30am-6pm late Oct.-late Mar.; €8; bus 435

The award-winning gardens are the main attraction at the 19th-century Monserrate Historic Park and Palace, 4 km (2.5 mi) west of Sintra town. The flora ranges from romantic to wild to exotic, with species from around the world. The estate was bought in 1856 by wealthy English textile magnate Francis Cook, who commissioned architect James Knowles to design the small palace with Gothic, Indian, and Moorish influences. From Sintra center or station take the 435 bus to Monserrate Palace.

Monserrate Historic Park and Palace

These buses run regularly and stop outside the main sights. Jump back on at the same spot for the return journey. It's worth buying a round-trip ticket or even a day pass for both the 434 and 435 buses.

Monserrate is part of the Sintra-Cascais Natural Park (tel. 219 247 200; www.cm-cascais.pt), which covers a third of the Cascais region, from Sintra to Cabo da Roca. It's a popular place for hiking, biking, horseback riding, and even zip-lining.

Food

Strong meaty flavors and delicious sweets are staples in this part of Portugal. Typical is vitela à Sintrense, a slow-roasted veal dish served with roast potatoes. The traditional queijadas de Sintra is a decadent sweet treat, with a creamy filling of fresh cheese and cinnamon wrapped in delicate, crisp pastry.

Nau Palatina
Calçada de S. Pedro 18; tel. 219 240 962; Tues.-Sat. 7pm-11pm; €10
Nau Palatina is a cute little place with scrumptious Mediterranean and Portuguese haute-rustic tapas, including regional specialties like pork cheeks, traditional Alentejo delicacies, oven-roast octopus and Tuna Muxama, and many vegetarian-friendly options.

Café Saudade

Av. Doutor Miguel Bombarda 6; tel. 212 428 804; Wed.-Sun. 8:30am-6pm; €10

The Portuguese word "saudade" roughly means "longing." This pretty eatery across from the train station fulfills longings for tasty meals and treats with an extensive menu that includes sandwiches, fresh soups and salads, coffee, and freshly baked pastries and snacks.

Tacho Real

Rua Ferraria 4; tel. 219 235 277; www.facebook.com/RestauranteTachoReal; Thurs.-Mon. noon-3:30pm and 7:30pm-10pm, Tues. noon-3pm; €20

A delightful little eatery serving typical Portuguese dishes in a historical building, complete with vaulted ceiling, azulejo-clad walls, a cobblestone patio, and echoes of Portuguese guitar strumming in the background.

O Lavrador

Rua 25 de Abril 36; tel. 219 241 488; http://restaurantelavrador.business.site; Tues.-Sat. noon-3pm and 7:30pm-10pm, Sun. noon-3pm; €20

Small, traditional Portuguese restaurant O Lavrador, on the main 25 de Abril road out of Sintra, has specialties that include naco de carne na pedra (chunks of beef on hot stone) and prawn and bacon skewers. Don't miss the Portuguese pottery hanging overhead.

SINTRA
FOOD

outdoor dining in Sintra

Incomum by Luis Santos

Rua Dr. Alfredo da Costa 22; tel. 219 243 719; www.incomumbyluissantos.pt; Thurs.- Tues. noon-midnight; €30

Contemporary cuisine in the historical heart of Sintra, this restaurant offers a exciting fusion of traditional Portuguese and modern Mediterranean fare that has taken the local culinary scene by storm.

Bars and Nightlife

Fonte da Pipa

Rua Fonte da Pipa 11-13; tel. 219 234 437; daily noon-1am

A popular meeting place for young people and locals, Fonte da Pipa, in Sintra's town center, is a lively, down-to-earth watering hole with a selection of Portuguese beer and wines.

Bar Saloon Cintra

Avenida do Movimento das Forcas Armadas N 5; tel. 914 462 761; https:// salooncompras.wixsite.com/website; Tues.- Fri. 8pm-2am and Sat.-Sun. 6pm-2am

Boasting a huge range of spirits, crafts beers, and cocktails, Bar Saloon Cintra, on the southern outskirts of town, is a quirky little bar with something for everyone, good music, and nibbles.

Accommodations

Although Sintra is only a short distance from Lisbon, staying overnight will allow you to fully experience the town after the sightseeing crowds have dispersed.

✪ NH Sintra Centro

Praça Da Republica; tel. 219 237 200; www.nh-hotels.com; €155 d

NH Sintra Centro is a gleaming and polished hotel located in the heart of Sintra, on the main square, near Sintra National Palace. Modern and modest, the cozy rooms have great views of the surroundings.

✪ Aguamel Sintra Boutique Guest House

Escadinhas da Fonte da Pipa 3; tel. 219 243 628; www.aguamelsintra.com; €120 d

In the heart of the historical center, family-run Aguamel Sintra Boutique Guest House offers a deluxe home-away-from-home experience. Contemporary on the inside, this cozy 19th-century property is a slice of history with a superb location in the town center.

Information and Services

- **GNR police station:** Terreiro da Rainha Dona Amélia (near Sintra National Palace in historical town center); tel. 217 653 240; www.gnr.pt; open 24/7
- **"Ask Me Sintra" tourism office:** Praça República 23; tel. 219 231 157 or 910 517 912; daily 10am-6:30pm
- **Main post office:** Praça da República 26; tel. 210 471 616; www.ctt.pt; Mon.-Fri. 9am-12:30pm and 2pm-5:30pm

Getting There and Around

GETTING THERE

Car

Sintra is 25 km (15.5 mi) west of **Lisbon** on the main **A16** motorway, a 30-minute drive. Taking the train is strongly recommended over driving to Sintra—the train is frequent, cost-efficient, and convenient. Parking is limited in the town center, restricted to residents, city buses, emergency services, commercial vehicles, and taxis. There are a few **parking lots** on the outskirts, a couple of which offer free parking, within walking distance of the historical center (www.cm-sintra.pt/car-parking-in-sintra). The roads to and in Sintra are rather narrow, and the center can become heavily congested, particularly in summer when the flux of traffic and tourists buses is at its peak.

Train

CP trains (tel. 707 210 220; www.cp.pt) to Sintra run from **Lisbon's Rossio, Oriente, and Entrecampos stations on the Sintra Line,** many times daily, roughly every half hour, for the 40-minute trip (€2.40 one-way). **Sintra train station** (Avenida Dr. Miguel Bombarda; tel. 707 210 220; ticket office Mon.-Fri. 6:45am-8:30pm, Sat.-Sun. and public holidays 7am-8:30pm) is approximately 1.5 km (1 mi) from town (about a 20-minute walk), but the **434 and 435 Sintra tourist buses** connect the station, the town center, and the main attractions such as Pena Palace.

GETTING AROUND

Sintra's compact town center can be covered **on foot,** but most sights are farther afield. For avid walkers who are happy to see Sintra's sights from the outside, there are various hiking trails through the lovely forested countryside, which run past main monuments. The Santa Maria 1-hour trail, for example, is suitable for hikers of all ages and fitness levels and climbs along paved roads to two of Sintra's most popular monuments—Pena Palace and the Moorish Castle—offering stunning views en-route. More information on hikes in Sintra can be found on the Parques de Sintra website (www.parquesdesintra.pt/media/qfidnhfn/brochura_percursos_pedestres.pdf). The main way to get to Sintra's sights is to take the Scotturb tourist buses. Other fun ways to explore Sintra include a tourist train and tuk-tuks, both found in the main town center.

Tourist Bus

The hop-on hop-off **Scotturb tourist buses** (tel. 214 699 125; www.scotturb.com) connect all the main sights, stopping in Sintra's historical town center and at the train station.

The 434 **'Pena Circuit'** route (€4.55 one-way to Pena Palace, €8.40 round-trip) includes stops at Sintra train station, the historical town center, Pena Palace, and Moorish Castle. In the summer, it departs roughly every 15 minutes between 9am-8pm (shorter hours in low season). The **435 '4 Palaces' route** (€6 round-trip) departs every 20 minutes from Sintra train station and goes to the Regaleira, Seteais, and Monserrate palaces, as well as Sintra National Palace. A full-day hop-on hop-off pass for both lines costs €13.50.

Tuk-Tuk

Operated by a number of private companies, such as **Turislua Tourist Entertainment** (tel. 219 243 881), the tuk-tuks can be rented for a single trip or for a full day's sightseeing—but this is a costly alternative to the bus, at around €30/hour. Tuk-tuks can be found near the train station and in the town center.

Tourist Train

The Sintra tourist train (tel. 918 258 001; www.comboiodesintra.pt), a miniature train on wheels, also takes visitors on a leisurely (and at times bumpy, thanks to the cobblestone roads) trip around the town and its attractions. It does a guided tour of the most emblematic locales in Sintra, including the National Palace, Quinta da Regaleira, Moorish Castle, and Pena Palace. The starting point is in the **old town center** (a 2-minute walk south from the National Palace), departing about once an hour between 10:30am-4.45pm, and there's a stop on Estrada da Pena for Pena Palace visitors. The complete circuit lasts 45 minutes and costs €10 (€6 children age 6-12). It takes passengers on a figure-eight loop from the historical center, north along Volta Duche (the scenic main road between the town center and Sintra train station), back around clockwise to the center, before climbing counterclockwise past the Regaleira Estate, Moorish Castle, and Pena Palace, and back down into town again.

Mafra and Ericeira

Mafra and Ericeira are day trips from Lisbon—with a difference. Distinct from each other and located just under an hour from the capital (with direct buses to both), their proximity means they can be combined into one day. Steeped in heritage, Mafra, some 40 km (25 mi) northwest of Lisbon in the Central Portugal region, is regal—a beautiful little town with one very big tourist attraction. The gargantuan Mafra National Palace is widely considered the most important example of Baroque

Highlights

✪ **Mafra National Palace:** One of the most extravagant examples of Baroque architecture in Portugal, the massive 18th-century Mafra National Palace complex rolls a palace, a monastery, and a basilica all into one outstanding package (page 164).

✪ **Mafra National Park:** The Tapado Nacional de Mafra is a magical forest teeming with wildlife; once a popular spot for royal recreation, nowadays it's frequented by active families (page 165).

✪ **Ericeira's Beaches:** A world surf reserve, this quaint fishermen's village has a life that revolves around the waves, the beach, and the local village square. Oh, and the "sea hedgehogs" (page 169).

architecture in Portugal, and the Tapada Nacional de Mafra hunting reserve, the palace's sprawling grounds, is open for visits too.

Ericeira, a 15-minute drive down the road from Mafra, is a laid-back surfy seaside town; it's a whitewashed suntrap piled on sheer cliffs that is famous for stunning ocean views and fresh seafood, not to mention world-class surfing. Attracting calm-seeking weekenders and wave-worshipers in droves, Ericeira is a barefoot beach retreat with a year-round summery vibe.

PLANNING YOUR TIME

Because of their proximity to Lisbon and direct public transport, **Mafra and Ericeira** can be combined into **one day,** especially if traveling by car. Mafra—about 40 km (25 mi) northwest of Lisbon on the A8 motorway—is home to the outstanding palace and national park; set aside a full morning to explore them.

Move on to Ericeira—15 minutes northwest from Mafra—for a seafood lunch. Spend the afternoon strolling the quaint streets and lazing on a beautiful beach, soaking

Previous: Ericeira sunset; **above:** Ericeira beach; Mafra National Palace.

up the surfy vibes. If you have the time, spend a night in Ericeira—especially if visiting during summer, when the village really comes alive after sundown—to allow time for a spot of surfing, or catch the last bus back to Lisbon (which leaves around 9:45pm).

Itinerary Idea

ESSENTIAL MAFRA AND ERICEIRA

Leave Lisbon as early as possible for Mafra. Buses depart about hourly from the **Campo Grande station,** or it's a 40-minute drive on the A8.

1 In Mafra, head straight for the vast **Mafra National Palace,** with its massive Baroque-style basilica and convent and twin bell towers. Plan to spend 1-2 hours here. Don't miss the library, one of Europe's most impressive Rococo libraries, whose ornate bookcases house a vast collection of rare books, manuscripts, and historical documents.

2 Enjoy a light lunch in Mafra at one of the atmospheric and cozy traditional Portuguese snack bars, such as **Fradinho** pastry shop.

3 Catch the bus (or drive) the short distance (10 km/6 mi) from Mafra to Ericeira, where you can amble the quaint streets, admire the whitewashed fishermen's cottages, and make your way to **Praia do Sul** beach for a spot of rest and relaxation.

4 Enjoy a fresh seafood lunch at **Marisqueira Furnas.** Try the local specialty, ouriço-do-mar (sea urchin), before making your way back to Lisbon.

Mafra

Just under 40 km (25 mi) northwest of Lisbon, Mafra is famous as the home of a large, extravagant palace, which makes it a popular stop between the capital and coastal surfing mecca Ericeira. The small rural town boomed in popularity as a commuter suburb after the completion of the A8 motorway in the 1990s. Mafra usually hums with a steady stream of page-turning tourists who stop there solely to take in the outstanding Mafra National Palace and Mafra National Park. The charming town center has plenty of little cafés and restaurants. Besides that, there is little else for visitors to do

Mafra and Ericeira

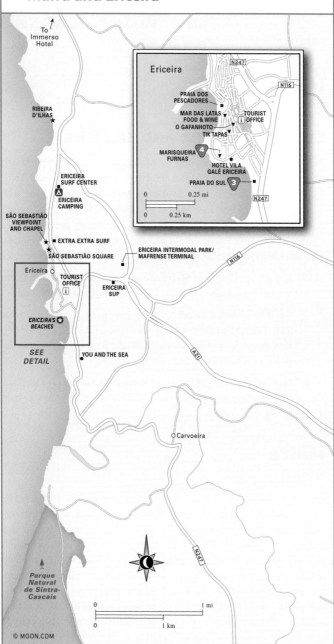

To Immerso Hotel

RIBEIRA D'ILHAS

Ericeira

PRAIA DOS PESCADORES
MAR DAS LATAS FOOD & WINE
O GAFANHOTO
TIK TAPAS
TOURIST OFFICE
MARISQUEIRA FURNAS 4
HOTEL VILA GALÉ ERICEIRA
PRAIA DO SUL 3

N247
N116

0   0.25 mi
0   0.25 km

ERICEIRA SURF CENTER
ERICEIRA CAMPING

SÃO SEBASTIÃO VIEWPOINT AND CHAPEL
EXTRA EXTRA SURF
SÃO SEBASTIÃO SQUARE

ERICEIRA INTERMODAL PARK/ MAFRENSE TERMINAL
N116

Ericeira
TOURIST OFFICE

ERICEIRA SUP

ERICEIRA'S BEACHES

SEE DETAIL

YOU AND THE SEA

A21

N247

Carvoeira

Parque Natural de Sintra-Cascais

0   1 mi
0   1 km

© MOON.COM

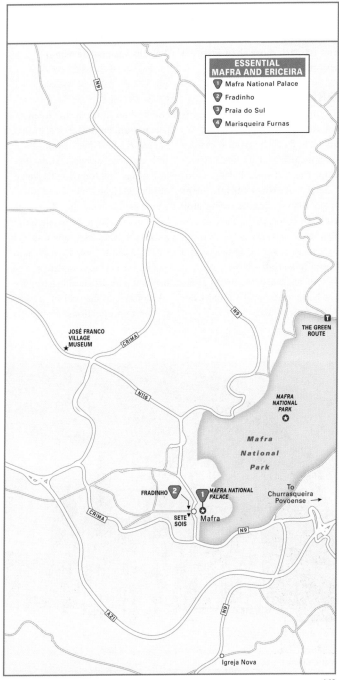

ESSENTIAL
MAFRA AND ERICEIRA
1 Mafra National Palace
2 Fradinho
3 Praia do Sul
4 Marisqueira Furnas

N9

JOSÉ FRANCO
VILLAGE
MUSEUM

CRIMA

N116

N9

THE GREEN
ROUTE

MAFRA
NATIONAL
PARK

Mafra
National
Park

FRADINHO 2

1 MAFRA NATIONAL
PALACE

CRIMA

SETE
SOIS

Mafra

To
Churrasqueira
Povoense →

N9

A21

N9

Igreja Nova

and see in Mafra, but the sheer size and sumptuousness of the palace and its park more than justify a visit to the town.

ORIENTATION

The main motorway to Mafra is the **A8**—tolls (approximately €4) apply, and can be paid in cash or with a card. Mafra's main attraction, the National Palace, is located in the **town center. Buses** from Lisbon conveniently stop right in front of the palace. The **Tapada Nacional** is best visited by car, as it would take over 1.5 hours to walk from the palace. It is a 10-minute drive north along the N9-2 road, or take a **taxi/Uber** from Mafra town.

SIGHTS
✪ Mafra National Palace
(Palácio Nacional de Mafra)

Terreiro Dom João V; tel. 261 817 550; www.palaciomafra.gov.pt; Wed.-Mon. 9:30am-5:30pm; €6

On a hilltop above the town center, the monumental Mafra National Palace is the finest example of 18th-century Baroque architecture in Portugal, built during the reign of John V (Dom João V) to fulfill a promise he made that if his wife bore him children, he would build a convent. The first stone was laid in 1717, and it took 13 years and 52,000 workers to complete it. The original plan was a monastery for 13 monks, but the project grew to immense proportions, eventually

Mafra National Palace

housing 300 monks and including a basilica and a royal palace. The sprawling monument's limestone facade measures 220 m (722 ft). Painted in sunny yellow, its beautiful exterior features twin bell towers that frame the central basilica. The lavish interior comprises 1,200 rooms and 5,000 windows and doors. The Old Library is a trove of 36,000 ancient books, and the basilica has no fewer than six organs. Outside, a lovely courtyard is frequented by wild birds, and the vast decorative patio creates a border between this national monument and the town. Guided tours of the palace are available with prior booking.

José Franco Village Museum
(Aldeia Tipica de José Franco)
N116; tel. 261 815 420; https://aldeiajosefranco.pt; daily 9:30am-7pm; free

Just 3.2 km (2 mi) north of Mafra town, in the village of Sobreiro, the José Franco Village Museum is made up of detailed miniature scenarios of typical Portuguese villages from the turn of the 20th century. This tribute to the local people and their customs, like an open-air museum, is the vision of renowned potter José Franco, who began building it in the 1960s. Among the buildings are a windmill, cottages, and a schoolroom, all of which are kitted out with genuine tools and paraphernalia from the era, and have life-like replicas of artisans hard at work inside.

The wood oven-baked chouriça sausage bread made in the on-site bakery is worth the visit. There's also an on-site restaurant, museum, ceramics shop, and petting zoo—plenty to keep the whole family entertained for a couple of hours. Public transport between Lisbon, Mafra, and Ericeira, stopping at Sobreiro, is operated by the Carris Metropolitana (tel. 210 418 800; www.carrismetropolitana.pt) buses, services 2740, 2741, 2132, 2751, 2803, 2137, 2140.

SPORTS AND RECREATION
⊙ Mafra National Park
(Tapada Nacional de Mafra)
Portão do Codeçal; tel. 261 817 050; www.tapadademafra.pt; daily 9:30am-6pm

A 10-minute drive northeast of Mafra town on the N9-2 road, the 8-sq-km (3-sq-mi) Mafra National Park is a sprawling royal game reserve created for the Mafra National Palace. Today it is still a verdant and varied habitat for free-roaming deer, wild boars, wolves, foxes, badgers, and birds of prey. Activities include **hiking, mountain biking, horseback riding, archery,** and **falconry,** staged mostly on weekends. For more information on how and where to join these activities, inquire at the main **ticket office** at the entrance (tel. 261 814 240; daily 9:30am-6pm) or see the **park website.**

There is no fixed entry fee to the Tapada, as prices are by activity. All entries pass through the main ticket office/visitors center.

deer in Mafra National Park

A "Walking in the Forest" day pass costs €5 on weekdays and €9.50 on weekends and includes access to hiking and mountain biking trails, a "Bees in the Forest," activity, and a Birds of Prey show.

BTT (mountain bike) routes are open 9am-4pm. There are three designated routes: **white** (8 km/5 mi), **yellow** (15 km/9.3 mi), and **red** (25 km/15.5 mi), which can be downloaded in advance from the Tapada de Mafra website (https:// tapadademafra.pt/percursos-pedestres). Rental bikes are available only for the white route and can be found at the trailhead (€16.50; max. 3 hours).

There are four different **hiking routes** of varying lengths, between 4 km-8.5 km (2.5-5.3 mi). The longer routes take hikers to farther-flung corners of the reserve, where spotting wild animals is more likely. Each route is marked out with a different color (blue, green, red, or yellow) in accordance with their respective length, level of difficulty, and slopes encountered. Maps are available at the main ticket office or online. **Guided Footpath Tours** are also available.

The Green Route

Hiking Distance: *8.2-km (5.1-mi) round-trip*
Hiking Time: *approx. 2 hours*
Trailhead: *Tapada Reception*
Information and Maps: *www.alltrails. com/trail/portugal/lisboa--6/percurso-verde-tapada-de-mafra*

The Green Route, an 8.2-km (5.1-mi) loop, is widely considered one of the most popular and scenic hiking trails in the Tapada. Described as moderately challenging, the hike takes visitors 2-2.5 hours. The trail is open in all seasons and passes through different areas of forest and woodland, where animals such as deer and wild boar can be spotted. Entry fee €5 weekdays, €9.50 weekends and holidays.

FOOD
Fradinho
Praça da República 28/30; tel. 261 815 738; daily 7am-8pm; €5

If it's a quick snack or a sugar boost you want, then this is the place to go. The Fradinho pastry shop and café has a wide selection of freshly baked regional sweets and delicacies, savory snacks, and sandwiches.

Churrasqueira Povoense
Rua 10 de Maio 2, Povoa da Galega; tel. 219 856 080; Tues.-Wed. noon-3pm, Thurs.-Sat. noon-3pm and 7:30pm-10pm; €10

Superb, unpretentious Churrasqueira Povoense specializes in grilled meats like the famous tirinhas de porco, delicious thin strips of pork grilled on charcoal and served with fries and salad.

Sete Sois
Largo Conde Ferreira 1; tel. 261 811 161; Wed.-Sun. noon-4pm and 7pm-11:30pm, Mon. noon-4pm; €20

Straight across the road from the National Palace, the cozy, elegant restaurant Sete Sois has a lovely little alfresco courtyard right in the middle of the town's action. It specializes in tasty grilled fish and meat dishes as well as local game specialties.

GETTING THERE
Car
Mafra is 40 km (25 mi) northwest of **Lisbon,** about a 40-minute drive. Follow the **A8** motorway from Lisbon, taking **junction 5** and then heading west on the **A21.** There is a spacious paid **parking lot** just next to the Mafra Palace (parking costs a couple of euros for a few hours) and also a large parking lot just outside the Tapada that is free for paying visitors.

Bus
Carris Metropolitana (tel. 210 418 800; www.carrismetropolitana.pt) buses run roughly every 20 minutes (less frequently in low season, on bank holidays, and on weekends) from Lisbon's **Campo Grande main bus station,** stopping in front of **Mafra National Palace.** The trip takes 1 hour each way and costs around €6. Carris Metropolitana also connects Mafra with Sintra, a 50-minute ride to the south.

GETTING AROUND
It is not recommended to walk between the Mafra National Palace and the Tapada—it's about 7 km (4.5 mi) each way; **drive** or take an **Uber/taxi,** which should cost around €15 one-way. The **palace** is located in the charming town center of Mafra.

Ericeira

On the coast, around 35 km (22 mi) north of Lisbon, the fishing village of Ericeira attracts surfers and big-name surfing competitions. The Save the Waves Coalition has even declared it a World Surfing Reserve, only the second in the world and the only one in Europe. Laid-back Ericeira is a little gem, not especially picturesque but with stunning ocean vistas and beautiful beaches. A jumble of white-washed fishermen's cottages piled atop high-backed cliffs that encircle the cove-like main beach and harbor, it is a place where you can walk around barefoot and carefree.

What Ericeira lacks in picturesqueness, it makes up for with vibrant nightlife and excellent seafood. Be sure to try the local specialty, the curiously named ouriço-do-mar (which literally translates as "sea hedgehog" but is better known as the sea urchin). Still not quite on the mass tourism radar, Ericeira has managed to strike the perfect balance between traditional and cool, which makes for a fun and heady combination that keeps visitors coming back.

ORIENTATION

Life in Ericeira centers around the **Praça da República** square, a cobbled hub fringed with lovely

São Sebastião beach below the chapel and viewpoint

cafés and cake shops, set back off the main **Praia dos Pescadores** (Fishermen's Beach). **Rua Dr. Eduardo Burnay** is the buzzing main street that runs south from the square to **Praia do Sul** (South Beach), lined with bars and seafood restaurants. At the northern end of the village is the **São Sebastião Square,** where the scenic São Sebastião **viewpoint** and **chapel** can be found.

The **bus terminal** is toward the top end of the village, opposite **North Beach** and the Praia dos Pescadores. Praça da República square is a 3-minute walk south from the bus terminal. Traversing the entire village is the main **N247 road,** which runs along the seafront. Most sights in Ericeira are within walking distance, and covering the entire length of the village—from São Sebastião viewpoint to South Beach—takes around 20 minutes (1.5 km/1 mi).

SIGHTS
São Sebastião Viewpoint and Chapel
Praia de São Sebastião

Peering over a beach that goes by the same name, the São Sebastião chapel is a small and simple whitewashed hermitage on the northern fringe of town. Its cliff-top setting offers panoramic views out to sea that are particularly spectacular at sunset.

✪ BEACHES

Ericeira has a mix of beaches that cater to most tastes, from small and secluded with calmer waters, to wide and open with powerful waves that challenge experienced surfers. Most have thick, soft sand, cliff backdrops, and the water can be pretty chilly. In terms of services and infrastructure (like beach bars, restaurants, public restrooms, and board rentals), the closer to the town center—or the more popular—the beach is, the better equipped it will be.

Pescadores Beach
(Praia dos Pescadores)
Largo das Ribas

Backed by a not-so-attractive high cement wall, Ericeira's Pescadores Beach is the town's most central and well-served beach in terms of services. Besides the droves of beachgoers who flock here, it is also a busy working harbor, a hive of activity for the local fishermen and their boats. Praia dos Pescadores's claim to fame is that it was from here that King Manuel II and his family fled on fishing boats to meet the royal yacht out at sea on October 5, 1910. Their departure into permanent exile signaled the end of the monarchy and the beginning of the Portuguese republic. Parking anywhere near here is virtually impossible, as the streets are narrow and heavily trafficked. The beachfront is, however, bookended by a number of parking lots all within walking distance of the old town center. The main parking areas on the fringes of town are near the São Sebastião shopping center, around

Praia dos Pescadores

the Vila Galé Ericeira hotel, and by the Municipal Market. These are mostly paid covered parking or metered street options.

South Beach (Praia do Sul)

Short walk south from the village center

Praia do Sul, near the village center, is the most popular beach in Ericeira. It is a crescent-shaped swath of golden sand sheltered by high cliffs, with clean seawater and mild waves, flat in summer, making it appropriate for sunbathing and swimming. Next to the beach is a little boardwalk with restaurants, esplanades, and showers.

Ribeira d'Ilhas

3 km (2 mi) north of village center

One of the top surfing spots in the region is Ribeira d'Ilhas, a regular fixture on the World Surf League Championship Tour, 3 km (2 mi) north of Ericeira town, a short 8-minute drive on the N247 road. It has strong surf most of the year and is where most of the local surfers head. It has good parking space as well as shower and rental facilities and year-round restaurants.

SPORTS AND RECREATION
Surfing

Ericeira has good surfing conditions year-round, with spots for beginners to experts. Dozens of different surf spots can be found on a relatively short stretch of coastline; if one doesn't suit you, you can find another. The **Ericeira Surf Center** (Estrada Nacional 247; tel. 925 062 012; www.boardculturesurfcenter. com) and **eXtra eXtra Surf** school (Av. São Sebastião 14I; tel. 962 603 192; www.extrasurfschool.com) are two well-established local companies that have boards, wetsuits, and other gear for rent. They also provide **lessons** and a wealth of information. Surfboard rentals start from €15 for a half-day; group lessons are €30-35 per person.

SUP

Stand-up paddleboarding (SUP) is popular in Ericeira and a nice alternative for non-surfers. The nooks and crannies of the coastline along Ericeira, a World Surfing Reserve, are perfect to explore by SUP. Local company **Ericeira SUP** (Rua dos Pocinhos, Rosa dos Ventos building; tel. 915 520 635; www.ericeirasup.com) organizes SUP excursions for paddlers of all levels of expertise, on the flat water of Ericeira harbor, the ocean, and along the bays and rock pools of the Ericeira coastline, as well as tours to nearby rivers and dams. Prices start from €30 and include paddleboard, paddle, wetsuit, and insurance.

FOOD

O Gafanhoto
Rua da Conceição 8; tel. 261 864 514; https://brunomata17.wixsite.com/gafanhoto; Wed.-Mon. noon-4pm and 7pm-10:30pm; €15

In the town center, O Gafanhoto (The Grasshopper) is typically Portuguese on the outside, with its azulejo tiles and sky-blue trim, and typically Portuguese on the inside, with a menu that features good old-fashioned favorites like cozido à Portuguesa (Portuguese stew), Portuguese-style liver, and the Transmontana bean stew. Daily special menus are available in full or half portions.

Tik Tapas
Rua do Ericeira 15; tel. 261 869 235; Tues.-Fri. 7pm-midnight, Sat.-Sun. 12:30pm-3pm and 7pm-midnight; €10

A rainbow of tasty meat, fish, and vegetarian tapas accompanied by great wines is served in this vibrant little eatery, with its bright-blue bar and tables and burnt-orange walls. Choco frito (deep-fried cuttlefish) is a popular option. This cozy and colorful little restaurant is one of the most popular in Ericeira and usually busy, so reservations are recommended. It has a handful of outside tables, and blankets at the ready for cooler evenings.

Marisqueira Furnas
Rus das Furnas 3; tel. 261 867 914; https://marisqueirafurnas.com; daily noon-10pm; €20

The oceanfront Furnas restaurant specializes in the freshest fish and seafood and is famous for its continual all-you-can-eat rodizio. Located near Ericeira's famous Furnas rocks, with a nautical-inspired decor, it has lovely sea views and a large outdoor terrace that can be closed in when the weather is cooler. Popular dishes include seafood stews and stuffed crab, to be washed down with a nice sangria or wine.

Mar das Latas Food & Wine
Rua Capitão João Lopes 24A; tel. 917 109 225; www.facebook.com/mar.das.latas; Mon.-Sat. 5pm-midnight; €30

This classy, modern-traditional eatery is a great place to head for fine wine, accomplished cuisine based on fresh local ingredients, and sunset drinks with a view. From the kitchen of a talented young chef come tasty starters such as ceviche, fried squid, and tuna tartar, while entrées range from delectable leg of lamb to cod curry, beetroot risotto, and Wagyu beef.

ACCOMMODATIONS

Ericeira offers a diverse range of accommodations to suit every budget. From large hotel resorts to boutique guesthouses and hostels geared specifically toward the surf and yoga crowds, there's an option for everyone, whether for a family vacation or traveling solo. Best to book well ahead though, as Ericeira can get very busy in summer and during surfing events.

You and the Sea

Rua das Silvas 2; tel. 261 243 370; www. youandthesea.pt; €200-300 d

Bright and modern holiday apartments with hotel service, You and the Sea is a popular option in Ericeira. With 35 units ranging from studios to four-bedroom apartments located right on the seafront, walking distance to Sul beach, a stay here also includes free access to a gym and spa. There's an on-site pool, restaurant, and parking.

Immerso Hotel

Rua da Bica da Figueir; tel. 261 104 420; https://immerso.pt; from €250 d (min. 3-night stay may apply)

Stylish and trendy throughout, from the contemporary architecture to the organic interior decor, Immerso Hotel is a laid-back, five-star hotel. Set back from town, some 6 km (4 mi) out, it is surrounded by natural countryside, with stunning views over rolling hills and out to sea. There's a free shuttle bus to Ericeira.

Hotel Vila Galé Ericeira

Largo dos Navegantes 1; tel. 261 869 900; www.vilagale.com; €100-200 d

A large, grand dame-style hotel on the Ericeira cliffs, facing South Beach on the southern edge of town, Vila Galé Ericeira has comfortable rooms and two pools, one of which is saltwater, both overlooking the ocean.

Ericeira Camping

Estrada Nacional 247; tel. 261 862 706; www.ericeiracamping.com; 2 people + 1 tent approx. €20 pp/night high season (July-Aug.), classic 4-person bungalow €110 pp/night (July-Aug.)

Free your inner adventurer and stay at the modern and well-equipped Ericeira Camping park. It offers traditional camping among shady trees, as well as bungalows and mobile homes. There is also catering and a surf school right next door.

INFORMATION AND SERVICES

- **GNR police station:** Rua Alto da Camacha; tel. 261 860 710; www.gnr.pt

- **Tourist office:** Praça da República 17; tel. 261 863 122; daily 10am-6pm

- **Main post office:** Rua do Paço 2; tel. 210 471 616

GETTING THERE
Car
Ericeira is 50 km (31 mi) northwest of **Lisbon,** 9.5 km (5.9 mi) west of **Mafra.** The quickest and easiest way to Ericeira from Lisbon is by car along the **A8** motorway, then the **A21** road west to the coast. It's about a 45-minute drive, and 15 minutes from Mafra, also on the A21.

Bus
Regular bus services operated by **Mafrense** (tel. 707 201 371; www.mafrense.com) run throughout the day between Lisbon's **Campo Grande terminal** and Ericeira (€8 one-way). Buses leave Campo Grande hourly, and the journey takes an hour; the bus drops off at the **Mafrense terminal** in the **Ericeira Intermodal Park** 250 m (275 yds) north of the Ericeira town center. Buses are less frequent on weekends.

GETTING AROUND
Getting around Ericeira is easy—most main beaches and amenities are within walking distance of the village center and bus terminal. **Parking,** however, is limited. Ericeira's streets are narrow and can get very crowded, especially during summer. But there is plenty of parking in **free parking lots** set back from the main beachfront, or limited paid parking within the village.

Tomar

A sense of history and grandeur

pervades the town of Tomar, which straddles the pretty Nabão River. Shrouded in mystery and packed with fascinating sights and ruins, the town was a key pillar in the formation of Portugal. During the 13th century, Tomar was a powerful town as the seat of the Knights Templar, a Catholic military order founded in 1119.

In addition to ruins with intriguing history, Tomar offers leisurely, picturesque walks along the Nabão River or a stroll through

Highlights

⭐ **Convent of Christ:** A UNESCO World Heritage Site, the Convent of Christ is a fascinating complex of ancient buildings once inhabited by the enigmatic Knights Templar (page 178).

⭐ **Almourol Castle:** Atop an island of rocky boulders in the middle of the Tagus River, Almourol Castle is a sight to behold and requires a fun boat ride to get there (page 180).

⭐ **Queijadas:** Finger-licking sticky and sweet, the delectable local queijada cakes are made from the unusual combination of almond and fresh cheese. Try one at **Café Estrelas de Tomar** (page 184).

lovely Mouchão Park. Browse the many traditional shops and cafés in the sleepy town center and indulge in one of Tomar's typical cakes, such as the almond and squash queijadas (sticky cakes) or the fatias de Tomar (Tomar slices) made with egg yolks, sugar, and water slowly cooked in a bain-marie in a special pan invented by a local tinsmith in the mid-20th century. As the locals say, the secret is in the pan.

ORIENTATION

The **Nabão River** flows tranquilly through the middle of Tomar. The town's main square, **Praça da República,** the **train station,** and other attractions such as the **Matchbox Museum** and the fascinating **Convent of Christ** are all on the western side of the river. The Convent complex is a 10-minute uphill hike from the main square, or a 15-minute walk from the train station, and the vistas en route are fantastic. Or take one of the tuk-tuks that can be found zipping around.

PLANNING YOUR TIME

Tomar is located approximately 140 km (87 mi) north of Lisbon (1.5 hours), and **a full day** should be allocated to exploring it. Tomar can be done as a day trip, by **car** or by **train,** although a car

---

Previous: Convent of Christ garden; **above:** Convent of Christ; Almourol Castle.

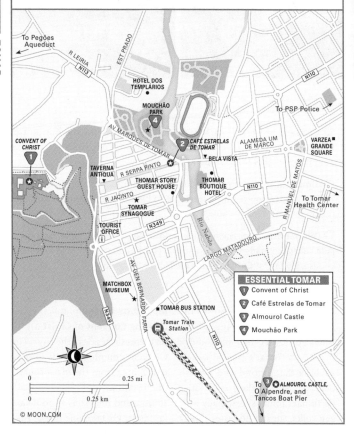

Tomar

To Pegões Aqueduct

R LEIRIA
N113

EST PRADO

HOTEL DOS
TEMPLÁRIOS

MOUCHÃO
PARK
4

AV MARQUES DE TOMAR

To PSP Police

N110

CONVENT OF
CHRIST
1

CAFÉ ESTRELAS
DE TOMAR
2

ALAMEDA UM
DE MARCO

VARZEA
GRANDE
SQUARE

BELA VISTA

TAVERNA
ANTIQUA

R SERPA PINTO

THOMAR STORY
GUEST HOUSE

R JACINTO

TOMAR
SYNAGOGUE

TOURIST
OFFICE
i

THOMAR
BOUTIQUE
HOTEL

N110

R MANUEL DE MATOS

To Tomar
Health Center

N349

Rio Nabão

LARGO MATADOURO

MATCHBOX
MUSEUM

AV GEN BERNARDO FARIA

N349

TOMAR BUS STATION

Tomar Train
Station

N110

ESSENTIAL TOMAR
1 Convent of Christ
2 Café Estrelas de Tomar
3 Almourol Castle
4 Mouchão Park

0   0.25 mi

0   0.25 km

© MOON.COM

To 3 ALMOUROL CASTLE,
O Alpendre, and
Tancos Boat Pier

is recommended if you want to visit the **Almourol Castle** too. The **Convent of Christ** alone warrants the journey. Spend a full morning or afternoon exploring the Convent of Christ, enjoy lunch in one of Tomar's many little local eateries, and use the rest of the day to wander around charming Tomar town or make the half-hour drive south to visit the Almourol Castle—a must-see when in this part of Portugal. Trains generally run once or twice an hour, and the last one back to Lisbon leaves around 10pm.

Itinerary Idea

ESSENTIAL TOMAR

Set off from Lisbon after an early breakfast and head for Tomar—aim to arrive mid-morning.

1 Head straight to the **Convent of Christ** and allow a good couple of hours to explore its nooks and crannies.

2 Make your way back down to the main town to enjoy lunch and a queijada at **Café Estrelas de Tomar.**

3 Make the half-hour drive south to **Almourol Castle,** a dramatic castle arrived at by boat (make sure you allow enough time for the last boat back!).

4 Stroll through Tomar's quaint streets, to the Nabão River and **Mouchão Park,** before heading back to Lisbon for dinner.

Tomar's main square

Sights

✪ CONVENT OF CHRIST

(Convento de Cristo)

Igreja do Castelo Templário; tel. 249 315 089 or 249 313 434; www.conventocristo. gov.pt; daily 9am-5:30pm Oct.-May, daily 9am-6:30pm June-Sept.; €10

The 12th-century Convent of Christ is a great work of Renaissance architecture, blending Romanesque, Gothic, and Manueline features in its remodeling over the centuries. The compound is on a hill overlooking Tomar, its lofty location dominating the skyline and enhancing the feeling of power and secrecy that cloaked the Order of the Knights Templar.

The Templars settled in Portugal in the early 12th century and built what is today the Convent of Christ in 1160 under the leadership of Gualdim Pais, provincial master of the order in Portugal. In the early days the convent was a symbol of the Templars' privacy and their desire to recapture the kingdom, but later, having been occupied by Henry the Navigator in the 15th century, it became an emblem for Portugal opening to the world.

The sumptuous interior outweighs the striking exterior and should be seen. The Convent of

Convent of Christ

Tomar and the Knights Templar

Knights Templar Festival

For at least 130 years, Tomar's Convent of Christ was the hub of the Templars in Portugal as they fought to free the country from Moorish control. In 1190 a Moorish invasion crossed the Tagus River and attacked Tomar, capturing nearby castles, but the Templars withstood a six-day siege and eventually claimed victory. With this and similar conquests in the region, the Templars gradually started the reconquest of Portugal from the Moors.

The Knights Templar order came to an abrupt end in the early 14th century when Philip IV of France, allegedly jealous of their prowess and conquests, convinced the pope to extinguish the order. While most Templars had their wealth and land repossessed, in Portugal they were spared that fate by King Dinis. He protected the Templars by persuading the pope to agree to a new order, renaming them the Order of Christ and moving their hub to Castro Marim. A century later, Tomar was restored to its full glory as the headquarters of the Order of Christ by Prince Henry the Navigator, an exceptional figure who played a pivotal role in the Age of Exploration.

Christ refers to a complex of buildings rather than just the convent used by the Templars (who later became the Order of Christ) for at least 130 years as their seat in Portugal, a mix of a classic 12th-century castle and eight cloisters added in the 15th and 16th centuries, plus vast gardens. The centerpiece is the castle's unusual **Charola,** the oratory of the Templars, an exuberantly decorated, light-filled church built by the first great master of the Templars and inspired by the architecture of the Holy Land. Outside,

✪ Almourol Castle

Almourol Castle

Set on a solitary islet that juts out into the Tagus River, in a parish known as Praia do Ribatejo (Ribatejo Beach), the **Almourol Castle** (Castelo de Almourol, Ilhota do Rio Tejo, Praia do Ribatejo, Vila Nova da Barquinha; tel. 927 228 354; www.igespar.pt; daily 10am-6:30pm; €6 includes boat trip) rises from a rocky outcrop. The castle dates to the 12th century, and its origins are shrouded in mystery. It is believed to have been built on the site of an ancient Lusitanian castro (a pre-Roman fortification) that

the church has a 16-sided polygonal structure, while inside it has a central octagonal structure, its lavish decor with floor-to-ceiling paintings indicative of the order's wealth and power.

It's possible to spend a few hours wandering this incredibly beautiful complex. Construction began in the 12th century on land donated by King Afonso Henriques to thank the Templars for their role in the reconquistas. It evolved into an impressive military complex. Henry the Navigator added a palace in the 15th century, when he was grand master of the order. He extended the monastic premises by adding two new cloisters and transformed the military house into a convent to be used by the clergy. The complex was completely remodeled in the 16th century by Manuel I, who also became master of the order, and was embellished throughout with elaborate sacred art, mural paintings, and decorative plasterwork. Classified a UNESCO World Heritage Site in 1983, it has intricate details and surprises around every corner, such as the many masons' inscriptions that linger from its days as the seat of the Templars.

Audio guides are available. A

was conquered by the Romans in the 1st century BCE and later held by invading Visigoths and Moors. It remains unclear when the structure was founded, although an inscription on the main entrance suggests it was circa 1171.

Enigmatic and powerful, Almourol is symbolic of the Christian reconquest, distinguished from other monuments by its riverside location on land that once fell under the protection of the Knights Templar. Almourol Castle forms part of a protective belt that was a frontline of defense along the Tagus River in the Middle Ages, along with the castles of Tomar, Zêzere, and Cardiga. It was abandoned with the extinction of the Knights Templar in Portugal, but in the 19th century it was rediscovered, and in the 20th century the castle was used by the government to host many important meetings.

GETTING THERE

Reach the castle from the nearby **Tancos boat pier,** in the parish of Vila Nova da Barquinha, sailing across the Tagus on a little boat to the islet. Boats depart hourly and allow visitors 40 minutes to wander the castle before the return trip. The castle is a magnificent fairy tale sight as the boat approaches. The views from the castle are phenomenal.

Vila Nova da Barquinha and Almourol Castle is a 25-minute, 22-km (13.6-mi) drive northeast from Tomar on the **N110** and **A13** roads.

CP (tel. 707 210 220; www.cp.pt) trains run six times daily from **Tomar** to Tancos train station (1-2 hours; €3.20); the journey may require a transfer at Entroncamento. Tancos train station is a 10-minute walk east of the boat pier.

combined ticket (€15) to the Convent of Christ, Alcobaça Monastery, and Batalha Monastery is valid for seven days if you have time to venture west of Tomar. Note that there are narrow, uneven passages, cobbled floors, and lots of worn stairs; accessibility could be problematic for people with limited mobility.

TOMAR SYNAGOGUE
(Sinagoga de Tomar)

Rua Dr. Joaquim Jacinto 73; tel. 249 329 823; www.cm-tomar.pt; Tues.-Sun. 10am-noon and 2pm-5pm Oct.-Mar., Tues.-Sun. 10am-1pm and 2pm-6pm Apr.-Sept.; free

Built in the 15th century in Tomar's historical center, the Tomar Synagogue is a rare example of a medieval Jewish temple in Portugal and is the best preserved. Tomar's Jewish community thrived until 1496-1497, when the Jews were forced to convert to Roman Catholicism or be expelled by Manuel I. Subsequently the synagogue served as a prison, a Christian chapel, a hay storehouse, and a grocery warehouse. From the outside, it blends in with the simple whitewashed houses on the street, distinguished by the blue Star of David above the door. Inside, Gothic vaulted ceilings connecting to the floor with spindly stone columns are an impressive sight. The synagogue's present-day north-facing entrance is not an original feature; the pointy Gothic east-facing arch was the main entrance in the Middle Ages. In 1921 the building was classified a National Monument, and it also houses a small Jewish museum, which hosts several medieval tomb slabs from across Portugal.

MATCHBOX MUSEUM
(Museu dos Fosforos)

Av. Gen. Bernardo Faria; tel. 249 329 823; Tues.-Sun. 10am-noon and 2pm-5pm; free

The quirky, colorful Matchbox Museum, located in the São Francisco convent, houses an extraordinary collection of 43,000 matchboxes, collected over 27 years from 127 countries and dating back to 1827, filling cabinets and creating a striking visual effect. The collection was started by local man Aquiles da Mota Lima and donated to the municipality in 1980. His fascination with matchboxes started when he traveled to the United Kingdom to attend the coronation of Queen Elizabeth II in 1953, and his first box features the British monarch.

MOUCHÃO PARK
(Parque do Mouchão)

Rua do Parque; tel. 249 313 326; open 24/7; free

Straddling the heart of Tomar town and a sliver of land called Mouchão Island in the Nabão River,

Mouchão Park is a public park with many trees for shady tranquility on hot days. Stroll the lovely gardens and hear the river running nearby. An old wooden waterwheel stands guard near one of the park's entrances, and a campsite is located nearby. The park is divided into two areas, with a playground, a sports field, and pavilion on one side and the verdant island on the other, connected by a bridge.

Mouchão Park

PEGÕES AQUEDUCT
(Aqueduto de Pegões)

Looming above the Ribeira dos Pegões valley, on the northwestern outskirts of Tomar, the 16th-century Pegões Aqueduct was originally built to supply the Convent of Christ with water. Like a caterpillar on long legs, the colossal water channel with its succession of lofty double-tiered arches winds around the hills for over 6 km (3.7 mi). Its highest point is 30 m (98 ft). Construction started in 1593 by Italian architect and engineer Filipe Terzi and was completed in 1641 by Portuguese architect Pedro Fernandes Torres.

Festivals and Events

Tray Festival
(Festa dos Tabuleiros)

June or July

One of Tomar's most ancient local traditions, the Tray Festival is a spectacle like no other. Staged every four years in June or July, it takes its name from the festival's high point: a procession of local girls wearing headdresses made from bread piled staggeringly high, parading through the streets with male partners as attendants. The headdresses, called tabuleiros, are decorated with colorful flowers and topped off with a white dove, symbolizing Christianity's Holy Spirit. The festival also features other traditional ceremonies and celebrations. The day after the procession, the pêza takes place, when bread and meat are shared among the local people. The festival is believed to have originated in rituals dating to the 13th century. Almost the entire local population—thousands of men, women, and children—takes part in this event.

Knights Templar Festival
(Festival dos Templários)

tel. 249 310 040; www.templarknights.eu;
July

The annual Knights Templar

Tray Festival

Festival is a series of celebrations dedicated to the Templars, held over four days at the beginning of July. These include a torchlit Knights Parade, medieval banquets, and a reenactment of the 1190 Moorish siege of Tomar. The festival dates to 2013, when Tomar was chosen to be world headquarters of the International Order of the Knights Templar (OSMTH)—the oldest Knights Templar organization in the world. The entire town dresses in its best medieval finery to recreate the mysticism and magic of the bygone era, with costumes, arts and crafts, and food and drink galore.

Food

✪ Café Estrelas de Tomar

*R. Serpa Pinto 12; tel. 249 313 275; www.
estrelasdetomar.pt; Thurs.-Tues. 8am-8pm;
€5*

Established in 1960, this riverfront café and bakery is one of the oldest and most celebrated in Tomar, producing fresh local sweets and "conventual" confectionary (traditional recipes that allegedly seeped down from the country's guarded convents), including Tomar's famous queijadas and fatias, every day. It is located on the west bank, near the Rua Marquês de Pombal Bridge.

Taverna Antiqua

*Praça da República 23-25; tel. 249 311 236;
www.tavernaantiqua.com; Tues.-Sun. noon-
3pm and 7pm-11pm; €15*

Fitting for a town so closely linked to knights, this medieval-themed restaurant, on the main Praça da República square, offers a unique dining experience with food, crockery, and entertainment of the era. Think banquet vibes, heavy wood tables, rock walls, and candlelight.

O Alpendre

*Rua Principal 13; tel. 919 562 990; https://
restaurante-alpendre.com; Mon.-Fri. noon-
2:30pm; €15*

Portuguese food doesn't get any better than at rustic O Alpendre, a homey, inexpensive eatery on the Nabão's east bank, with rich regional favorites including excellent beef dishes and homemade desserts.

Bela Vista

*Rua Marquês de Pombal 68; tel. 249 312
870; http://abelavista.pt; Wed.-Mon. 11am-
11pm; €15*

Sitting pretty on the Nabão riverbank, Bela Vista serves authentic regional meat and fish dishes like octopus rice and roast goat. Founded in 1922, it boasts stunning views over the river, Mouchão Park, and the convent hill from the outdoor esplanade—a lovely spot for a memorable meal.

Accommodations

Thomar Story Guest House

Rua João Carlos Everard 53; tel. 925 936 273; www.thomarstory.pt; €75 d

In the heart of historical Tomar, modern little Thomar Story Guest House occupies a late-19th-century building that oozes character and charm. Each of the 12 tastefully decorated rooms is designed to reflect the town's history.

Thomar Boutique Hotel

Rua Santa Iria 14; tel. 249 323 210; www.thomarboutiquehotel.com; €100 d

This chic and contemporary urban boutique hotel is within walking distance of Tomar's main sights. Located on the Nabão riverside, it has a nice rooftop with great views over the historical town center.

✪ Hotel dos Templários

Largo Candido dos Reis 1; tel. 249 310 100; www.hoteldostemplarios.com; €160 d

Overlooking the Nabão River, at the foot of the Convent of Christ hill, the central, four-star Hotel dos Templários has spacious rooms and sizable indoor and outdoor pools. Its great location makes a good base for exploring the region.

Information and Services

- **National emergency number:** tel. 112
- **PSP police:** Rua Dom Lopo Dias de Sousa 8D; tel. 249 413 900; www.psp.pt
- **Tourist office:** Av. Dr. Cândido Madureira 531; tel. 249 329 800; www.cm-tomar.pt, daily 8am-6pm
- **Tomar Health Center:** Rua Nabância 14; tel. 249 329 720; Mon.-Fri. 9am-noon and 2pm-5:30pm

Getting There and Around

GETTING THERE

Car

Tomar is a 1.5-hour, 140-km (87-mi) drive north from **Lisbon** on the **A1** motorway.

Bus

Rede Expressos (tel. 707 223 344; www.rede-expressos.pt) runs four daily buses between Lisbon's **Sete Rios** hub and Tomar (1 hour 45 minutes; €12). **Rodoviária do Tejo** (tel. 249 810 700; www.rodotejo.pt) has seasonal buses (May-Oct.), a special "Leisure" sightseeing line that links Tomar to Nazaré, stopping in Fátima, Batalha and Alcobaça along the **IC9** road. Tomar's **bus station** (Avenida Combatentes da Grande Guerra; tel. 249 787 878) is located on the west side of the Nabão river, a 15-minute walk south of the Convent of Christ.

Train

CP (tel. 707 210 220; www.cp.pt) trains run from Lisbon stations including **Santa Apolónia, Entrecampos, Cais do Sodré,** **Sete Rios, Rossio,** and **Oriente** stations to Tomar (2 hours; €11) roughly every couple of hours. Tomar's **railway station** is adjacent to the bus station on Avenida Combatentes da Grande Guerra, a short walk from the historical city center.

GETTING AROUND

Tomar is easy to navigate, with most of the main sights and transport terminals being packed into town on the west side of the river. The town is easily (and best) covered **on foot.**

There is plenty of **parking** in Tomar, such as the free parking lot in the **Varzea Grande square** in front of **Tomar Station** and an **underground parking garage** on the opposite side of the river. However, seeing as the Covent is somewhat of an uphill hike (albeit a relatively short one), driving up or even getting a local **tuk-tuk** is also an option (Tuk Lovers, Praça da República main square; tel. 918 541 229 or 918 350 329; www.tuk-lovers.com; from €10).

Costa da Caparica

Located just south of Lisbon, on the other side of the Tagus River, Costa da Caparica is a sun-and-fun destination geared largely toward Portuguese tourists. Born from a traditional fishing village, it is still very much a working fishermen's town, and colorful little fishing boats can be seen going out to sea and coming in with their loads on a daily basis. Being a more recent resort, Costa da Caparica lacks some of the traditional charm and character that other popular beach resorts like Cascais and Estoril offer but makes

Highlights

✪ **Costa da Caparica Promenade:** Walk off the ice cream with a scenic stroll along the seafront promenade that hems Costa da Caparica town (page 192).

✪ **Transpraia Mini Tourist Train:** See the best of Costa da Caparica's many beaches on this fun little tourist train (page 193).

✪ **Praia Fonte da Telha:** Spot ancient fossils in the cliffs surrounding Fonte da Telha beach (page 195).

up for it with space and competitive prices.

Famous for its beaches, Caparica has the longest continuous stretch of sand in Europe, a 30-km (19-mi) strip of coastline that extends along the entire western fringe of the Setúbal Peninsula. Popular with seaside loving Lisboetas, Costa da Caparica is still relatively undiscovered by foreign tourists. In summer the resort area comes alive with cool sunset parties at busy beach bars. Luxury villas sit alongside neat apartment blocks, hotels, and traditional fishermen's huts. With its consistent rolling waves and Portugal's original nudist beach (Meco), Costa da Caparica is a hip melting pot of families, in-crowds, surfers, and free-spirits. The further south you head, the wilder and more rugged the scenery becomes.

ORIENTATION

Costa da Caparica is a knife-shaped strip of coast that extends from the top of the **Setúbal Peninsula,** narrowing off toward **Meco Beach** at the bottom. The resort's **town,** the heart of Costa da Caparica, with its shops, bars, restaurants, and hotels, is located toward the top of the coastal strip. The **bus station** is located about 1 km (0.6 mi) southeast of the main town center, and 500 m (0.3 mi) from the beachfront. A 2-km (1.2-mi) **promenade** runs along the seafront. Toward the bottom end

Previous: surfer on the beach along Costa da Caparica; **above:** Costa da Caparica's promenade; Transpraia train.

of the promenade is the **Bairro dos Pescadores,** the old fishermen's quarters, where the local fishermen go about their daily lives in their whitewashed houses.

The busy north end of Costa da Caparica is family-friendly and developed for tourism. Farther south, you'll find vast, spacious stretches of sand where nudism becomes the norm. At the far southern end, the beaches are pristine, fringed by rugged reedy dunes and accessible only by **car** or by the **tourist train.** Also along this stretch of coast is the **Costa da Caparica Fossil Cliff Protected Landscape** (Paisagem Protegida da Arriba Fossil da Costa da Caparica)—around 10 km (6 mi) south of Costa da Caparica town, reachable by walking from **Fonte da Telha** village—a nature preserve rich in ancient fossils and rocks. Blanketing the cliffs that shelter the southern beaches, this natural area is a protected zone that sprawls over 1,000 hectares (2,500 acres). It is rich in ancient fossils and rocks, some of which are more than 15 million years old.

The **N377-2** is the main road that runs through the town and along the seafront.

PLANNING YOUR TIME

A 20-minute drive from Lisbon (17 km/10.5 mi), the Caparica Coast is a great place to head—especially in summer—for a few hours at the beach or a fun weekend away from the flurry of the city. It is easy to reach by **car** from Lisbon, over the **25 de Abril Bridge,** and there is regular and inexpensive **public transport** between Lisbon and Costa da Caparica. A **direct bus** is one option, while taking the **ferry** from Cais do Sodré to Cacilhas, and from there an **express bus** to Costa da Caparica, is another. The ferry operates daily 5am-1:20am. Buses run at least once an hour, pretty much around the clock, seven days a week. In **summer** Costa da Caparica will be busy but seldom feels crowded or overrun. If you have a car, Costa da Caparica can also be combined with a day trip to other parts of the peninsula, such as Setúbal or Sesimbra. By public transport the journey becomes lengthy and time-consuming.

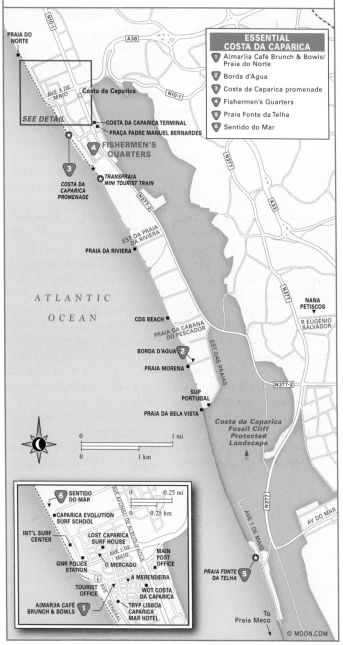

Costa da Caparica

PRAIA DO NORTE

A38

N10-1

AVE 1 DE MAIO

Costa da Caparica

SEE DETAIL

COSTA DA CAPARICA TERMINAL

PRAÇA PADRE MANUEL BERNARDES

FISHERMEN'S QUARTERS 4

3

COSTA DA CAPARICA PROMENADE

TRANSPRAIA MINI TOURIST TRAIN

N377-2

EST DA PRAIA DA RIVIERA

PRAIA DA RIVIERA

ATLANTIC OCEAN

N377

NANA PETISCOS

R EUGÉNIO SALVADOR

CDS BEACH

PRAIA DA CABANA DO PESCADOR

N33

BORDA D'AGUA 2

PRAIA MORENA

EST DAS PRAIAS

N377-2

SUP PORTUGAL

PRAIA DA BELA VISTA

Costa da Caparica Fossil Cliff Protected Landscape

N377

0 ___ 1 mi
0 ___ 1 km

AVE 1 DE MAIO

AV DO MAR

To Praia Meco

ESSENTIAL COSTA DA CAPARICA

1. A(mar)ia Café Brunch & Bowls/ Praia do Norte
2. Borda d'Agua
3. Costa da Caparica promenade
4. Fishermen's Quarters
5. Praia Fonte da Telha
6. Sentido do Mar

Detail inset

6 SENTIDO DO MAR

CAPARICA EVOLUTION SURF SCHOOL

INT'L SURF CENTER

LOST CAPARICA SURF HOUSE

AVE AFONSO DE ALBUQUERQUE

0 ___ 0.25 mi
0 ___ 0.25 km

AVE 1 DE MAIO

MAIN POST OFFICE

GNR POLICE STATION

O MERCADO

A MERENDEIRA

i TOURIST OFFICE

WOT COSTA DA CAPARICA

AVE GENERAL

1 A(MAR)IA CAFÉ BRUNCH & BOWLS

TRYP LISBOA CAPARICA MAR HOTEL

PRAIA FONTE DA TELHA 5

© MOON.COM

Itinerary Idea

ESSENTIAL COSTA DA CAPARICA

Make your way from Lisbon to Costa da Caparica after breakfast, by either driving over the 25 de Abril Bridge or taking public transport. If driving, you can park in the northern end of town, in the **parking lots** near the Inatel campsite and Praia do Norte beach. It's a good idea to pack **towels and swimsuits** for a trip to Costa da Caparica, but don't worry too much if you forget—there's no shortage of shops selling such paraphernalia in town. There are also plenty of beach concessions with sun beds and umbrellas for rent for around €7-10 a day.

1 For a chilled-out late breakfast or brunch, head to **A(mar)ia Café Brunch & Bowls,** in the heart of Costa da Caparica town, before spending a few hours people-watching and soaking up the sun on **Praia do Norte.**

2 For a waterfront lunch, sample freshly caught seafood at **Borda d'Agua.**

3 Walk lunch off with a stroll along the **Costa da Caparica promenade,** admiring the fishing boats, hotels, and vistas en route.

4 Head to the **Fishermen's Quarters** to explore this traditional neighborhood with its typical shack-like houses, characterful inhabitants, and fishing equipment strewn along the streets.

5 Jump on the Transpraia mini tourist train to see Costa da Caparica's southern beaches, such as **Praia Fonte da Telha,** famed for its healing mud.

6 Return to town on the Transpraia just in time for a sunset dinner at **Sentido do Mar** before heading back to Lisbon.

Sights

⚙ COSTA DA CAPARICA PROMENADE

Avenida General Humberto Delgado; limited parking along this strip

Costa da Caparica's long promenade is the perfect spot for a refreshing stroll any time of year. It runs north to south, parallel with the beach and the main coastal through-road, Avenida General Humberto Delgado. Soak up the sun and the sea breeze as you walk along the seafront, past colorful beach shacks and hip bars; make way for the rollerbladers and cyclists and joggers. It's a 2.6-km (1.6-mi) stroll from North Beach at the top end of town to the Fishermen's Quarters and beach train at the bottom. The trailhead is at the top of town near the P2 parking lot, and the walk along the promenade takes around 30 minutes to complete, one-way.

FISHERMEN'S QUARTERS
(Bairro dos Pescadores)

Rua Parque de Campsimo de Almada; on-street parking

This part of town is not as easy on the eye as Costa da Caparica's beautiful beaches, but it is an important piece of the local fabric and history. Built to house the town's traditional

Costa da Caparica's promenade

fishing families, the Fishermen's Quarters is a raw and authentic government-funded social housing neighborhood. Its inhabitants still live off the sea and are mostly active fisherfolk. Their neighborhood is a mishmash of different sized boxy buildings, with corrugated iron trimmings, colorful clothing flying from washing lines, authentic characters in the street, and plant pots and fishing paraphernalia strewn out front.

Transpraia train

✪ TRANSPRAIA MINI TOURIST TRAIN

Rua Parque Infantil; tel. 212 900 706; www. transpraia.pt; daily 9am-8pm June-Sept.

The Transpraia mini tourist train carries beachgoers from one end of Costa da Caparica to the other. It's a bumpy but scenic way to discover Costa's best beach spots. It runs 9 km (5.6 mi) from Caparica town, starting at **Praia do Norte,** the beach in front of the fishermen's quarters, down to its southernmost stop at Fonte da Telha, which takes around 25 minutes, with four little stations and 15 stops en route. The track is divided into **zone 1** (€5 round-trip) and **zone 2** (€8.50

round-trip). The train operates only in high season (June-September). There are two departures per hour from each end, one on the hour and the other at half past. In Caparica, the Transpraia train leaves from in front of the children's beachside play park in the main town center.

COSTA DA CAPARICA FOSSIL CLIFF PROTECTED LANDSCAPE

(Paisagem Protegida da Arriba Fossil da Costa da Caparica)

Rua Dom João V, 17, Aroeira, Estrada Florestal da Costa de Caparica - Praia da Rainha

This protected area, about 12 km (7.5 mi) south of Costa da Caparica town, near Fonte da Telha beach, and covering 1,570 hectares (3,880 acres), centers on a ridge of unusually shaped cliffs, rich in fossil fauna. A marked nature trail runs along the foot of the cliffs, which are swaddled by a blanket of woodland, scrubland, and pine trees that form the basis of a botanical reserve. It was designated a

Costa da Caparica Fossil Cliff

protected landscape in 1984 for the purpose of preserving its geomorphological and geological characteristics, and is currently one of about 30 officially protected areas in Portugal. Dating back some 10 million years, these cliffs and their surroundings are among the most important examples of their kind in Europe.

Beaches

TOP EXPERIENCE

Costa da Caparica is famous for its beaches, and with good reason. Boasting a coastline of golden sandy shore that stretches over 30 km (19 mi), it has an entire spectrum of beaches for all purposes and ambiences: surfing, naturist, families, gay, you name it, Costa da Caparica has a beach for it. A lively resort in summer and peaceful but still popular in winter, its beaches are sought by sun-lovers and surfers alike. The sea here is cool, and waves can be powerful and of a good size, but not on the same scale as in Nazaré or Peniche. Most of these beaches will have some form of beach bar or restaurant providing service, and usually a concession with beds and umbrellas, while parking is generally available along the roads leading to the beaches or in dusty parking lots.

There are more than a dozen beaches making up the Costa da Caparica coast, starting with the northernmost, the aptly named **Praia do Norte** (North Beach). The stretch of sand immediately fronting the Costa da Caparica resort is segmented by tidal piers to protect the coastline from rough tides. This creates a series of small beaches, locally named after the bars that serve them. From there a long stretch of beach extends over 24 km (15 mi) to the southernmost Caparica beach, **Meco,** which is Portugal's original and most famous nudist beach. The best-known beaches along the coast are usually sought-after for their easy access and space. Most will have a lifeguard on duty during the main beach months, loosely May/June to September. The cute **Transpraia beach train** (www. transpraia.pt; €3-5 one-way) connects over a dozen of the beaches, starting in Costa da Caparica town near Praia do Norte.

North Beach
(Praia do Norte)
Rua Manuel Agro Ferreira 1, off Costa da Caparica main town; parking lots nearby

A thin sliver of sand at the top end of Costa da Caparica, Praia do Norte is one of the busier beaches, frequented by locals, tourists, working fishermen, and surfers. Flanked by two pontoons, this strip of beach all but disappears when the tide is high.

Morena Beach
(Praia Morena)

6 km (3.7 mi) south of Costa da Caparica town

Just before Bela Vista Beach, Morena Beach is renowned for being a quiet, tranquil beach with plenty of space, easy parking, and translucent, calm waters that make it ideal for stand-up paddleboarding.

Bela Vista Beach
(Praia da Bela Vista)

7 km (4.3 mi) south of Costa da Caparica town

An official nudist beach, Praia da Bela Vista is a wide, peaceful beach of fine white sand, flanked by cliffs and dunes. It is accessed by a dirt road and has its own parking lot.

✪ Fonte da Telha Beach
(Praia Fonte da Telha)

10 km (6 mi) south of Costa da Caparica town

Fonte da Telha beach, the last stop on the Transpraia train, is a vast, spacious beach made up of soft white sand and cool, clean seawaters, as famous for being an unofficial naturist beach as it is for being walking distance to the Lagoa de Albufeira tidal lagoon. It fronts a beach town made up of fishermen's huts, local cafés, and holiday homes that grew from a tiny fishing community. There are plenty of pockets for parking alongside the beach.

Sports and Recreation

SURFING AND STAND-UP PADDLEBOARDING

Waves along this stretch are consistent but not in the same category as Guincho or Ericeira, which makes Costa da Caparica perfect for less-experienced surfers. Top spots for surfing are **CDS Beach** (Costa da Caparica town, off the main avenue) and **Praia da Riviera** (2 km/1.2 mi south of CDS Beach). Local surf schools, shops, and guesthouses have flourished in the vicinity.

Most establishments will generally charge around €15 for 2-hour board plus wetsuit rentals.

Caparica Evolution Surf School

Estrada da Muralha, Marcelino Beach-K bar; tel. 939 124 758; http://www.kevolutionsurf.com; daily 9am-8pm May-Oct., daily 10am-6pm Nov.-Apr.

Local surf schools, shops, and guesthouses have flourished in the vicinity, including the Caparica Evolution Surf School.

surfing off Costa da Caparica

International Surf Center

Muralha da Praia, Apoio 10; tel. 935 528 383; www.centrointernacionaldesurf.com; daily 9am-8pm

Located on Costa da Caparica's main town beachfront, the International Surf Center organizes lessons and rentals of all types of boards and surf equipment.

SUP Portugal

Praia da Bela Vista; tel. 967 697 039; www. sup-portugal.com; daily 10am-7pm

Located on Bela Vista beach, SUP Portugal is a stand-up paddleboard school that runs courses, tours, and board rentals.

Food

Costa da Caparica excels in seafood. Canja de carapau (mackerel soup) is a local specialty.

A(mar)ia Café Brunch & Bowls

Largo Vasco da Gama 1; tel. 931 751 589; Tues.-Sun. 10am-6:30pm; €10

This is the best place for a chilled-out breakfast or brunch in Costa da Caparica. The highly-rated A(mar)ia Café is a quaint little house along the seafront serving everything from the traditional full English to continental platters, fruit and açaí bowls, and trendy avocado toast. Enjoy a healthy shake or snack in one of the cool macramé hanging chairs, or tuck into a taco, poke bowl, or waffle.

196

Sentido do Mar

Rua Muralha da Praia, Apoio 7, Praia do Norte 278; tel. 212 900 473; https://sentidodomar.pt; daily noon-3:30pm and 6:30pm-10:30pm; €10

Funky and modern, Sentido do Mar has menus covering sushi to grilled fresh fish, complemented with fantastic sunset views.

O Mercado

Avenida 1 de Maio 36D; tel. 218 235 099; www.facebook.com/omercadocc; Tues.-Sat. 12:30pm-3pm and 7:30pm-10pm; €15

A rustic-chic gastropub in the center of Costa da Caparica, O Mercado serves typical Portuguese fare made from the freshest market produce, with a contemporary international flourish; don't miss the octopus tempura.

A Merendeira

Rua dos Pescadores 20; tel. 212 904 527; www.amerendeira.com; daily 10am-1am; €6

A Merendeira's wholesome soups, freshly baked chouriço rolls, and traditional puddings make it the perfect pit stop for a quick lunch.

NANA Petiscos

Rua Eugénio Salvador 23; tel. 933 240 178; www.nanapetiscos.pt; Wed.-Sun. 3pm-11:30pm; €8

Typical tasca (a simple, small Portuguese eatery), NANA Petiscos serves a rainbow of petiscos (tapas)—tasty fish and meat snacks perfect for sharing.

Borda d'Agua

Praia da Morena; tel. 212 975 213; www.bordadagua.com.pt; daily 10am-midnight May-Oct., 10am-7:30pm Nov.-Apr.; €15

The name of Borda d'Agua translates as "waterside," and it makes the most of its beachside location, with a large deck for alfresco dining as well as enclosed indoor seating for breezier days. It's a must-visit for delicious fresh fish with a sea breeze.

Accommodations

Hotels in Costa da Caparica are varied and cheaper than most accommodations in central Lisbon.

Lost Caparica Surf House

Rua Dr. Barros de Castro 17; tel. 918 707 779; www.lostcaparica.com; €40 pp shared, €70 d private room

Surfers will love Lost Caparica Surf House, whose accommodations range from a shared six-bed room to private rooms with single or double beds. An added bonus is the on-site surf school and rental equipment.

WOT Costa da Caparica

Av. Dr. Aresta Branco 22; tel. 926 250 786; www.wotels.com; €100 d

Set a few streets back from the beach, small, simple WOT Costa da Caparica is unfussy and clean, with a good breakfast included in the rates.

✪ Tryp Lisboa Caparica Mar Hotel

Av. Gen. Humberto Delgado 47;
tel. 212 918 900;
www.tryplisboacaparica.com;
from €138 d

The ultimate beachfront hotel, four-star Hotel Costa da Caparica is family-friendly, with a nice swimming pool. Some of the 354 rooms over seven floors have views over the Atlantic.

Information and Services

- **GNR police station:** Rua Pedro Álvares Cabral 29; tel. 265 242 590, www.gnr.pt
- **Tourist office:** Av. da República 18; tel. 212 900 071; Mon.-Sat. 9:30am-1pm and 2pm-5:30pm
- **Main post office:** Praça de 9 de Julho

Getting There and Around

GETTING THERE
Car

Costa da Caparica is roughly 16 km (10 mi) from downtown **Lisbon.** From Lisbon, take the **A8** motorway over the **25 de Abril Bridge** southbound, before heading west on the **A38** to Costa da Caparica. This is the fastest road route between Lisbon and Costa da Caparica and takes around 20 minutes if traffic is flowing normally. Be warned that on good-weather weekends and in summer, the traffic across the bridge can get very congested.

Bus

There are two ways of getting from Lisbon to Costa da Caparica by public transport. The most direct is by taking the frequent **3710 bus** operated by **Carris Metropolitana** (tel. 210 410 400; www.carrismetropolitana.pt; daily) from **Praça do Areeiro** (Metro Green line), the 3708 line from Cais do Sodré, or 3709 service from Marquês do Pombal (weekdays only, less frequent). Note that the Carris network covers inside the city centre, while Carris Metropolitana covers the area outside the main city centre. All terminate in Costa da Caparica near the Argolas Tower in Praça Manuel Bernardes. Tickets cost around €3 and the journey takes approximately 40-45 minutes.

Alternatively, a more roundabout, but possibly more fun journey, involves taking the **ferry** from **Cais do Sodré** (Metro Green line) to Cacilhas, and catching the 3011 bus from **Cacilhas** to Costa da Caparica. The ferry costs €1.50

one-way and terminates at the Cacilhas main transport hub. From there take the 3011 bus (www.tsuldotejo.pt) to Costa da Caparica.

GETTING AROUND

Costa da Caparica's main sights—the main beach and town center, **Fishermen's Quarters,** and **tourist train**—are all within walking distance. During peak season, the little **Transpraia** beach train connects 15 different stops along a 9-km (5.5-mi) stretch of coast. It departs from **Praia do Norte,** the beach in front of the Fishermen's Quarters, and runs to **Praia Fonte da Telha.**

A long road, the N377, runs parallel to the stretch of coast south of Costa da Caparica town, to Fonte da Telha beach. Driving from Costa da Caparica to Fonte da Telha takes just under 20 minutes.

Setúbal Peninsula

Comprising several municipali-ties and cities, the Setúbal Peninsula is an en-thralling, underexplored region just a stone's throw from Lisbon, reached by crossing ei-ther the 25 de Abril Bridge or the Vasco da Gama Bridge. An hour's drive south from the capital, Setúbal is home to a dolphin-inhab-ited estuary, famed natural landscapes, and a folklore-infused cape where dinosaurs once roamed. Its golden beaches and freshest sea-food are the cherry on top.

Wedged between the Arrábida Natural

Highlights

✪ Dolphin-Watching in Sado Estuary: Enjoy one of Setúbal's most unique and popular attractions with a boat trip to meet the Sado Estuary's friendly community of wild bottlenose dolphins (page 209).

✪ Seafood in Sesimbra: Sesimbra's seafood isn't famed for nothing; tuck into heaped platters of the freshest delicacies straight from the Atlantic Ocean at a picturesque port-side restaurant—make sure to try the local specialty, grilled black scabbard fish (page 216).

✪ Cabo Espichel Promontory and Lighthouse: There's something alluringly eerie about the barren Espichel Cape with its abandoned sanctuary, dinosaur footprints embedded in the cliff tops, and the tiny chapel solemnly overlooking the endless Atlantic (page 218).

✪ Setúbal-Troia Ferry Crossing: Enjoy unique views of the Sado Estuary and Troia from one of the bright green ferries that make the regular daily crossings between the two. If you're lucky, you might even spot dolphins (page 222).

✪ Cetobriga Roman Ruins: Tour the ancient houses and Roman thermal baths of Cetobriga, a settlement originating in the 1st century (page 223).

✪ Troia Beaches: You'll find plenty of space to stretch out on one of Troia's long, golden beaches (page 224).

✪ Horseback Riding on Comporta Beach: Some very famous faces are said to have enjoyed a horse ride down the soft, white stretch of Comporta Beach, one of the area's top activities (page 232).

Park and the Sado Estuary Natural Reserve, the main city, Setúbal, a 50-minute drive south of Lisbon, is an industrialized working port, home to the country's largest fish market. Setúbal makes no apologies for its unrefined, unpolished character, but the unbridled natural beauty that surrounds the city eclipses what it lacks in airs and graces. A few kilometers west of Setúbal city is the sprawling

Arrábida Natural Park, where wild birds of prey soar over dramatic coastal scenery. Farther on, toward the western tip of the Arrábida Park, are charming fishing town Sesimbra and vertiginous Espichel Cape. A major draw to Setúbal is its estuary, one of few water inlets in Europe to be inhabited by wild dolphins, which happily make appearances for eager tourists.

ORIENTATION

Setúbal city is situated 54 km (33.5 mi) south of Lisbon, across the Tagus River. It is sandwiched by two expansive natural beauty spots: **Arrábida Natural Park** to the west and **Sado Estuary Natural Reserve** to the east. Heading west, through the Arrábida Park, you reach **Sesimbra,** and further on still, at the very westernmost tip of the peninsula, is **Cabo Espichel,** the Espichel Cape. The region's most popular tourist activity, dolphin-watching trips depart from Setúbal waterfront and Sesimbra's little port.

The Troia Peninsula is a long sandbank situated 1 hour 45 minutes south of Lisbon, or a 25-minute ferry ride across from the port city of Setúbal. Passenger ferries frequently cross from Setúbal to the tip of the peninsula, Troia town, with its modern marina and white sand beaches. Vehicle ferries sail to and from another port, a little further down on the east side of the peninsula. **Troia** is a place where visitors can really unwind, taking a boat trip to see the dolphins, enjoying a stroll along the beach or a cycle without heaps of traffic, or tucking into a good meal at one of the upmarket eateries around the marina.

Troia Peninsula separates the Atlantic Ocean to the west from the Sado Estuary Nature Reserve to the east. Measuring approximately 17 km (10.5 mi) in length, it is easy to navigate and has good infrastructure. At its base, a 20-minute (17 km/10.5 mi) drive from Troia Marina, is the Alentejo village of **Comporta.**

PLANNING YOUR TIME

A day trip to Setúbal is highly recommended to see a rawer, unadulterated side of Portugal's seafaring soul, and the Sado dolphins never fail to bring a smile to those who catch one of the many boat trips that run from the city. **Setúbal** is an easy 50-minute drive (54 km/33.5 mi) south of Lisbon, following either the main **A2** or **A12** motorways. Allow a full day to explore its attractions; the dolphin trips usually take around 3 hours. Book trips online beforehand to secure places.

Also set aside a couple of hours to explore the **Arrábida Natural Park,** just west of Setúbal. While all this and more can be done in one

---

Previous: fishing boats docked at Setúbal; the ferry in Setúbal; Cabo Espichel Promontory and Lighthouse.

day, spending a night in quaint **Sesimbra,** a short drive west of Setúbal, is highly recommended. There you can enjoy a romantic seafood dinner and a trip to **Cabo Espichel.** The last bus back to Lisbon from Setúbal leaves at around 8:30pm most of the year, later in summer; the last train departs slightly later, at 8:48pm.

Troia is an excellent day-trip destination with a jaw-dropping backdrop. Unless your purpose is a beach holiday—in which case, plan to spend a full day, or maybe even a night in Troia—its main attractions can be covered in a few hours while passing through the peninsula. Set aside at least a morning or afternoon to enjoy a walk along one of its scenic trails, explore the town, and enjoy a coffee on the attractive marina. The last ferry leaves Troia at 10:40pm; the last pedestrian catamaran sets off at 4:30am. Schedules may change depending on season. The ideal itinerary would be to tack a trip to Troia and **Comporta** on to a visit to Setúbal.

Itinerary Ideas

DAY 1

Leaving Lisbon for Setúbal in your rental car, take either the **A2** motorway over the **25 de Abril Bridge** or the **A12** over the newer **Vasco da Gama Bridge.**

1 In Setúbal, head straight to the waterfront for a morning Sado Estuary dolphin-watching trip with **Vertigem Azul;** book your tickets in advance.

2 Enjoy lunch at **Batareo,** one of Setúbal's many great seafood restaurants, a typical fishermen's tavern famed for its charcoal-grilled fresh fish, scallops, and octopus salad.

3 After lunch, take the **Setúbal-Troia Ferry** across to Troia. Keep an eye out for dolphins as the ferry crosses the Sado Estuary.

4 Stroll along Troia's **beachside walkways** and stop at a beachside café for an afternoon coffee.

5 Drive 20 minutes south on N253-1 to **Comporta** to relax beside the crystal clear waters of Comporta Beach.

6 Enjoy a sunset dinner at **Sublime Comporta's Country Retreat & Spa,** then head back to Setúbal or Lisbon.

Setúbal Peninsula

DAY 2

1 Walk around Setúbal town center, taking in sights such as the recently revamped waterfront and the **Monastery of Jesus of Setúbal.**

2 Sample local produce for lunch at the busy and bustling **Livramento Market.**

3 Jump in the car and head 2.5 km (1.5 mi) west to the Arrábida Natural Park, spending a couple of hours exploring this beautiful area with a hike and visiting the **Our Lady of Arrábida Fort.**

4 Before heading back to town, visit the 16th-century **Arrábida Monastery.**

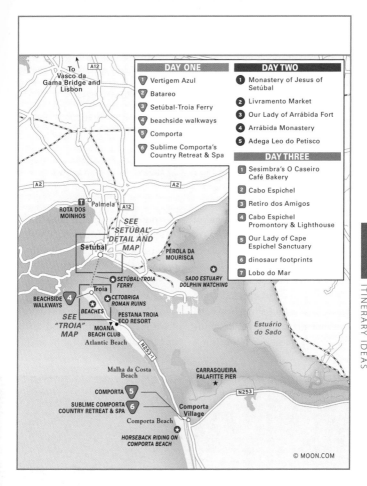

Within the map image:

DAY ONE
1. Vertigem Azul
2. Batareo
3. Setúbal-Troia Ferry
4. beachside walkways
5. Comporta
6. Sublime Comporta's Country Retreat & Spa

DAY TWO
1. Monastery of Jesus of Setúbal
2. Livramento Market
3. Our Lady of Arrábida Fort
4. Arrábida Monastery
5. Adega Leo do Petisco

DAY THREE
1. Sesimbra's O Caseiro Café Bakery
2. Cabo Espichel
3. Retiro dos Amigos
4. Cabo Espichel Promontory & Lighthouse
5. Our Lady of Cape Espichel Sanctuary
6. dinosaur footprints
7. Lobo do Mar

© MOON.COM

---

5 Tuck into fried cuttlefish (choco frito), a local specialty, at **Adega Leo do Petisco,** in the town center.

DAY 3

1 For a spot of breakfast, drive to **Sesimbra's O Caseiro Café Bakery.**

2 Keep driving west along Av. 25 de Abril toward **Cabo Espichel,** the westernmost point of the Setúbal Peninsula.

3 Pop in to the simple and friendly **Retiro dos Amigos** for lunch.

4 Stroll around the blustery **Cabo Espichel Promontory** toward the **lighthouse.**

5 Explore the ghost town **Our Lady of Cape Espichel Sanctuary,** an eerie and largely abandoned site of religious, historical, and cultural interest overlooking the tumultuous ocean. As well as the Sanctuary itself, the spot is famous for fossilized dinosaur footprints.

6 Walk along the cliffs to see the **dinosaur footprints.**

7 Head back to Sesimbra to enjoy more fresh seafood for dinner at **Lobo do Mar.** Be sure to try grilled scabbard fish, a local specialty.

Setúbal and the Sado Estuary

The unpolished port town of Setúbal is divisive. Many are charmed by its lovely old town square, busy waterfront, and unrepentant lack of pretension; others are unable to see past its industrial facade. Colorful fishing boats and commuter ferries run beside leisure vessels, a sure sign that tourism is buoying the city. With good hotels and restaurants, Setúbal is well placed as a base for exploring the wildlife-heavy Sado Estuary.

Originating in the deep Alentejo, in the Vigia mountain range, the Sado River flows into the sea south of Setúbal. The humid and fertile Sado Estuary Natural Reserve

town center of Setúbal

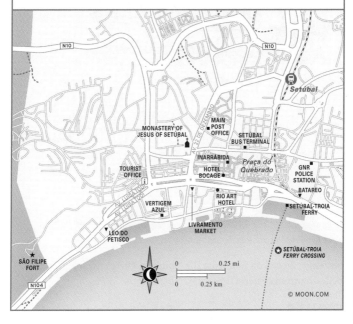

Setúbal

MONASTERY OF JESUS OF SETÚBAL

MAIN POST OFFICE

SETÚBAL BUS TERMINAL

TOURIST OFFICE

INARRÁBIDA

HOTEL BOCAGE

Praça do Quebrado

GNR POLICE STATION

BATAREO

VERTIGEM AZUL

RIO ART HOTEL

SETÚBAL-TROIA FERRY

LÉO DO PETISCO

LIVRAMENTO MARKET

SETÚBAL-TROIA FERRY CROSSING

SÃO FILIPE FORT

0   0.25 mi

0   0.25 km

N104

N10

N10

AV. 22 DE DEZEMBRO

AV. LUÍSA TODI

AV. LUÍSA TODI

Setúbal

© MOON.COM

covers 230 sq km (89 sq mi) of rich wetlands. It is a protected nature reserve, one of 30 officially protected areas in the country, where mirrorlike wetlands and surrounding banks and thickets host more than 200 bird species, including white storks and pink flamingos. Once one of the most important salt-producing areas in the country, it is a hot spot for bird- and dolphin-watching. A pod of bottlenose dolphins has long resided in the estuary's calm waters, a phenomenon unique in Portugal and rare in the world.

ORIENTATION

Sustained by the Sado River, Setúbal formed on the river's bay-like western bank, an industrious, underrated port city that is surprisingly appealing once you scratch past its unpolished surface. It sits on the southern fringe of the Setúbal Peninsula, wedged between the **Arrábida Natural Park** and the **Sado Estuary.** Located along the waterfront is the **ferry terminal,** and set back from the waterfront is the historical **old town** and its maze of quaint cobbled streets dotted with hip boutiques and eateries. Setúbal's main **bus terminal** is set a few streets back from the waterfront, about 150 m (500 ft) from the city center, while the **train station** is just under a kilometer (0.5 mi) north of the center. Most of Setúbal's main sights can

a dolphin-watching cruise on the Sado Estuary

be easily reached on foot from the pedestrianized center.

SIGHTS
Monastery of Jesus of Setúbal
(Convento e Igreja de Jesus)

Rua Acácio Barradas 2; tel. 265 537 890; www.mun-setubal.pt; Tues.-Sat. 10am-6pm, Sun. 3pm-7pm; free

Designed in 1494 by architect Diogo de Boitaca (best known for his work on Lisbon's emblematic Jerónimos Monastery), the austere gray Monastery of Jesus of Setúbal is one of the earliest examples of Manueline architecture in Portugal. Among its distinguishing features are soaring spiral granite pillars and typical azulejo murals. Outside, gargoyles and twisted pinnacles perforate an otherwise plain facade. Inside, an intricate ribbed vaulted ceiling in the main chapel and twisted-rope columns of pink and beige Arrábida stone are highlights.

São Filipe Fort
(Forteleza de São Filipe)

Estrada do Castelo de São Filipe; tel. 265 545 010; www.mun-setubal.pt/forte-de-sao-filipe; daily 10am-8pm

Sitting atop a swollen mound on the western skirts of the city center, the 16th-century São Filipe (Saint Phillip) Fort (also referred to as Setúbal Castle) is one of Setúbal's top attractions. Peering over the city, its fishing port, and the Sado beyond, it is an imposing sight, with its austere, sturdy ramparts and solid battlements. It's a 30-minute hike up from the town, but the persistent are rewarded with stunning sights and a quaint little chapel with a fascinating azulejo wall. Currently housing a luxury hotel, the battlements and grounds are open to the public.

SPORTS AND RECREATION

✪ Dolphin-Watching in Sado Estuary

Dolphin-watching cruises (3 hours; from €40) are available from companies including **Vertigem Azul** (tel. 265 238 000; www.vertigemazul.com), **Portugal Sport and Adventure** (tel. 910 668 600; www.portugal-sport-and-adventure.com), and **Sado Arrábida Nature Tourism** (tel. 265 490 406 or 915 560 342; www.sadoarrabida.pt).

Tourists cruise the Sado aboard a restored sal galleon.

Galleon Sal Sado Trips

tel. 265 227 685; www.sal.pt; 3 hours; from €28 (min. 35 passengers)

A different way to explore the Sado is aboard a historical sal (salt) galleon. These wooden ships were converted from small fishing vessels, first used to transport salt and later used for fishing and cargo. The restored boats are now used for coastal and estuary cruises. Sal Cruises runs trips on the Sado, Tagus, and Zêzere Rivers.

FOOD

You'll often see locals sitting alfresco, sharing a plate of local specialty choco frito (fried squid) with a cold beer.

Livramento Market (Mercado do Livramento)

Avenida Luísa Todi 163; tel. 265 545 392; Tues.-Sun. 7am-2pm

One of the most famous markets in Portugal, lively Mercado do Livramento bursts with fantastic fresh produce and buzzes with activity. Regional cheeses, the freshest fish and seafood, and fruit and vegetables galore are all in their finest glory to be seen and sampled. Originally inaugurated in 1876, it houses a diversity and character that visitors would be hard-pressed to find elsewhere in Portugal. Widely considered one of Portugal's best markets, it is also one of the biggest.

✪ Leo do Petisco

Rua da Cordoaria 33; tel. 265 228 340; Mon.-Sat. noon-2:30pm and 7pm-9:30pm; €8

Head for the simple café-snack bar Leo do Petisco in Setúbal's town center to try local delicacy choco frito served on a plate or—interestingly—in a sandwich.

Batareo

Rua das Fontainhas 64; tel. 265 234 548; Tues.-Sun. noon-3:30pm; €25

Small, simple dockside Batareo

does only fish and shellfish—mostly on the charcoal grill. Fish move straight off the boat and into the glass display case, creating a fresh, seasonal menu that changes daily.

Pérola da Mourisca

Rua da Baía do Sado 9; tel. 265 793 689; Wed.-Mon. noon-10pm; €10

With the best sea and river produce, down-to-earth Pérola da Mourisca to the east of town is best known for its shellfish tapas but also cooks seafood-based rice and pasta dishes.

ACCOMMODATIONS

Hotels in Setúbal are located in and around the town center and the port.

Hotel Bocage

Rua de São Cristóvão 14; tel. 265 543 080; www.hoteisbocage.com; €80-100 d

Just off Setúbal's main drag, Avenida Luísa Todi, in the heart of the historical part of town, two-star Hotel Bocage provides an unfussy, comfortable stay. Its sister, Bocage Guest House, is on a side street just around the corner.

Rio Art Hotel

Av. Luísa Todi 117; tel. 965 801 988; www. rioarthotel.pt; €100-150 d

In the heart of Setúbal, the Rio Art Hotel retains some original features of its historical exterior. The renovated interior is gleaming and contemporary, with 23 colorful, spacious rooms and vintage-chic touches.

INFORMATION AND SERVICES

- **GNR police station:** Av. Jaime Cortesão; tel. 265 242 500; www.gnr.pt

- **Tourist office:** Casa da Baía – Tourism Promotion Center; Avenida Luísa Todi 468; tel. 265 545 010 or 915 174 442; www.mun-setubal.pt/postos-de-turismo; daily 9am-8pm

- **Main post office:** Av. Mariano de Carvalho; tel. 210 471 616; Mon.-Fri. 9am-6pm

GETTING THERE AND AROUND

Setúbal's downtown area, with the main sights, attractions, and restaurants, can easily be explored **on foot.** The main **bus terminal** (Avenida 5 Outubro/Av. Dr. Manuel de Arriaga 2; tel. 265 525 051; www.carrismetropolitana.pt) is closer to the old town center than the **train station** (Praça do Brasil; tel. 707 210 220; www.cp.pt), which is to the north of the city, about 1 km (0.6 mi), a 14-minute walk, to Praça de Bocage, Setúbal's main square, or 1.3 km (0.8 mi) to the waterfront **ferry terminal.**

The **Sado Natural Reserve** is located approximately 90 km (56 mi) south of Lisbon; it envelops the immediate fringes of Setúbal, and is about 38 km (24 mi) east from Sesimbra. The best way to explore the protected wetlands is with an **excursion** from Setúbal or Sesimbra, and most people plan on staying and eating in Setúbal or Sesimbra.

Car

Located 50 km (31 mi) south-east of Lisbon Airport, Setúbal is a 45-minute drive from Lisbon. By car the main route is over the **25 de Abril Bridge,** following the **A2** motorway.

Train

There is direct public transport between Lisbon and Setúbal. **CP trains** (tel. 707 210 220; www. cp.pt) run every hour from Lisbon's **Santa Apolónia** and **Cais do Sodré stations,** among others, and take around 2 hours. Single-trip tickets cost in the region of €13-17, depending on the service. The train station is about 1 km (0.6 mi) east of the main town center in **Praça do Quebrado** (Quebrado Square), near the main bus stops on **Avenida 5 de Outubro.**

Ferry

Alternately, take the **Transtejo & Soflusa ferry** (tel. 808 203 050; www.transtejo.pt) from Lisbon's **Terreiro do Paço** terminal to **Barreiro** (€2.65), with up to seven crossings per hour; then catch a CP train from the station next to the ferry terminal to **Praça do Quebrado** in Setúbal (twice per hour, 30 minutes; €2.30).

Bus

Carris Metropolitana buses (tel. 218 418 800; www. carrismetropolitana.pt) also run directly from Lisbon's Oriente (lines 4720 and 4715) and Sete Rios (line 4725) stations, departing once an hour; the trip takes about an hour and costs €4.50 one-way. National express-bus company **Rede Expressos** (tel. 707 223 344; www.rede-expressos.pt) operates a dozen buses per day between Lisbon's Sete Rios terminal and Setúbal (45 minutes; €6).

Arrábida Natural Park

Blanketing a chunk of coastline between the city of Setúbal and the village of Sesimbra, the Arrábida Natural Park (Parque Natural da Arrábida) covers 165 sq km (64 sq mi). A rugged belt of deep green, the Serra da Arrábida mountain range is separated from the Atlantic by thin, white-gold beaches. Its tallest peak stands at 499 m (1,637 ft), and the chalky Arrábida massif is covered by a thick rug of plant life, including rare species like rockroses and purple star thistle, as well as typical Mediterranean maquis and garigue scrubland. To protect the vegetation, some areas can only be accessed with an authorized guide.

Opt for a leisurely activity such as biking or hiking, or join certified guides who lead mountain climbing, caving, and diving excursions.

SIGHTS

Our Lady of Arrábida Fort

(Forte de Santa Maria da Arrábida)

Portinho da Arrábida; tel. 265 009 982; Tues.-Fri. 10am-4pm, Sat. 3pm-6pm; €3.50; access via the park's narrow, winding roads; roadside parking available near the fort

Perched above translucent seawater and overlooking one of the prettiest beaches in the region, Portinho da Arrábida, the Arrábida Fort was built in 1676 as part of a strategic coastal defense line. An **oceanographic museum** now occupies the historical cliff-foot Fort. Inside, make sure to visit the chapel and its stone image of Our Lady, then take a refreshing dip in the sea below.

Portinho da Arrábida

Arrábida Monastery

(Convento da Arrábida)

tel. 212 197 628; www.foriente.pt; on-site parking

The park is also home to the enigmatic Arrábida Monastery (Convento da Arrábida). This 16th-century complex, a hub of small white houses, is situated higher in the hills above the fort, amid 25 hectares (62 acres) of dense shrubbery and uninterrupted sea views. The cluster of religious buildings includes two former convents, chapels, a garden, and a sanctuary. **Tours** (Wed. and Sat.-Sun.; €5) are available if you reserve in advance. You'll need your own car to get here, as there is no public transport to the monastery.

SPORTS AND RECREATION

Blanketed with thick, verdant indigenous vegetation, the Arrábida Natural Park's rugged coastal terrain and its stunning views are conducive to a menu of physical outdoor activities that range from leisurely **hikes** to radical sports. The translucent turquoise waters along the jagged coast are also perfect for **stand-up paddleboarding, kayaking,** and **canoeing.**

Several accredited companies organize more radical activities in the park, such as coasteering (hiking, rappelling, cliff diving), diving, and mountain climbing. Certain areas of the park are accessible only when accompanied by an official guide. For more information, contact the **main park headquarters** (Praça da República, Setúbal; tel. 265 541 140).

The following companies are among the various outfitters based in Setúbal and Sesimbra that organize guided activity excursions in the par, as well as equipment rentals:

Arrábida Monastery in the Arrábida Natural Park

- **InArrabida** (Setúbal; tel. 919 442 488; www.inarrabida.pt)
- **Vertente Natural** (Sesimbra; tel. 210 848 919; www. vertentenatural.com)
- **Discover the Nature – Outdoor and Events** (Sesimbra; tel. 925 437 916 or 212 100 189; www. discoverthenature.com)

Hiking

The park itself is crossed by sign-posted footpaths, tailored to varying degrees of physical aptitude. There are three main hikes.

Formosinho Peak

Hiking Distance: *6.6 km (4.1 mi) round-trip*

Hiking Time: *4 hours*

Trailhead: *Arrábida Monastery*

Information and Maps: *Arrábida Park Office; tel. 265 541 140*

This is a demanding 6.6-km (4.1-mi) trail to the highest point of the Arrábida mountain range, Formosinho Peak (500 m/1,640 ft), which takes around 4 hours to complete. The trail climbs 398 m (1,247 ft) from the trailhead at the **Arrábida Monastery.** Up a small staircase from the woods, hikers pass through woodland and a clearing often used for camping, after which the trail veers to the right, up to the top of the mountain and panoramic views of the surroundings. Coming down, much of the hike passes through overgrown shrubbery, so it's advisable to wear sturdy shoes and trousers. The trail is open year-round with facilities available at the trailhead.

Risk Point

(Serra do Risco)

Hiking Distance: *8 km (5 mi) round-trip*

Hiking Time: *2.5 hours*
Trailhead: *The little parking lot on road to Mina de Brecha da Arrábida viewpoint*
Information and Maps: *Arrábida Park Office; tel. 265 541 140*

A strenuous, scenic route popular with mountain bikers and hikers is the roughly 8-km (5-mi) loop that starts at a little parking lot on the road down to the **Mina de Brecha da Arrábida viewpoint,** to Serra do Risco (Risk Point). The hike follows along mountain passes and plenty of scenic views, past a cave, and to an information point at 302 m (991 ft) near a quarry. The terrain is rocky and can be slippery on wet or damp days. There's also some high, scrubby vegetation to pass through, so wearing long sleeves and trousers is recommended, even in summer. Bring plenty of water, as none is available on the trail. You'll find facilities at the trailhead.

Windmill Path
(Rota dos Moinhos)
Hiking Distance: *10.9 km (6.7 mi) round-trip*
Hiking Time: *2.5 hours*
Trailhead: *Palmela parish, near bus station*
Information and Maps: *Arrábida Park Office; tel. 265 541 140*

An easy hike is the Rota dos Moinhos (Windmill Path) loop, which takes hikers from the village of **Palmela** along a path dotted with traditional, old but well-preserved windmills in the Serra do Louro mountain range. Starting and ending near the bus terminal in Palmela, this trail is popular with dog walkers and birdwatchers, but sadly much of it, especially at the start of the trail, was charred by the fires of 2022. Nonetheless, the landscape is still scenic and interesting, with views of Lisbon on one side and mountains and distant snatches of the sea on the other. The trail is easy and enjoyable, although a buddy system is recommended for some steeper inclines. The trail is open year-round, and you'll find an excellent bakery at the trailhead.

INFORMATION AND SERVICES
Arrábida Park Office
Praça da República, Setúbal; tel. 265 541 140; Mon.-Fri. 9am-12:30pm and 2pm-5:30pm

Contact the park office for more information on attraction opening times, hiking and cycling routes, and other park activities.

GETTING THERE AND AROUND
Arrábida Natural Park is 2.5 km (1.6 mi) west of **Setúbal,** a 5-minute drive along the **Avenida General Daniel de Sousa** and the **N10 road.** A taxi from Setúbal should cost around €15.

From **Sesimbra,** the 10-km (6.2-mi) drive east takes about 20 minutes on the N378 road and Avenida 25 de Abril. A taxi should cost in the region of €20.

Public transport is infrequent; the best way to reach the Arrábida Natural Park is **by car,** or by asking at your hotel or the local tourist office what excursions are available.

The Arrábida Natural Park is located approximately 40 km (25 mi) south of **Lisbon;** the fastest route is following the **A2** motorway connecting over the **25 de Abril Bridge** (50 minutes).

Sesimbra

At the foot of the Arrábida Mountain Range (Serra da Arrábida) in a protected bay, the authentic fishing town of Sesimbra (seh-ZEEM-brah) has marvelous beaches but remains largely undiscovered, allowing its genuine seaside charm to shine. It's also located at the western edge of the Arrábida Natural Park, making it a gateway to unspoiled natural beauty.

Praia do Ouro

ORIENTATION

Sesimbra is a small seaside town nestled at the foothills of the Arrábida mountain range. The outskirts of town step down toward the **main center,** which is centered on the **beach.** At the western tip of town is the small **fishing port** and its authentic **fresh fish restaurants,** while at the opposite end are a couple of swanky modern hotels. The two ends are bound by a sweep of golden sand and a pretty seafront road and promenade, **Avenida dos Naufrágios,** with all the other main hotels, bars, and restaurants found in between them. The small, open-air bus terminal is on **Avenida da Liberdade,** one of the main avenues that run down into Sesimbra, perpendicular to the beachfront. It is approximately 0.3 km (0.2 mi) to the beach.

BEACHES

With fine sand and crystalline waters, Sesimbra's beaches are glorious.

Ouro Beach
(Praia do Ouro)
Avenida dos Náufragos

Praia do Ouro (just west of the town center) is a generous strand of golden sand sloping gently toward calm, clear water, along Sesimbra's main seaside avenue. Find comforts like sun beds, beach bars, and a children's play area.

Ribeiro do Cavalo Beach
(Praia do Ribeiro do Cavalo)
Rua Baía de Sesimbra

Smaller Praia do Ribeiro do Cavalo is on a cove with rocky

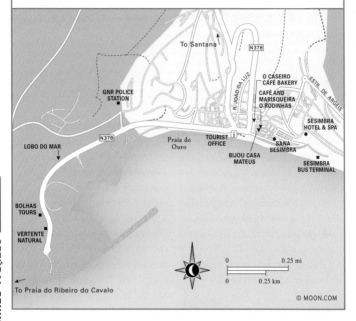

Sesimbra

To Santana

N378

O CASEIRO
CAFÉ BAKERY

CAFÉ AND
MARISQUEIRA
O RODINHAS

ESTR. DE ARGEIS

R. JOÃO DA LUZ

GNR POLICE
STATION

SESIMBRA
HOTEL & SPA

N378

Praia do
Ouro

TOURIST
OFFICE

SANA
SESIMBRA

LOBO DO MAR

BIJOU CASA
MATEUS

SESIMBRA
BUS TERMINAL

BOLHAS
TOURS

VERTENTE
NATURAL

← To Praia do Ribeiro do Cavalo

0   0.25 mi

0   0.25 km

© MOON.COM

SETÚBAL PENINSULA
SESIMBRA

beds teeming with sea life, making it perfect for diving or snorkeling. There are no diving outfitters on the beach, so bring your own gear. It's a 3-km (2-mi) drive west of town, but you can reach it by **boat** from Sesimbra's port for €10 round-trip.

SPORTS AND RECREATION
Fishing

Fishing trips are the main excursions in Sesimbra, and deep-sea fishing is the most popular. Tours vary but generally last around 5 hours and are suitable for the whole family.

Bolhas Tours—Follow Sensations

tel. 910 658 555 or 912 265 834; www.bolhastours.com; $35 pp

Bolhas Tours—Follow Sensations operates from Sesimbra Marina with sightseeing boat trips, fishing trips, and dolphin-watching, as well as boat rentals and diving.

✪ FOOD

Sesimbra's gastronomy is all about the sea. Local specialties include arroz de marisco (a rich, well-sauced rice stew packed with gently boiled seafood and spices) and peixe-espada preto (black scabbard fish).

✪ Café and Marisqueira O Rodinhas

Rua Marques de Pombal 25; tel. 212 231 557; www.marisqueiraorodinhas.pt; Fri.-Tues. 12:30pm-10:30pm; €12

Unpretentious Café and Marisqueira O Rodinhas serves seafood delights in a cozy and casual interior. Fried cuttlefish, snails, and "Francesinha" sandwiches are the house specialties, as well as a rainbow of fresh seafood.

Café and Marisqueira O Rodinhas

Bijou Casa Mateus

Largo Anselmo Braamcamp 4; tel. 963 650 939; Wed.-Sun. noon-3pm and 7pm-10pm, Tues. 7pm-10pm; €15

With its charming worn tile facade and simple wooden tables, acclaimed Bijou Casa Mateus puts all the focus on the seafood. Offerings include caldeirada (fish stew) and arroz de marisco, along with seafood delicacies such as razor clams, Sesimbra lobster, and cockles.

✪ Lobo do Mar

Av. dos Náufragos, Porto de Abrigo; tel. 965 853 167 or 212 235 233; www. lobodomar.com; Tues.-Sun. noon-4pm and 7pm-11pm; €15

Simple seaside Lobo do Mar is famous for its grilled fish. No frills, the plain and clean interior is unremarkable, but it's usually busy and buzzing, and it's the food here that sings. A bit of a local institution, Lobo do Mar is the place to try grilled black scabbard fish, the local specialty, a rich Caldeirada fish stew, or a fresh-as-it-gets octopus salad.

O Caseiro Café Bakery

Rua da República 8-10; tel. 212 280 963; daily 8am-7pm

If you plan to explore Cabo Espichel Promontory, O Caseiro Café Bakery is a lovely breakfast spot to fuel up on sweets and savories freshly baked on-site.

ACCOMMODATIONS

Sesimbra has only a handful of hotels, including newish middle-size units and charming guesthouses.

Sana Sesimbra

Av. 25 de Abril; tel. 212 289 000; www. sanahotels.com; €150-250 d

On the beach in the heart of Sesimbra village, upscale hotel Sana Sesimbra brings the luxury of an acclaimed chain to a small town. Its central location and fabulous views enhance the hotel's cool retro look.

✪ Sesimbra Hotel & Spa

Rua Navegador Rodrigues Soromenho; tel. 212 289 800; www.sesimbrahotelspa.com; €200-300 d

Built on a cliff overlooking Califórnia Beach and the Atlantic, modern Sesimbra Hotel & Spa has panoramic views from all rooms as well as from its infinity pool. Its plush interior and stylish seaside decor are relaxing and refreshing.

INFORMATION AND SERVICES

- **GNR police station:** Rua 4 de Maio; tel. 217 657 700; www.gnr.pt
- **Tourist office:** Rua da Fortaleza; tel. 212 288 500; daily 9:30am-8pm
- **Main post office:** Av. Padre António Pereira de Almeida 8

GETTING THERE
Car

Sesimbra is 40 km (25 mi) south of **Lisbon**, a 50-minute drive. By car, take the **A2** motorway over the **25 de Abril Bridge** and head southwest toward Setúbal. At the junction of the **N378** road, head directly south to Sesimbra. From **Setúbal,** Sesimbra is 30 km (19 mi) west, a 45-minute drive along the **N10** road and **Avenida 25 de Abril.**

Bus

Public transport between Setúbal and Sesimbra is frustratingly sparse, with around a dozen departures a day on weekdays and just four or five on weekends, making a day trip difficult via public transport. The service, **line 4642,** is operated by **Carris Metropolitana** (tel. 218 418 800; www.carrismetropolitana.pt) and costs €2-3. In **Sesimbra** the bus stops at the main terminal on the **Avenida da Liberdade,** 0.3 km (0.2 mi) from the beach.

Carris Metropolitana (tel. 218 418 800; www.carrismetropolitana. pt) runs an inexpensive express-bus service (line 3721) between Lisbon's Sete Rios terminal and Sesimbra (1 hour; €4.50); tickets can be purchased from the driver.

Cabo Espichel

Wind-battered and rugged, Cabo Espichel is the Setúbal Peninsula's most southwesterly headland, a barren cape with massive cliffs and an eerie, desolate feel. Everything about Cabo Espichel is wild—the waves roar, the scenery is untamed, and there are few modern comforts.

SIGHTS
✪ Cabo Espichel Promontory and Lighthouse
(Promontório e Farol do Cabo Espichel)

EM 569 Cabo Espichel; tel. 214 157 600; www.visitsesimbra.pt/to-visit/90/farol-do-cabo-espichel-; lighthouse Wed. 2pm-5pm; promontory open 24/7

Perched on the promontory, this hexagonal lighthouse guards the entire Setúbal Peninsula. The structure stands 32 m (105 ft) tall but is still dwarfed by the sheer size of the cliffs. On a clear night, sailors can see the powerful beam from the lighthouse 40 km (25 mi) out to sea. The lighthouse is open to the public Wednesday 2pm-5pm only. Entry is €4.50 (prior booking required), and visitors can climb to the top to see the lamp.

Dinosaur Footprints
(Pegadas dos Dinossauros)
open 24/7; free
Within walking distance of the lighthouse is a unique sight: dinosaur footprints. Likely made by sauropods, theropods, and ornithopods that inhabited the area millions of years ago, two sets of prints can be clearly seen in the cliffs. Directly above the prehistoric prints, the isolated 15th-century Chapel of Ermida de Memória perches perilously close to the cliff's edge. The chapel's interior is clad in traditional tile depicting "The Lady of the Cape"—the Virgin Mary is said to have appeared to an elderly couple in that spot in 1410.

Our Lady of the Cape Sanctuary
(Santuário da Nossa Senhora do Cabo)
tel. 214 157 600; Tues.-Sun. 10:30am-1:30pm and 2:30pm-5pm; free
Built in 1701, the Baroque Our Lady the Cape Sanctuary was designed first as a place of defense, then to provide shelter. Two long arms stretching out from either side of the church include rooms that housed pilgrims. The church itself has a simple marble interior.

BEACHES
Meco Beach
(Praia Meco)
11.6 km (7.2 mi) north of Cabo Espichel
Wide and rugged, Meco, the Costa's original and most famous nudist beach, is 24 km (15 mi) from Costa Caparica town, or a short drive north from Cabo Espichel.

FOOD AND ACCOMMODATIONS
There's not much by the way of places to eat and drink or stay in the vicinity of Cabo Espichel and its main attractions. Most visitors plan on meals and lodging in nearby Sesimbra or Setúbal, though there are a few eateries in the area.

Retiro dos Amigos
Av. 25 de Abril; tel. 210 847 536; Thurs.-Tues. 8am-10pm; €12
On the main road down toward Cabo Espichel is Retiro dos Amigos, a small and simple place that serves great seafood at good prices. Friendly and welcoming, this spot is a find for anyone wanting to try typical home-cooked Portuguese dishes. Fish options can be a little different from the norm, such as pink swordfish and local clam dishes.

Hotel dos Zimbros
Facho de Azóia; tel. 210 405 470; www. hotelzimbros.com; €150-200 d
Incongruous with the wild

landscape of the Arrabida Natural Park, the sleek 38-room Hotel dos Zimbros is on the main road into Cabo Espichel. Complementing spacious, stylish rooms, some of which have sea views, are a nice, large pool and spa area, on-site parking, and a gym.

GETTING THERE

Taking public transport to Cabo Espichel is difficult, so most visitors **drive.** Cabo Espichel is 14 km (8.7 mi) west from **Sesimbra** via the **N379 road** (20 minutes) and 40 km (25 mi) west from **Setúbal** via the main **Avenida 25 de Abril** (50 minutes).

A public bus, **line 3205,** operated by **Carris Metropolitana** (tel. 218 418 800; www.carrismetropolitana. pt), runs between **Sesimbra's main bus** station and Cabo Espichel three or four times a day, usually around 8am, noon, 3pm and late evening, depending on the time of year. The journey takes approximately 30 minutes and tickets cost about €3 one-way.

From Costa da Caparica, catch the Carris Metropolitana bus 3710 (www.carrismetropolitana.pt; 22 mins) to Lisbon (Areeiro), transferring at the Pragal (Portagem) stop to the 3721 line to Sesimbra (55 mins). From Sesimbra, take the 3205 to Cabo Espichel.

The last bus back from Cabo Espichel to Sesimbra is at 5:40pm, year-round.

Troia Peninsula

A brief and highly scenic boat ride across from Setúbal is the Troia Peninsula—a 17-km-long (11-mi) slither of pine-studded sand dunes, modern hotels, and pristine beaches, embraced as a high-end alternative to time-honored and more touristy coastal destinations. This slinky stretch of tranquil paradise connects seamlessly at its base to the top end of the Alentejo coastline, an under-explored, up-and-coming part of Portugal known for its boho-chic vibes, untouched villages, and authentic charm.

Located 1 hour 45 minutes south of Lisbon, or a 25-minute ferry ride from Setúbal, the Troia peninsula unfolds into sandy dunes separating the Atlantic Ocean from the Sado Estuary Nature Reserve, adorned with pristine beaches and a modern town at the tip. Originally conceived in the 1970s with the ambitious goal of becoming one of Europe's premier tourism destinations, Troia faced setbacks to its initial plans from the 1974 Revolution. Over subsequent years, however, Troia gradually took shape, tempting Portugal's elite away from time-honored bourgeois destinations such as Estoril and Cascais.

Despite the challenges faced in its early years, Troia in recent times has witnessed a surge in

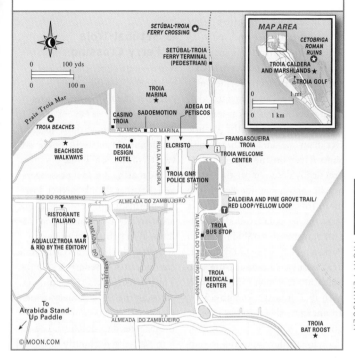

Troia

SETÚBAL-TROIA FERRY CROSSING

SETÚBAL-TROIA FERRY TERMINAL (PEDESTRIAN)

MAP AREA
- CETOBRIGA ROMAN RUINS
- TROIA CALDERA AND MARSHLANDS ★
- TROIA GOLF

TROIA MARINA ★

Praia Troia Mar

TROIA BEACHES ★

CASINO TROIA

SADOEMOTION

ADEGA DE PETISCOS

ALAMEDA DO MARINA

BEACHSIDE WALKWAYS ★

TROIA DESIGN HOTEL

RUA DA AROEIRA

ELCRISTO

FRANGASQUEIRA TROIA

TROIA WELCOME CENTER

TROIA GNR POLICE STATION

RIO DO ROSAMINHO

ALMEADA DO ZAMBUJEIRO

CALDEIRA AND PINE GROVE TRAIL/ RED LOOP/YELLOW LOOP

RISTORANTE ITALIANO

ALMEADA DO ZAMBUJEIRO

ALMEADA DO PINHEIRO MANSO

TROIA BUS STOP

AQUALUZ TROIA MAR & RIO BY THE EDITORY

TROIA MEDICAL CENTER

To Arrabida Stand- Up Paddle

ALMEADA DO ZAMBUJEIRO

TROIA BAT ROOST ★

© MOON.COM

international visitors. Conjoined at its base to the Alentejo coastline, namely at the village of Comporta, the peninsula also serves as a gateway to a series of untouched, authentic Alentejo villages that stand in contrast to modern, human-made Troia, offering a glimpse into bygone Portugal. Today this elongated stretch is experiencing substantial investments in luxurious resorts tailored for the global elite.

More recently, the top end of the Alentejo coastline has attracted numerous global celebrities and dignitaries who seek refuge in its peaceful ambiance, discretion, and relative anonymity of its hidden gems. Cool food trucks and chic wine bars now sit side by side with quaint churches and whitewashed village houses, with their typical brightly colored bands around the windows and doors. The unspoiled natural charm woven into every unassuming detail of this region enhances its allure, making it a destination that is off the beaten track and captivating, for both its tranquility and burgeoning sophistication.

SIGHTS

This stunning, slender sandbar is famous for being where Portugal's wealthy choose to holiday. Away

221

from the throngs of tourists who fill up mainstream beach destinations in summer, Troia offers plenty of manicured peace and space, as well as swish attractions such as a casino, a top-class golf course, and a small but perfectly formed marina. Renowned for its breathtaking natural beauty, this 17-km-long (11-mi) stretch, flanked by the Atlantic Ocean on one side and the tranquil Sado River on the other, boasts practically deserted pristine white beaches and crystalline waters. The main-town end of the peninsula faces the Serra da Arrábida mountain range and Arrábida Natural Park, a region of breathtaking natural beauty. The peninsula also holds archeological importance, with its Cetobriga Roman Ruins, an ancient fish-salting site, being one of its major attractions. The main town's developments are surrounded by either manicured gardens or sandy pine forests, giving the area a cool and leafy feel. Troia Peninsula's sheltered location between the sea and the Sado gives it a unique microclimate and calm waters that, for much of the year, make it an ideal spot for all types of outdoor sports. Its scenic coastline and extensive beaches make Troia a particularly pretty destination for stand-up paddleboarding. The nearby Sado Estuary and Protected Nature Reserve is a playground for the resident pod of bottlenose dolphins.

◐ Setúbal-Troia Ferry Crossing

www.atlanticferries.pt; light passenger vehicle €19.60, pedestrian €5.60; catamaran €8.80 per passenger Setúbal-Troia; Troia-Setúbal trip free

The ferry trip from Setúbal to Troia is a highlight in itself. There are two terminals on Troia: one next to the marina, for foot passengers, and the other slightly farther down the peninsula for vehicles. There are also two types of craft: a traditional ferry that carries foot passengers and vehicles, and a modern catamaran for pedestrians only. The trip itself takes 15-20 minutes, crossing the Sado Estuary, which means passengers could see one of the local resident dolphins. The car ferry sails almost hourly in winter season, 7:30am-10pm, and more frequently in summer. The catamarans run 6am-4am.

Setúbal-Troia ferry crossing

Cetobriga Roman Ruins

⊛ Cetobriga Roman Ruins

Troia, post code 7570-789; tel. 939 031 936; www.troiaresort.pt/ruinas-romanas-de-troia; Wed.-Sat. (Tues.-Sat. June-Aug.) 10am-1pm and 2:30pm-6pm; €6 normal entry, €7.50 guided tour

Evidence of human presence in Troia extends back centuries. A notable historical relic, and one of the peninsula's main attractions, is the Cetobriga Roman Ruins, believed to originate from the 1st century. These ruins constitute the site of one of the largest complexes dedicated to fish salt-preservation in the Western Roman Empire. Located on the northwest side of the peninsula's tip, just above the car-ferry port, a few minutes' drive from the town center, the open-air site is approximately a 2-km (1.2-mi) walk from the main road. Occupied until the 6th century, the site today contains the remnants of factories, houses, tombs, tanks, and hot and cold Roman thermal baths.

Troia Marina
(Marina de Troia)

Rua da Aroeira; tel. 935 784 746; www.troiaresort.pt/troia-marina; open 24/7; free

Offering beautiful views over the Sado Estuary to Setúbal and Serra da Arrabida, the 180-berth Troia Marina is hemmed by swanky restaurants and trendy coffee shops. A short walk though lovely gardens to the town's hotels and developments, the Marina is at the heart of life on Troia and can get quite busy in the height of summer. It's also from here that the dolphin-watching boat trips depart. On the left-hand-side of the marina, when facing Setúbal, are the casino and the scenic wooden boardwalk that runs along the northwest coastline and Troia's main beach, Praia Troia Mar. To the right is the dock from where the passenger-only ferry departs. From the marina, you can access the **beachside walkways** (passadiços).

Troia Caldera and Marshlands
(Caldeira de Troia)
Galé Coast; open 24/7; free

Located on the peninsula's eastern coast, just above the southern car ferry dock, is the Troia Caldera and marshlands, a protected lagoon that mixes freshwater from the river with salt water from the sea. Low tide reveals the rusty skeletons of sunken ships and the muddy, marshy bottom of the Sado Estuary. Surrounded by sandy pine groves, the caldera fills and empties twice a day with the tides, exposing the secrets beneath. It's also a popular bird-watching spot.

Troia Bat Roost
(Morcegário)
Troia, post code 7570-789

Approximately 0.5 km (0.3 mi) from Troia center is one of the peninsula's more unusual attractions, a bat roost. Built in 2003, it is a human-made sanctuary for bats, an artificial shelter to rehome and protect a local bat population identified during a phase of planning for extensive changes in Troia. Bats are protected by law in Portugal, with some species considered at risk of extinction. This colony of European free-tailed bats (*Tadarida teniotis*) was identified in a tower building marked for demolition. At night the bats emit audible echolocation signals, "chatter," that can be heard by humans. Bats are nocturnal animals and will usually be most active at night, leaving the roost at dusk to find water and feast on bugs.

✪ BEACHES
Praia Troia Mar
access via Alameda do Salgueiro; open 24/7

Wrapping around Troia's tip, Troia Mar beach (Praia Troia Mar) is the Peninsula's main beach. A long stretch of pristine shimmering sands and transparent calm waters, it runs around the tip of the peninsula, from the marina, around the northwest flank. Facing the Atlantic Ocean, it offers stunning views across the water to the Arrabida mountain range. This beach is close to all the main hotels and amenities, as well as being easy walking distance to the passenger ferry dock, and is easy to access via a raised wooden walkway that runs along much of it. It offers plenty of space for everyone to enjoy and has

Praia Troia Mar

a simple beach kiosk selling cold drinks and ice cream.

Bico das Lulas
access via Alameda do Zambujeiro; open 24/7

Also situated on Troia's west coast, Bico das Lulas beach is a long expanse of fine white sand and clean, clear, almost waveless water. Wide, long, and quiet, it is also walking distance to the main town and its amenities. Facilities on the beach include public toilets and a beach bar.

Atlantic Beach
(Praia Atlântica)
Grândola; open 24/7

Atlantic Beach is one of Troia's longer beaches, a vast expanse of white gold sand that extends as far as the eye can see. It runs roughly from the spot of coast directly opposite the car-ferry pier south to almost halfway down the peninsula. As the name indicates, it faces the Atlantic, has sun beds and umbrellas available, and is backed by a large development comprising elegant residential and holiday properties. There's plenty of parking and a café nearby.

Malha da Costa Beach
(Praia da Malha da Costa)
access between the Soltroia resort and Comporta; park along the main N253 road; open 24/7

Praia da Malha da Costa is one of the last beaches before reaching Comporta village, toward the base of the Troia Peninsula. Its secluded, dune-backed location in an undeveloped spot means it's also one of Troia's quieter beaches. Untouched, without beach bars or other amenities, it is a deserted paradise with pristine sand and crystalline water. Access requires a walk through the dunes.

SPORTS AND RECREATION
Hiking
Caldeira and Pine Grove Trail (Caldeira e Pinhal Trilha)
Hiking Distance: *2.3-4.7 km (1.4-2.9 mi) round-trip*
Hiking Time: *approx. 1-2 hours*
Trailhead: *P3 parking lot near Troia Caldera*
Information and Maps: *www.troiaresort.pt/wp-content/uploads/Caldeira-Lagoon-and-Pinewood-trail.pdf*

To see two of Troia Peninsula's most distinctive features, this is the hiking trail to follow. It takes hikers through two distinct terrains: around the marshy caldera, and through the pine groves that swaddle it. Starting and ending in the P3 parking lot, there are two routes to follow: a circular 2.3-km (1.4-mi) **Red Loop** that hugs the caldera shore and takes around 1 hour to complete, returning along the cycle track further inland, or a longer, 4.7-km (2.9-mi) **Yellow Loop** that prolongs the Red Loop through pine forests. Both trails are marked out with stakes. Wear sturdy footwear and take water.

Golf
Troia Golf
Carvalhal GDL; tel. 265 494 024; www. editoryhotels.com/troia-golf; daily 8am-5pm; from €50

Widely described as one of Europe's finest golf courses, Troia Golf is an 18-hole, par 72 course inaugurated in 1980 and designed by the North American golf architect Robert Trent Jones Sr. It stands out for highly scenic rounds of golf, with views to the Atlantic Ocean and the stunning Serra da Arrabida as a backdrop. Two holes deserve special mention: the 3 and the 18, the former considered by Robert Trent Jones Sr. himself one of his best designs, the latter, a par 5 featuring a leftward dog-leg, an elevated green, safeguarded by three bunkers at the front. Sitting seamlessly with its natural surroundings, it has hosted a number of top-flight events, including the Portuguese Open. Challenging and exciting, Troia Golf should be on the list of any golf enthusiast visiting Portugal.

Stand-Up Paddleboarding
Arrabida Stand-Up Paddle
Troia Mar Beach; tel. 963 927 951; www. arrabidasup.com; daily 9am-2:30pm; from €25

Enjoy fabulous views of Troia Peninsula as you glide along its turquoise waters and tranquil caldera on a stand-up paddle excursion with Arrabida SUP. Departing from Setúbal quayside, the 2-hour excursion includes all equipment and boat transfers.

Dolphin Watching
Sado Emotion
Alameda da Marina de Troia; tel. 930 569 493; www.sadoemotion.pt; daily 10am-6pm; from €40

Leaving from Troia Marina, Sado Emotion dolphin-watching boat trips give visitors the unique chance to get up close to the Sado Estuary's famous resident pod of bottlenose dolphins. Providing an opportunity for passengers of all ages to enjoy a memorable experience with the graceful, playful mammals, Sado Emotion's smaller boats and personalized service also include a guided tour along the Arrabida coast and its beautiful bays.

Dolphin-watching trips leave from the Troia Marina.

FOOD
For a small town Troia has a nicely varied food scene with everything from high-end, international restaurants to low-key local favorites.

Ristorante Italiano

Rua do Rosmaninho; tel. 935 209 035; www.editoryhotels.com/aqualuz-troia-marrio/restaurante-bar/ristorante-italiano; daily noon-3pm and 7pm-10:30pm; €20

A stone's throw from the beach with lovely floor-to-ceiling glass windows, elegantly modern Ristorante Italiano is about as close to Italy as you can get without leaving the country. It specializes in typical Italian food—pastas, wood-oven-baked pizzas, and stuffed calzones.

Frangasqueira Troia

Troia Marina; daily noon-3pm and 7pm-10:30pm; €15

Sometimes, for all the bells and whistles, all you want is something simple. And that's what Frangasqueira Troia offers: wholesome, down-to-earth charcoal-grilled chicken and chips (and other meats and sides), which can be enjoyed inside or outside the bright and immaculate restaurant.

Elcristo

Alameda da Marina LM-1; tel. 265 490 705; https://restaurante-elcristo-troia.negocio.site; Tues.-Mon. noon-11pm; €35

El Cristo is a funky marisqueira (seafood restaurant) with an eye-catching neon and monochrome interior and views over the marina. It serves grilled fresh fish and shellfish (prices usually by the kilo), as well as filling comfort dishes like prawn lasagna and creamed codfish, rounded off with specialty desserts.

Adega de Petiscos

Alameda da Marina Loja LM 3A; tel. 960 401 859; https://adegadepetiscos.pt; Thurs.-Tues. noon-midnight; €20

If it's tasty fare-to-share that floats your boat, try Adega de Petiscos, where Mediterranean-Portuguese tapas take pride of place. On the menu are deep-fried croquettes, cold charcuterie and cheese boards, fresh squid salads, shellfish, and steaks, plus a range of indulgent sweets, and a vast variety of wines to perfectly pair.

ACCOMMODATIONS

Troia has a good mix of plush and contemporary hotels and resorts to choose from, most of which are either beachfront or easy walking to the beach.

Troia Design Hotel

Marina de Troia; tel. 265 498 000; www.troiadesignhotel.com; €300 d

Troia Design Hotel is instantly recognizable thanks to its contemporary, wavy front that dwarfs the marina. Inside, this five-star hotel is equally polished and swanky, with facilities including wellness and entertainment centers, outdoor pools, restaurants, and stylish ocean-view rooms with glass-enclosed bathrooms.

Aqualuz Troia Mar & Rio by The Editory

Alameda do Zambujeiro; tel. 265 499 000; www.editoryhotels.com; €131 d

Clean and modern, four-star Aqualuz Troia Mar & Rio by The Editory offers bright and spacious rooms. Overlooking Troia Mar beach, on-site facilities include a large pool and pool bar and restaurants.

Pestana Troia Eco Resort

Via Longitudinal de Troia 253-1; tel. 265 240 150; www.pestana.com; approx. €600/night

Located about a third of the way down the peninsula, on the Galé coast, near Atlantica beach, Pestana Troia Eco Resort fuses style with eco-friendly practices to produce a stunning nature experience. It comprises 360 units (apartments and villas), surrounded by sandy pine groves. Right on the beach, with wood decks and rustic touches, this low-rise, four-star resort has more than a hint of adventure about it. Minimum 2-night stays may apply.

INFORMATION AND SERVICES

- **Atlantic Ferries:** tel. 265 235 101; www.atlanticferries.pt

- **Troia GNR police station:** Rua da Aroeira; tel. 265 249 760; www.gnr.pt

- **Troia Medical Center:** Alameda do Pinheiro Manso; tel. 933 338 932; www.troiaresort.pt

- **Troia Welcome Center:** Alameda do Salgueiro; tel. 936 547 536; www.troiaresort.pt

- **Troia-Comporta Transfers EuropaTaxis:** tel. 964 398 527; europataxis. pt/servicos/transfer/ transfer-troia-comporta

GETTING THERE AND AROUND

Car

From Setúbal port, take the vehicle ferry to Troia (tel. 265 235 101; www.atlanticferries.pt; 25 minutes; car plus 1 driver €19.60; additional passenger €5.60). Alternatively, Troia can be reached by road, without crossing by ferry, driving an inverted *C* inland around the Sado estuary, along the A2 motorway and N253 roads.

Bicycle

The main nucleus of Troia is walkable. To explore the further afield, either a car or a bicycle will be useful. Operating in both Troia and Comporta, Grândola-based bike hire company **Passeios e Companhia** (https:// passeiosecompanhia.com) rents bikes from €25/day, or €13/day if rented for 1 week (minimum 5 days required).

Bus

Take the direct bus line from Troia, across the street from the Welcome Center, to Comporta Village. Look for line **8148** (www.rodalentejo.pt). The journey takes 20 minutes and costs around €3 one-way.

Train

There are no direct trains between Setúbal and Troia or Comporta. There are no trains on the Troia Peninsula.

Comporta

Situated within the Sado Estuary Nature Reserve, Comporta, the name of a parish and its main village in the municipality of Alcácer, is located on the wild Alentejo coastline, at the base of the Troia Peninsula. It boasts an impressive array of untouched natural landscapes, from wide, wild beaches, famed for horseback riding, to shady pine forests, marshy rice paddies, and rugged dunes, all home to a wealth of flora and fauna.

One hour 20 minutes south of Lisbon, sleepy Comporta has been dubbed Europe's Hamptons. With its effortless Alentejo authenticity and mild Mediterranean climate,

Comporta has, until recently, remained something of a secret refuge favored by those in the know, mainly wealthy city-dwellers and few international visitors prizing the coastal Alentejo's peace and privacy. But that's changing; significant investment is being poured into developing high-end resorts to accommodate the region's growing number of discerning visitors, eager to sample a slice of an unspoiled, upscale Portugal.

Following its metamorphosis into one of Portugal's trendiest boho-chic retreats, Comporta today oozes low-key luxury. Royalty from all realms—fashion,

Comporta Village

movies, music, and even real royals—have forayed into the area, via holidays or investment ventures, further raising the profile of the Alentejo's most famous hidden gem.

SIGHTS
Comporta Village

Surrounded by splendid rice paddies that are sandwiched between the land and the coast, Comporta sits at the foot of the Troia Peninsula. Lined with boutique-y handicraft shops, gleaming restaurants, and trendy hangouts, compact Comporta village is a hub of cultural chic-ness, the ultimate rural hamlet for the hip crowd. It is an interesting mix of locals and international visitors, with languages from the four corners of the world heard throughout its streets. Local artisans display their wares in stylish craft shops. In one corner, storks' nests top the village church, which sits next to the local café. Across the road, a swish wine and tapas bar hums with lively conversation, and music floats over from the trendy food truck and summer DJ spot. Brunch cafés and a poke house are recent additions to the otherwise traditional village. Comporta is small enough to walk around but has lots to see, especially in terms of arts and nature. Within walking distance from the center of the hamlet are the local winery, rice museum, and cultural center. The village center itself is a melting pot of regional foods and products and an international palette of dining options.

Comporta Cultural Centre
(Casa da Cultura da Comporta)

Rua Do Secador 8; tel. 265 497 514; www. fundacaohdc.pt/casa-da-cultura; Tues.- Sun. 10:30am-2pm and 4:40pm-9pm; free

Created to showcase Portuguese arts, crafts, and culture, the Comporta Cultural Centre, or Alma da Comporta (Soul of Comporta), is a little nook of all things local, regional, and national. A great place to find a souvenir, it was born from the renovation of the local cinema and an adjacent rice bar. A gallery section houses changing exhibitions, while the grand hall is home to around a dozen stalls featuring artisans and crafts.

Comporta Rice Museum

Rice Museum
(Museu do Arroz)

N261 Herdade da Comporta; tel. 965 280 465; www.herdadedacomporta.pt/pt/ museu-do-arroz; Wed.-Sun. 10am-7pm; from €7.50 (min. groups of 10)

Housed in an old rice-husking

factory, the Comporta Rice Museum tells all about how rice and the magnificent Comporta rice paddies are at the heart of local livelihoods. The museum explores rice-growing and its traditions, houses exhibitions and workshops, and also gives visitors the opportunity to sample it in the on-site restaurant. A visit to the Rice Museum can also be combined with a visit to the local winery.

Comporta Vineyard
(Adega da Herdade de Comporta)

Espaço Comporta, EN 253, Km 1; tel. 965 280 465; www.herdadedacomporta.pt/en; daily 10am-9pm; visit €7.50, visit plus tasting (3 wines) €20

With around 35 hectares (85 acres) of sandy, sea-salt-kissed vineyard, the Adega da Comporta winery works year-round to produce the Herdade da Comporta wines. Visitors have the opportunity to see how wines are made, as well as enjoy a tasting of whites, reds, and rosé, in the elegantly decorated winery.

Comporta Vineyard

Carrasqueira Palafitte Pier
(Porto Palafitte da Carrasqurira)

Carrasqueira; open 24/7; free

Located between the neighborhoods of Carrasqueira and Moitinha, a few kilometers behind Comporta, is the Carrasqueira Palafitte Pier, perhaps one of the most iconic and photographed spots in the region. Still used by local fisherman, these ramshackle wooden piers, built in the 1950s and 1960s, perch over the water on their stilts. Best visited at sunset, it's like a little spot that time forgot, with colorful fishing boats and storage huts adding to the charm.

BEACHES
Comporta Beach
(Praia da Comporta)

access via N253-1; open 24/7; free

Widely considered one of the finest and prettiest beaches south of Lisbon, Comporta Beach is a long, wide, rugged stretch of fine white sand with crystal clear, cool water, backed by rice paddies. Underdeveloped and stretching as far as the eye can see, it has plenty of space for everyone, even in the height of summer. The surf is usually gentle in summer, and it's also a popular spot for horseback riding, an activity the region is famed for. There is plenty of parking and a few beach cafés around, but they can be expensive. Wooden walkways lead from the main car park off of N253-1 to the beach.

SPORTS AND RECREATION

Cycling

Comporta Electric Bikes

Lagoa Formosa, Rua da Praia; tel. 938 295 365; www.instagram.com/comporta_electric_bikes; daily 9am-5pm; €25/hour, €85/day

Head south of Comporta Village to rent an electric bike and enjoy a scenic cycle along the coast. E-bikes are a fun and comfortable way to explore Comporta's off-road attractions, like the rice paddies and the beach.

✪ Horseback Riding

Cavalos na Areia

Estrada Nacional 261 Km 6; tel. 913 181 844; www.cavalosnaareia.com; daily 9am-6pm; from €70 pp

Well-known company Cavalos na Areia, just south of Comporta Village, specializes in horseback rides through Comporta's rice paddies and pine groves to the beach, or along the banks of the Sado River. Rides can be enjoyed with or without extras, like picnics. A hat, long pants, and closed-toe shoes are recommended. Advance reservations required.

Buggy Tours

Feel Comporta

Tv. das Laranjeiras; tel. 968 996 173; www.feelcomporta.com; daily 8am-10pm; €160 2-people buggy tour

Discover Comporta on an exciting 4x4 buggy tour. Experience the thrill of off-road exploration and learn about the area from locals who know Comporta like the backs of their hands. Tours run twice a day for just under 2 hours. Helmets and goggles provided.

FOOD

Comporta has a varied dining scene, from contemporary regional fare to poke bowls and brunch spots, catering to an international crowd.

Cavalariça Comporta

Rua Do Secador 9; tel. 930 451 879; www.cavalarica.com; Wed.-Sun. 1pm-2:30pm and 7pm-10:30pm; €40

Cavalariça Comporta embodies local essence: a refined culinary experience based on seasonal products, housed in charmingly converted old horse stables, located in the heart of the hamlet. The clever conversion from stables to restaurant boasts an elegant decor that incorporates unique traditional features. The dishes are equally creative—contemporary regional cuisine with a twist, perfect for sharing. Reservations recommended.

Be Comporta

Rua Beco da Comporta; tel. 265 523 209; https://becomporta.eatbu.com/?lang=en; Sat.-Thurs. 9:30am-8pm; €15

Be Comporta is a great place for a healthy breakfast, brunch, or light snack. The breakfast/brunch menu covers a mouthwatering range of options, from breakfast bowls and pancakes to smoothies and egg dishes, while snacks include bagels and pizzas.

Restaurante São João

*Rua 24 de Junho 2; tel. 960 314 173; www.
instagram.com/restaurantesaojoao; Fri.-
Wed. noon-4pm and 7pm-10pm; €30*

A very pretty restaurant with a cool rustic-chic, beachy vibe, Restaurante São João takes inspiration from Comporta's decoration and flavors. It serves typical regional and Portuguese cuisine, in steel pots, on wooden plates, and on arty ceramic tableware. Choices include fresh fish, grilled meat, seafood rice pot stews and cataplanas, and traditional specialties like fried cuttlefish with coriander dressing.

Gomes Casa de Vinhos & Petiscos

*Largo Luis de Camões; tel. 265 497 748;
www.facebook.com/gomes.casa.vinhos.
petiscos; Wed.-Mon. 5pm-10pm; €25*

Artisanal cheeses and meats, pâtés, and preserves are all waiting to be sampled at Gomes Casa de Vinhos & Petiscos, as well as hearty traditional dishes like bean stews and oven-baked meats. Comfort food in all shapes and sizes can be enjoyed in the classically elegant restaurant, a former barn, or in its gorgeous alfresco garden setting.

ACCOMMODATIONS

Places to stay in Comporta village are limited to smaller guesthouses and private lodgings, although on the outskirts there are larger units and resorts.

Almalusa Comporta

*Rua Pedro Nunes 3; tel. 265 098 600;
www.almalusahotels.com/comporta;
€300-500 d*

In the heart of Comporta village, near the cultural center, four-star Alma Lusa is a celebration of local arts and traditions. Born from the reconversion of a preexisting hotel, the 53 modern rooms and suites are decorated with locally sourced materials and decorative pieces. A rooftop bar offers panoramic views of the endless rice paddies.

Quinta da Comporta Wellness Boutique Resort

*Rua Alto do Pina, 2; tel. 265 112 390; www.
quintadacomporta.com; €800 d*

South of Comporta Village, overlooking Comporta's magnificent rice paddies, set out around a long, narrow infinity pool, Quinta da Comporta Wellness Boutique Resort is constructed largely from wood and natural materials. It has an understated, cabana-chic appeal— a sprawling luxury lodge-style resort inspired by its location. The main building has soaring ceilings, flanked by outbuildings comprising single rooms and suites, to townhouses and pool villas. Eco-conscious, it sits in harmony with the surroundings and has an on-site restaurant and spa for a deeply restful retreat. Minimum 5-night stay may apply.

Sublime Comporta Country Retreat & Spa

EN 261-1 Muda; tel. 269 449 376; www. sublimecomporta.pt; €785-1,000

Offering five-star luxury in a secluded rural retreat, Sublime Comporta is nestled on a large estate of pine and cork trees south of Comporta Village. The estate comprises rooms, suites, and villas, distributed over several buildings. Oozing a rustic-chic decor steeped in nature, the resort has a pool, restaurant, and spa, and is just a stone's throw from the beach. Minimum 3-night stay may apply.

INFORMATION AND SERVICES

- **Comporta GNR police station:** tel. 265 249 750; www.gnr.pt
- **Comporta Health Center:** Rua 24 de Junho 13; tel. 265 490 520; Mon-Fri 9am-5pm

GETTING THERE AND AROUND

Car

Comporta is a short 20-minute drive south from Troia, along the N253-1 road. Alternatively, Comporta can be reached by road, without crossing by ferry, driving an inverted C inland around the Sado estuary, along the A2 motorway and N253 road.

Bicycle

Comporta Village can be easily explored on foot. Venturing further afield will require either a car or a bicycle. Grândola-based bike hire company **Passeios e Companhia** (https://passeiosecompanhia.com) covers both Comporta and Troia. Hires start from €25/day, or €13/day for 1 week (minimum 5 days required).

Bus

There is a direct bus line between Troia and Comporta, line **8148** (www.rodalentejo.pt). The journey takes 20 minutes and costs around €3 one-way. Catch the bus from the Troia bus stop, across the way from the Troia Welcome Center, to Comporta Village. The bus departs daily, twice a day, morning and evening, at around 8:45am and 6:15pm.

Train

The closest train station to Comporta is Grândola, approximately 31 km (19 mi) south of Comporta, which serves as a sort of hub for the area. Trains between Lisbon (Cais do Sodré/Entrecampos/Sete Rios/Oriente/Rossio/Santa Apolónia) and Grândola (www.cp.pt) cost €14-20 and take just over 1 hour. From Grândola, there is a bus to Comporta, operated by Rodoviária do Alentejo (www.rodalentejo.pt; lines 8346 and 8360), approximately four times a day, which takes around 20 minutes and costs €2-4 one-way. A taxi (tel. 966 924 696; www.taxisemgrandola.pt) will cost in the region of €25-30.

Melides

A little over 130 km (81 mi) from Lisbon (just under 30 km/19 mi south of Comporta and 45 km/28 mi south of Troia) is Melides, a tiny Alentejo hamlet that shares a reputation similar to that of its northern neighbor Comporta, despite not yet having quite the same noise about it.

An authentic Alentejo seaside village where life moves at a relaxed pace, it has also long been a destination of choice for Portuguese holidaymakers looking to steer clear of over-crowded beaches and mainstream holiday

Highlights

✪ **Fonte dos Olhos:** Cool off with a dip or picnic at this lovely park on the edge of town (page 238).

✪ **Melides Beach:** Marvel at incredible natural scenery at this rugged beach, the perfect spot for horseback riding or a sunset dinner (page 239).

✪ **Melides Lagoon:** Enjoy a paddle or bike ride along the bird-rich lagoon (page 239).

resorts. A few high-profile visitors and glossy travel spreads later, and this former hidden gem is trending, evident in the contemporary construction mushrooming in the region. But the village itself remains pretty much unperturbed (barring a brand-new boutique hotel by shoe legend Christian Louboutin), a humble hamlet with a handful of restaurants, a quaint village church, and picturesque attractions. It is home to a blended community of locals and creatives, attracted by Melides's light and tranquility. Melides's major draw, however, is its magnificent, wild beach—an endless stretch of golden sand, backed by windswept dunes and lagoons. This is the Alentejo Coast experience in a pure, unadulterated form.

ORIENTATION

The hamlet of Melides is located on the Alentejo coastline, a 1.5-hour drive south of Lisbon and 1 hour south from Setúbal. Fronted by the crashing Atlantic Ocean, Melides comprises a village and a beach, and it's about a 10-minute (6-km/3.7-mi) drive from the village to the beach. Melides is also roughly 1.5 hour by car southwest from Évora, the Alentejo region's biggest city.

Previous: Melides village; **above:** Fonte dos Olhos; Melides Lagoon.

Melides

ESSENTIAL MELIDES

1. Pottery Museum & Ceramics Workshop
2. O Melindense
3. Arroz Viewpoint
4. Blue Melides

© MOON.COM

PLANNING YOUR TIME

Set aside **a full morning or afternoon** for Melides, especially if you want to enjoy the beach. It can be visited in conjunction with Comporta, tacked on to a longer itinerary including Troia and Setúbal, or Évora. The last bus from Melides back to Troia leaves at 5:19pm, the journey takes around an hour, and it's a 40-minute ferry trip from Troia back to Setúbal.

Itinerary Idea

ESSENTIAL MELIDES

1 Begin your time in Melides by having a wander around the quaint whitewashed hamlet, exploring the peaceful streets and craft shops. Admire the local church and square, and pay a visit to the nearby **Pottery Museum & Ceramics Workshop.**

2 Make the short walk down to the Fonte dos Olhos for a dip and a moment's contemplation before heading back to the village to enjoy lunch at quirky **O Melindense.**

3 After lunch, head to the beach and lagoon, stopping at the **Arroz Viewpoint** en route. At the beach, revel in its endless wild beauty and its tranquil lagoon, and if the weather allows, have an hour or two relaxing under the sun.

4 Round off your visit with a refreshing drink or ice cream at one of the pretty beach cafés before making your way back to base, or enjoy dinner with a memorable sunset from the rooftop of **Blue Melides.**

Sights and Beaches

VILLAGE
Pottery Museum & Ceramics Workshop
(Núcleo Museológico da Olaria de Melides)

Rua da Fonte; tel. 269 908 058; www. visitgrandola.com/conhecer/museus/ poi/nucleo-museologico-da-olaria-de-melides-78; Tues.-Sat. 9:30am-1pm and 2pm-5pm; free

Besides rice and beaches, the region is also known for its pottery, and Melides was once one of the most important producers in the area. A visit to Melides's local ceramics museum, housed in an old pottery, sheds light on its history and traditions in ceramics through an exhibition, documentary, and working artisans who keep the traditional craft alive.

✪ Fonte dos Olhos

Rua da Fonte 3; www.cm-grandola.pt/o-que-fazer/turismo-de-natureza/parques-de-merendas/poi/fonte-dos-olhos-melides; open 24/7; free

A short walk west from the village center, the Fonte dos Olhos (Fountain of the Eyes) is enchanting, like something out of a children's book. Built in the 1960s to supply the village with water, it features a mini waterfall with a

Melides Lagoon

covered picnic spot and a pretty stream to splash along that flows into the rice paddies.

Arroz Viewpoint
(Miradouro do Arroz)

Rua da Fonte; 24/7; free

On the way to Melides Beach from the village, it's worth stopping at the Arroz Viewpoint, a scenic deck overlooking the sprawling rice paddies that characterize this part of Portugal. It's a great photo op and also a popular hiking area.

BEACH
✪ Melides Lagoon
(Lagoa de Melides)

access via Estrada Da Praia de Vigia; www. cm-grandola.pt/o-que-visitar/patrimonio/ patrimonio-natural/poi/lagoa-de-melides; open 24/7; free

Separated from the ocean by a wide strip of golden sand, Melides Lagoon is a tranquil trove of biodiversity. A long wooden walkway runs the length of the lagoon, from the parking lot to the beach, providing plenty of opportunity for bird-watching and photo-taking. Classified a Protected Area of National Interest since 2010, it is a distinguishing feature of Melides and home to a wide variety of bird-life, as well as being a perfect spot for activities like canoeing and stand-up paddleboarding. From the village, drive about 10 minutes west to the car park on Estrada Da Praia de Vigia.

✪ Melides Beach
(Praia de Melides)

Estrada de Melides; open 24/7; free

Following Estrada de Melides some 6 km (4 mi) from the village west to the coast, you'll arrive at Melides Beach. Untamed and naturally beautiful, the long swathe of fine, golden sand separates the spirited

Atlantic Ocean from the tranquil lagoon. Devoid of development with the exception of a little cluster of reasonably priced cafés and craft stalls, next to a large, free parking area, Melides Beach is spacious and scenic. It's an idyllic spot for long walks and also popular with local horseback riding operators. The water along this open coastline can be rougher and cooler than the sheltered southern coast.

Melides Beach

Galé-Fontainhas Beach
(Praia da Galé-Fontainhas)

access via the N261 road; open 24/7; free

A 12-minute drive or 35-minute cycle from Melides village is Praia da Galé-Fontainhas, north of Melides's main beach. After parking in a residential area just before the beach, a brief walk leads you to this breathtaking, rugged stretch of coast. The beach can be accessed via a pathway through sandy dunes from the parking spot. Rolling waves undulate the turquoise water, and there's plenty of flat golden sand to stretch out on. The Blue-Flag beach is backed by dunes and fossil-laden cliffs, including the **Galé Fossil Cliffs Natural Reserve** (Arriba Fóssil da Galé), whose formations date back millions of years.

Sports and Recreation

Melides's natural attributes make it a strong contender for scenic outdoor sports and activities. Horseback riding, hiking, cycling, bird-watching, and water sports are just a few to be enjoyed.

HORSEBACK RIDING
Horses by the Beach
Estrada da Praia de Melides; tel. 918 124 490; horsesbythebeach.com; daily 7am-8pm; €65

From the ranch through pine forests to the beach, Horses by the Beach shows off Melides from the saddle. Treks usually take 1.5-2 hours with an experienced guide. Advanced reservations are required.

STAND-UP PADDLEBOARDING
Surf in Comporta / Melides Sports Center
Melides Lagoon; tel. 962 475 961 or 967 566 192; www.surfincomporta.com; daily 8am-8pm; group surf lessons from €45, SUP lesson/tours €40

A local-family-run business with over 14 years' experience teaching, nearby Surf in Comporta covers everything from surf lessons to board rentals, as well as SUP and kayak tours on scenic spots including Melides Lagoon and through rice paddies.

CYCLING

If you want to leave the car parked, jump into the saddle and enjoy a scenic cycle from Melides village to the beach. It's a 20-minute (6.3 km/3.9 mi) ride along the Estrada da Praia de Melides.

Melides by Bike

Rua do Parque; tel. 965 171 178; www. electrica.pt; €15 half-day, €25 full day

Explore Melides on two wheels and save on the legs with a comfy e-bike. Local bike rental company Melides by Bike offers both independent rentals and cycling tours of the local attractions.

Food

In the village, Melides's food scene is low-key and local, with typical restaurants showcasing regional fare. At the beach is a cluster of laid-back beach bars, cafés, and cool restaurants.

VILLAGE

Anguilla Surf Café

Travessa do Futuro 1A; tel. 962 475 961; Wed.-Mon. 10am-6pm; €10

Run by the family who owns Surf in Comporta, Anguilla Surf Café

O Melidense

was established to offer Melides options for vegetarian and healthy eating. A newer addition to the local food scene, this pretty café in the middle of the village is a pleasant spot for a snack or light meal like a fresh sandwich, gluten- and lactose-free pancakes, gluten-free avocado toast, or tasty poke bowl.

O Melidense

EN 261-2; tel. 269 907 288; Thurs.-Tues. noon-10pm; €20

A meal at O Melidense is a must when visiting the hamlet. Located in the heart of the village, it's hard to miss, quirky on the outside and eclectic on the inside—with a trove of curious knickknacks. The menu is an uncommon variety of proper, old-fashioned Alentejo dishes, like tomatoes with eggs, lamb stew, and broad beans with chorizo sausage.

Quinta do Lourenço

EN 261, Saibreira; tel. 269 907 329; Thurs.-Mon. 10am-10pm; €20

Just north of the hamlet, Quinta do Lourenço is a simple eatery ideal for a light meal, or something a little more filling, with no frills. This is a good place to try homemade local dishes, like eel stew and pork Alentejo-style.

BEACH

Sem Nexo

Estrada da Praia de Melides 4; tel. 964 797 883; www.semnexo.pt; Tues.-Sun. noon-11pm; €25

Facing Melides Beach, Sem Nexo is a classy little seaside restaurant with dainty fairy lights and a chic-shack feel. A pleasant spot for a bite at sunset, the menu is based on tapas and sharing plates inspired by fresh produce from the coast.

Blue Melides

Melides Beach; tel. 913 603 366; www.bluemelides.pt; Fri.-Mon. 1pm-11:30pm, Tues. and Thurs. 1pm-5pm; €30

Blue Melides restaurant and lounge bar is hard to miss, as it is, as the name suggests, bright blue. Located at the entrance to Melides Beach, at the top of the wooden walkway that runs along the lagoon, its menu is just as bold—an intriguing fusion of fresh local products with a Belgian twist. It also has a cool rooftop offering amazing sunset views.

Accommodations

Melides has an interesting but limited mix of places to stay, from local lodgings to exclusive boutiques. Due to demand, peak seasons can be pricy.

VILLAGE

Vermelho Melides

Rua Dr. Evaristo Sousa Gago 2; tel. 915 280 511; www.vermelhohotel.com/hotel-melides; €600-800/night (min. 3-night stay may apply, prices vary in peak season)

When it opened it caused quite a bit of a buzz, as Vermelho Melides, in the heart of the village, is the creation of none other than eminent designer Christian Louboutin. With 13 individually styled rooms, Vermelho (Red) Melides is extravagant, eccentric, flamboyant, and a celebration of Portuguese heritage.

Nômade Melides Eco Lodge

Cerca do Barranco; tel. 938 281 953; https://nomademelides.com; €270/night (min. 4-night stay may apply in peak season)

Situated 5 km (3 mi) northeast of Melides, Nômade Melides Eco Lodge is a rural retreat that comprises single-story apartments in one long outbuilding positioned next to a natural pool. Cozy and

Montum Farm Living

quirky, they are fully equipped to cater for longer stays and have log-burners for cooler months, as well as lovely alfresco porches overlooking the garden for lazy summer evenings.

Montum Farm Living

EN261 Km 30.7; tel. 915 266 199; www.montumfarmliving.pt; €205-260/night (peak season)

Experience the real rural Alentejo with a stay in individual country cottages. Built on 42 hectares (100 acres) of land owned by the family for over 200 years, the luxury cottages south of Melides have access to private pools and hot tubs, and a fresh breakfast basket is delivered to the door every morning. Prices in the low season can be considerably lower.

Information and Services

Most main services and amenities, like police, health, and municipal services, and larger supermarkets, are located in nearby Grândola.

- **Melides Mobile Health Unit**: tel. 269 907 123; Mon. 9am-1pm and 2pm-3pm, Tues.-Wed. 9am-1pm and 2pm-5pm, Thurs. 9am-1pm, Fri. 8am-1pm and 2pm-4pm

- **Pharmacy Silva Ângelo**: Rua de Santo António 4; tel. 269 907 118; Mon.-Fri. 9am-1pm and 3pm-7pm, Sat. 9am-1pm

- **GNR Police Station Grândola:** Rua da Raínha Dona Leonor 10; tel. 269 249 170; www.gnr.pt

Getting There and Around

GETTING THERE
Car
From Setúbal port, take the vehicle ferry to Troia (tel. 265 235 101; www.atlanticferries.pt; 25 mins; car plus 1 driver €19.60, additional passenger €5.60). Melides is a 40-minute drive south from Troia, and 20 minutes south from Comporta, along the N253-1 road. Alternatively, Melides can be reached by road, without crossing by ferry, driving an inverted C inland around the Sado estuary, along the A2 motorway and N253 roads. From Lisbon, it's a 1.5-hour drive (132 km/82 mi) south along the 2 motorway.

Bus
There is a direct bus line, twice daily, between Troia, Comporta, and Melides, line **8148** (www.rodalentejo.pt; morning and late afternoon). The journey from Troia to Melides takes just under an hour and costs about €6 one-way. The same bus line from Comporta to Melides takes 30 minutes and costs around €4. From Grândola, where the closest train station is located, there is a bus service to Melides, operated by **Rodoviária do Alentejo** (www.rodalentejo.pt; lines 8346 and 8360), but it may require a change in nearby hamlet Pinheiro da Cruz (to line 8148). In total the trip takes around 1 hour 40 minutes and costs around €7. A taxi from Grândola (tel. 966 924 696; www.taxisemgrandola.pt) is the quickest option at approximately 17 minutes and costs around €16. By bus, there's a direct service from Lisbon's Sete Rios station to Grândola with **Rede Expressos** (www.rede-expressos.pt; 1 hour 45 minutes; €14). From

Grândola, the easiest way to travel to Melides is by taxi (17 mins; approx. €25-30). The local bus takes a long, indirect route.

Train

There are no direct trains between Setúbal and Troia or Melides. There are also no trains on the Troia Peninsula. The closest train station to Melides is Grândola, approximately 17 km (11 mi) east of Melides, which serves as a sort of hub for the area. Trains between Lisbon (Entrecampos/Sete Rios/Oriente) and Grândola (www.cp.pt) cost €16-17 and take around 1 hour. From Grândola take a bus or taxi to Melides.

GETTING AROUND

Melides village can be easily covered on foot. There is a parking lot in the middle of the village. A car, bicycle, or horse trek will be required for making the short journey (6 km/3.7 mi) to the beach.

Évora

In the heart of the Alentejo, Évora (EH-voh-rah) is the region's biggest city, built on a small hill amid the surrounding plains 133 km (82 mi), or a 1.5-hour drive, from Lisbon. Wonderfully preserved, Évora is home to unusual historical monuments and leading wine producers, and it is a university city that blends the old with the demands of modern youth.

Often called the megalithic capital of Iberia, Évora, a UNESCO World Heritage

Highlights

✪ **Chapel of Bones:** The chilling Chapel of Bones is a gruesome but unmissable highlight of Évora (page 250).

✪ **Megaliths at Almendres Cromlech:** This Neolithic-era site comprises mysterious menhirs that predate England's Stonehenge (page 253).

✪ **Cartuxa Estate:** Learn about the essence of the Alentejo's famous wines at the iconic Cartuxa vineyards (page 254).

Site, has sites that date from pre-history. The most famous is Almendres Cromlech, on the city's outskirts, with menhirs (standing stones) that predate England's Stonehenge. Évora's city center is well preserved. First inhabited by Celts, the city was conquered by the Romans in the 1st century BCE, and relics of their occupancy, such as the Roman Temple, remain along with surviving architectural influences from the subsequent Moorish occupancy. In the 15th century, Évora was home to Portugal's kings, which brought great wealth, and more prestige came in the 16th century when Évora was elevated to an ecclesiastical city.

ORIENTATION

Évora is not that big, and its main sights can be covered **on foot** in one day. Central **Giraldo Square (Praça do Giraldo)** is the city's main meeting point. Flanked by historical monuments and buildings and lined with elegant cafés and restaurants, it has a grand feel, with the **Bank of Portugal** at its southern end and a charming church and marble fountain at the northern end. The **Roman Temple of Évora, Évora Cathedral,** and **Évora University** are all northeast from the square; the **Chapel of Bones** is in the opposite direction, southwest of the square. Évora's historical center is encircled by strapping 14th-century **walls,**

Previous: Évora Cathedral; above: Chapel of Bones; Cartuxa Estate.

and the city itself is encircled by the busy IP2 main ring road. The **aqueduct** is outside the city, on the other side of the IP2, north of Évora, and the **Cartuxa wine estate** is just a little further in the same direction.

PLANNING YOUR TIME

Plan to spend at least one day in Évora exploring the **monuments,** mazelike **cobbled streets,** and the many excellent **cafés** and **restaurants.** Allow another day or two to venture outside the city center and discover a host of acclaimed **vineyards** and quaint **villages.** As Évora is a 1.5-hour drive east of Lisbon (about 140 km/87 mi), an overnight stay is ideal. The city can be eye-wateringly hot in summer, so if visiting in summer, plan activities outside midday and 4pm, which are the times of most intense heat. Be aware that Évora's **historical center** (inside the walls) can be very busy with traffic; parking is limited and mostly paid. There are free **parking lots** outside the city walls. The last train back to Lisbon from Évora departs at around 7pm; the last bus leaves about 30 minutes later.

Itinerary Ideas

ESSENTIAL ÉVORA

Leave Lisbon nice and early to make the 1.5-hour drive to Évora.

Day 1

1 Start your exploration of Évora in its heart, enjoying a coffee in the bustling **Giraldo Square.**

2 Head south to the creepy **Chapel of Bones.**

3 Afterward, follow the walls northeast to see the **Aldeia da Terra** miniature sculptures, a lighthearted take on Portuguese village life.

4 Enjoy lunch at **Chão das Covas Café,** one of Évora's many excellent restaurants.

5 Walk off lunch by following the walls to the **Roman Temple.**

6 From here, make the short walk to **Évora Cathedral,** whose terrace marks the highest point in the city.

7 Wrap up Day 1 with a romantic dinner at **Taberna Típica Quarta Feira.**

Évora

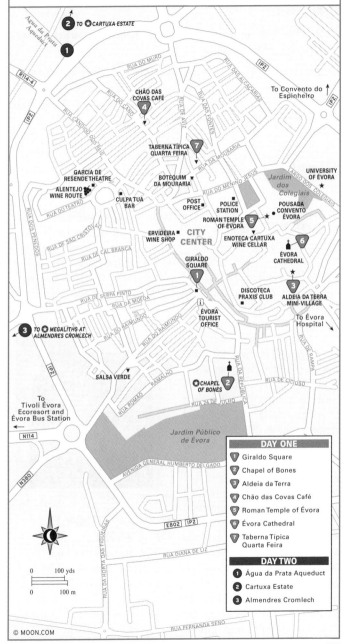

Água da Prata Aqueduct

R114-4

IP2

RUA DO MURO

RUA DAS ALCARIAS

IP2

2 TO ★ CARTUXA ESTATE

1

IP2

RUA CÂNDIDO DOS REIS

RUA DO CANO

CHÃO DAS COVAS CAFÉ **4** ▼

RUA DE AVIZ

RUA DAS FONTES

To Convento do Espinheiro ↑ IP2

TABERNA TÍPICA QUARTA FEIRA **7** ▼

RUA DA MOURARIA

UNIVERSITY OF ÉVORA ★

GARCIA DE RESENDE THEATRE ■

BOTEQUIM DA MOURARIA ▼

RUA DO MENINO JESUS

Jardim dos Colegiais

LARGO DOS COLEGIAIS

ALENTEJO WINE ROUTE ■

CULPA TUA BAR ■

POST OFFICE ■

POLICE STATION ■

ROMAN TEMPLE OF ÉVORA **5**

★

POUSADA CONVENTO ÉVORA

RUA DO TEATRO

RUA DE SÃO CRISTÓVÃO

ERVIDEIRA WINE SHOP ■

CITY CENTER

ENOTECA CARTUXA WINE CELLAR ■

★

ÉVORA CATHEDRAL **6**

RUA DE CAL BRANCA

GIRALDO SQUARE **1**

RUA DE SERPA PINTO

RUA DA MOEDA

i

ÉVORA TOURIST OFFICE

DISCOTECA PRAXIS CLUB ■

★

ALDEIA DA TERRA MINI-VILLAGE **3**

To Évora Hospital ↘

3 TO ★ MEGALITHS AT ALMENDRES CROMLECH

RUA DO RAIMUNDO

RUA DA RAMPA

IP2

SALSA VERDE ■

RUA ROMÃO

RAMALHO

★ CHAPEL OF BONES **2**

RUA 24 DE JULHO

RUA DE CICIOSO

To Tivoli Évora Ecoresort and Évora Bus Station ←

N114

Jardim Público de Évora

RUA DA REPÚBLICA

AVENIDA GENERAL HUMBERTO DELGADO

N380

0   100 yds

0   100 m

🌙

E802 IP2

RUA DIANA DE LIZ

RUA DA HORTA DAS FIGUEIRAS

RUA FERNANDA SENO

© MOON.COM

DAY ONE	
1	Giraldo Square
2	Chapel of Bones
3	Aldeia da Terra
4	Chão das Covas Café
5	Roman Temple of Évora
6	Évora Cathedral
7	Taberna Típica Quarta Feira

DAY TWO	
1	Água da Prata Aqueduct
2	Cartuxa Estate
3	Almendres Cromlech

Day 2

1 Make the short trip north outside the city to see the **Água da Prata Aqueduct.**

2 Then, keeping in the same direction, head to the **Cartuxa Estate** for a tour of the vineyards.

3 After your tour of Cartuxa, where you can accompany wine tastings with regional products like cheeses, sausages, and jams for a light lunch, start heading south back to Lisbon, stopping at the **Almendres Cromlech** en route.

Sights

✪ CHAPEL OF BONES
(Capela dos Ossos)

Praça 1 de Maio 4; tel. 266 704 521; www. igrejadesaofrancisco.pt; daily 9am-5pm winter, daily 9am-6:30pm summer; €6

The odd and chilling Chapel of Bones is next to the entrance of the Church of Saint Francis (Igreja de São Francisco) in the heart of the city. The inner walls and pillars of this 16th-century chapel are clad with the tightly packed human bones and skulls of 5,000 local residents who were exhumed from the overcrowded cemeteries that once sprawled on the city's fringes. Local monks decided to put their remains on display as a warning about the superficiality of materialism and the certainty of death. This is explained in a message above the chapel door: "Nós ossos que aqui estamos, pelos vossos esperamos," or "We bones that are here are awaiting yours." The visit to Chapel of Bones is a self-guided walkthrough, although guided

tours to Évora's monuments can be previously arranged with a certified tour guide through the local **tourist office** (Praça do Giraldo 73; tel. 266 777 071; Mon.-Fri. 9am-7pm and Sat. and Sun. 10am-2pm and 3pm-7pm).

entrance to the Chapel of Bones

ROMAN TEMPLE OF ÉVORA
(Templo Romano de Évora)

Largo do Conde de Vila Flor; tel. 266 769 450; www.visitevora.net/templo-romano-evora-diana; open 24/7

A sacred site dating from the 1st century CE, the Roman Temple of

Roman Temple of Évora

Évora is one of the best-preserved Roman temples on the Iberian Peninsula. Also referred to incorrectly as the Temple of Diana, it is one of Portugal's most recognizable landmarks. The temple is believed to honor Emperor Augustus, who was worshipped as a god. Its remains are a series of Corinthian stone columns on a solid base, but the Roman architecture is still evident. In the historical center, near the cathedral, the temple is on the highest point in the city in front of the manicured public Garden of Diana (Jardim de Diana), pleasant for a shady stroll and with a café with glorious views over Évora.

ÉVORA CATHEDRAL
(Catedral de Évora)
Largo do Marquês de Marialva 809; tel. 266 759 330; www.evoracathedral.com; daily 9am-6pm; cathedral, cloister, and panoramic rooftop €3.50 (€4.50 including museum)

The grand Évora Cathedral, or Sé, is the largest medieval cathedral in Portugal. Similar to Lisbon's monumental cathedral, Évora Cathedral has two massive towers, Gothic cloisters, a Manueline chapel, and a magnificent Baroque chapel. Also of note, among many other unique features, are the striking six-turret lantern-tower and the main portal, whose huge marble columns have impressive carvings of the apostles.

Built on the highest ground in the city, near the Roman Temple, the Gothic structure also bears Romanesque, Manueline, and Baroque architectural touches in its add-ons over the centuries. Construction ran from 1280 to 1350 to mark the victory of the Christian Crusaders over the Moors. The cathedral has the look of a fortress, evident in features such as the battlement-encircled terrace. Its main facade is made of rose granite. Inside are ornamental cloisters and beautiful rose windows that give an ethereal feel, a contrast to the simple exterior.

Évora Cathedral rooftop

Évora Cathedral also houses a **museum** packed with religious art and has the only Gothic statue of the pregnant Virgin Mary in Portugal, over a gilded altar inside the church. An added bonus is the view from the rooftop; the climb up is via a narrow 135-step spiral staircase through the bell tower, suitable only for the agile.

UNIVERSITY OF ÉVORA

(Universidade de Évora)

Largo dos Colegiais 2; tel. 266 740 800; www.uevora.pt; Mon.-Sat. 9:30am-5pm; €3 (audio guides €1.50), children under 12 free; all visits (guided or self-guided) should be booked in advance via email: visitas@ uevora.pt

The University of Évora is monumental but overshadowed by the city's more famous attractions. Founded in the 16th century,

the university comprises several restored historical structures around the city, identified with a dove sculpted into a marble circle above the main entrance. The university's main building is the spectacular square Espírito Santo College, a magnificent edifice with an imposing facade of successive grand arches on marble columns, encasing a courtyard and central fountain. Construction took place 1550-1559. Visitors can explore on their own the lecture halls and hidden works of art, which include ancient tile plaques and an old bookshop with a mural.

ÁGUA DA PRATA AQUEDUCT

(Aqueduto da Água de Prata)

Supplying drinking water over a length of 9 km (5.6 mi), this 16th-century stone aqueduct, literally "Silver Water Aqueduct," was a complex and challenging construction project for its era. Massive arches, at points 25 m (82 ft) high, rise from the ground. The main arches are located outside the city walls, north of Évora near the ring road. In the city's core it blends in seamlessly, fused to houses and shops. Originally the aqueduct ran to a marble fountain in the main Giraldo Square, with a series of public fountains along the way.

It is possible to follow the route of the aqueduct by foot or bicycle through the city on the **Água de Prata Route** (Percurso da Água de Prata), which leads to the outskirts of the city, through farms and cork

☉ Almendres Cromlech

Almendres Cromlech

As well as its plethora of incredible monuments, Évora is home to another intriguing attraction, the **Megalithic Route,** a trail through the megalithic sites throughout the region. The finest and largest of these is the famous Almendres Cromlech, a Neolithic complex located in the deep Alentejo.

This circular twin set of prehistoric standing stones (or menhirs) is said to predate the world's most famous megaliths, Stonehenge in England, reportedly erected over several periods. It is the largest site of such structures on the Iberian Peninsula, which, along with Évora's other smaller sites throughout the region, gives it its nickname "the megalithic capital of Iberia." Comprising 95 standing stones arranged facing downhill in two oval rings, many of which have enigmatic engravings whose meanings remain unknown, the mysterious Almendres site's construction is said to date back to the 6th millennium BC. While its purpose is not certain, it is believed to be a ceremonial site for celestial worship or a form of astronomical observatory.

GETTING THERE

The Almendres Cromlech is located near the village of Nossa Senhora de Guadalupe on the outskirts of Évora (30 minutes, 18 km/11 mi west from Évora). It is situated off the national roadway (N114) from Évora to Montemor-o-Novo, just after the village of Guadalupe, in the Herdade dos Almendres (Almendres Estate), a scenic hillside location swaddled by olive and cork trees.

Public transport to the site is sparse, but it is open 24/7 and there is no entry fee. Visitors are free to wander and touch the stones at leisure.

oaks. A shorter route is from **Porta da Lagoa,** where the aqueduct crosses the R114-4 road from Évora to Arraiolos, into the city center; follow the aqueduct and enjoy the sights along the way. Charming little shops have been built beneath some of the arches, and there is a Renaissance-style water box with a dozen Tuscan columns on Rua Nova. Other streets where you can see the aqueduct are Rua do Cano, Rua do Salvador, and Travessa das Nunes.

Wine Routes and Tours

Alentejo Wine Route
Wine Tasting Center
(Rota dos Vinhos do Alentejo)

Rua 5 de Outubro 88; tel. 266 746 498 or 266 746 609; www.vinhosdoalentejo. pt; Mon-Fri. 10am-1pm and 2pm-6pm; tastings €5

Wine lovers are spoiled for choice with Alentejo wines, and the Alentejo Wine Route (Rota dos Vinhos do Alentejo) Center takes visitors through the region's various wine-growing areas, listing dozens of wineries. It aims to promote regional wine-making as well as other aspects of regional culture. The headquarters are just outside the historical city center, between the hospital and the train station. Staff can help organize a trip and winery visits.

Ervideira Wine Shop

Rua 5 de Outubro 56; tel. 266 700 402; www.ervideira.pt; daily 11am-7pm

Housed in a traditional building in the heart of Évora, this smart store exclusively sells wines produced by the family-run Ervideira estate, whose history dates back to 1880, when the illustrious Count D'Ervideira began producing wine in the Évora region. Tastings are also available.

✪ Cartuxa Estate

Quinta de Valbom; tel. 266 748 383; www. cartuxa.pt; daily 10am-7pm

One of Évora's most iconic vineyards is the Cartuxa Estate, 1.7 km (1.1 mi) from the town center, a 30-minute walk, a 5-minute drive, or €5 by taxi. Producing iconic EA, Foral de Évora, and Pêra-Manca wines, the century-old 15-hectare (37-acre) organic vineyard offers guided tours (1 hour, in English, by appointment only), as well as wine and olive oil tasting (from €10). Just next door is the Cartuxa Convent, built between 1587 and 1598, which houses monks.

Sports and Recreation

Skydive Portugal

Évora Municipal Airdrome;
tel. 910 999 991; www.skydiveportugal.pt;
from €149

Adventurous travelers can take their trip to Évora to new heights and enjoy bird's-eye views of the region with an adrenaline-charged skydive. The basic Silver Pack includes a 10-minute panoramic airplane flight over the historical city of Évora to an altitude of around 2,700 m (9,000 ft), 20 seconds of freefall at 200 km/h (124 mph), then 5 minutes of gentle parachuting, sailing through the skies of Alentejo, admiring the Alentejo plains.

Balonissimo

tel. 935 646 124; www.balonissimo.com;
from €170

Enjoy the beauty of the Alentejo from the serenity of a hot-air balloon. Watch the sunrise as you glide over Évora, the aqueduct, and the rolling plains and vineyards with a glass of champagne in hand. Balonissimo offers free pickup from anywhere in Évora. Flights last about an hour, with the full excursion taking 3-4 hours.

Arts and Entertainment

Garcia de Resende Theatre
(Teatro Garcia de Resende)

Rua do Teatro 10; tel. 266 703 112;
www.cendrev.com

This magnificent century-old building is worth a look, if only to admire the simple granite exterior, behind which hides an opulent Italian-style theater. Shaped like a horseshoe, the main concert hall has three tiers of balconies; their deep red lining, gold-trimmed rims, and incredible painted ceiling give the main room a regal, Baroque feel. Inaugurated in June 1892, the theatre is named after Évora-born poet, designer, and architect Garcia de Resende, who was an esteemed figure on Portugal's Renaissance scene. The playhouse has a busy year-round program of national and international plays and performances.

Food

Évora's food scene spans rustic restaurants to fine dining, centered on hearty, meaty regional dishes, although international cuisine and vegetarian restaurants can be found. The Alentejo is famous for its porco preto (black pig) and excellent wines, and most restaurants in Évora will serve both. Many of the city's best-known restaurants are in the **Moorish Quarter** (centro histórico).

Chão das Covas Café

Largo Chão das Covas Évora; tel. 266 706 294; Wed.-Sat. noon-3pm and 7pm-10:30pm, Sun. noon-3pm, Tues. 7pm-10:30pm; €10

Don't be misled by the "café" in the name of Chão das Covas Café; this cute little eatery might be small, but its home-cooked Alentejano dishes and tapas are huge in flavor.

Salsa Verde

Rua do Raimundo 93A; tel. 266 743 210; www.salsa-verde.org; Mon.-Fri. noon-3pm and 7pm-9:30pm, Sat. noon-3pm; €10

Vegetarian restaurant Salsa Verde is an airy, colorful setup in a former convent, a true haven for veggie fans in a land of meat lovers. Meat-free twists on traditional Portuguese dishes use fresh local produce and herbs. There are no

an outdoor café in Évora

fixed menus; every day the offerings are fresh and different.

Botequim da Mouraria

Rua da Mouraria 16A; tel. 266 746 775; Mon.-Fri. 12:30pm-3pm; €15

One of Évora's most popular restaurants, Botequim da Mouraria is small, rustic, and tavern-like, run by a husband-and-wife team who prepare simple, unfussy, traditional Portuguese food. Be sure to try the presunto cured ham.

Pastelaria Conventual Pão de Rala

Rua de Cicioso 47; tel. 266 707 778; Mon.-Fri. 8am-6pm, Sat.-Sun. 8am-5pm; €5

Treat yourself to a coffee and a delicious pastry at the Pão de Rala cake shop. Small and cozy, tucked away on a backstreet, it specializes in typical local "conventual sweets"—sweets and desserts believed to have been made by nuns and monks in convents and monasteries during the Middle Ages and Renaissance periods—and traditional Portuguese confectionary.

✪ Taberna Típica Quarta Feira

Rua do Inverno 18; tel. 266 707 530; Tues.-Sat. 12:30pm-2:30pm and 7:30pm-9:30pm; €20

Unpretentious and atmospheric, the family-run Taberna Típica Quarta Feira serves tasty local and regional specialties such as Alentejo-style pork meat and grilled black pork chops.

Enoteca Cartuxa Wine Cellar

✪ Enoteca Cartuxa Wine Cellar

Rua de Vasco da Gama 15; tel. 266 748 348; www.cartuxa.pt; daily 12:30pm-3pm and 7:30pm-10pm; €20

Cosmopolitan Enoteca Cartuxa Wine Cellar is a polished restaurant by the producers of the famous Cartuxa vineyard wines. The estate's wines are paired with Portuguese regional dishes such as cow tongue, pork cheek, sheep and goat cheese, smoked sausages, and cured meats.

Local Specialties

Two local delicacies are porco preto (black pig) and the sweet treat queijada d'Évora. **Black pig,** also known as Alentejano pig, is a darker-skinned animal than its relatives. Its origins can be traced to wild boars. The black pig is traditionally free-range and feeds on acorns, so the meat is moister, more succulent, and more fragrant, with a nutty taste.

Queijada d'Évora is a small, sweet tartlet with a thin, crispy pastry crust and a creamy filling made from egg yolks and fresh sheep-milk cheese. It is a form of doçaria conventual, traditional Portuguese sweets whose closely guarded recipes come from convents.

Bars and Nightlife

Évora has a vibrant alfresco social scene. In summer especially, locals socialize in the cooler temperatures after dark, giving the city a bustling café-culture feel, topped with the energetic vibe of the university students.

Discoteca Praxis Club

Rua Valdevinos 21; tel. 965 566 620; www. instagram.com/praxisclub_oficial; Tues.-Sat. midnight-6am

Many of the city center hotels have upscale wine and cocktail bars, while the other bars around the historical center buzz with students and younger people, particularly on Wednesday night. Discoteca Praxis Club has four bars and two dance floors popular with the younger crowd. Its packed calendar features resident and guest DJs, live bands, and themed evenings.

Culpa Tua Bar

Praça Joaquim António de Aguiar 6; tel. 965 435 209; www.facebook.com/ Culpatuabar; daily 6pm-3am

The rustic Culpa Tua Bar is a busy little bar showcasing great local liquor, wine, and fruity cocktails. The bar is in a characterful old building with a vaulted ceiling, brick arches, and a cobbled floor.

Accommodations

Tivoli Évora Ecoresort

*Quinta da Deserta e Malina; tel. 266 738
500; www.ecorkhotel.com; €100-200*

Built using natural materials, refined countryside Tivoli Évora
Ecoresort has an eco-friendly ethos
with 56 private suites a 10-minute
drive from the city center in the
rolling Alentejo plains.

✪ Convento do Espinheiro

*5.2 km (3.2 mi) north of Évora city
center; tel. 266 788 200; www.
conventodoespinheiro.com; €150-250 d*

Luxury boutique hotel Convento
do Espinheiro, converted from
a 15th-century convent, is one
of Portugal's most famous and
emblematic hotels. Surrounded
by gardens, it offers 92 rooms (including 5 suites), divided between
sumptuous conventual rooms and
a modern wing with midcentury-
inspired decor.

Pousada Convento Évora

*Largo do Conde de Vila Flor; tel. 266 730
070; www.pousadas.pt/en/hotel/pousada-
evora; €200-300 d*

The serene 36-room Pousada
Convento Évora, with a swimming
pool, is in Évora's historical center,
converted from a low-rise, whitewashed monastery dating to 1487.
The luxurious rooms are former
monks' cells.

Information and Services

- **PSP police station:** Rua
  Francisco Soares Lusitano;
  tel. 266 760 450; www.psp.pt
- **Main post office:** Rua
  Olivença; tel. 266 745 480
- **Évora Hospital:** Largo Senhor
  da Pobreza; tel. 266 740 100

- **Évora Tourist Office:** Praça do
  Giraldo 73; tel. 266 777 071;
  Mon.-Fri. 9am-7pm, Sat.-Sun.
  10am-2pm and 3pm-7pm

Getting There and Around

GETTING THERE

Car

Évora is 1.5 hour drive east of **Lisbon,** about 140 km (87 mi), following the **A6** motorway.

Bus

Évora's main **bus station** (Av. Tulio Espanca; tel. 266 738 120) is a 10-minute walk west of the walled city center.

Rede Expressos (tel. 707 223 344; www.rede-expressos.pt) runs air-conditioned buses almost every half hour from Lisbon's **Sete Rios** bus station (1.5 hours; from €8-12.50) and **Flixbus** runs from **Oriente** station (https://global.flixbus.com; 1 hour 20 minutes; €5). Tickets can be bought at the stations' ticket office or booked online.

Train

CP (tel. 707 210 220; www.cp.pt) trains run four times daily from Lisbon stations including **Oriente, Sete Rios, Cais do Sodré,** and **Entrecampos** (2 hours 12 minutes; second class €14.80, first class €19.15).

The train station in Évora, **Largo da Estação,** is outside the city walls, 1 km (0.6 mi) south, a 15-minute walk. The station is simple, but look for the old azulejo tile murals depicting local life.

GETTING AROUND

Most of Évora's sights can be covered **on foot,** but the old cobbled streets can be slippery and uneven.

Car

Rent a car to explore the surrounding wine farms, villages, and Almendres Cromlech. Hotels work with local car rental companies; ask at reception. South of the walled city, between the IP2 road and the Circular de Évora ring road, are a number of car rental offices, including **Europcar Évora** (Rua da Horta das Figueiras 140; tel. 266 742 627; www.europcar.pt; Mon.-Sat. 9am-12:30pm and 2pm-6:30pm), **Hertz** (Hertz Building, Rua do Centro de Formação Profissional 5; tel. 219 426 300; www.hertz.pt; Mon.-Fri. 9am-1pm and 2pm-6pm), and **Drivalia** (Rua Vitor Branco dos Santos 9A; tel. 932 403 022; www.drivalia.pt; Mon.-Fri. 8:30am-12:30pm and 2:30pm-6:30pm, Sat. 9am-12:30pm).

Finding **parking** within the city walls can be difficult and must be paid for weekdays 8:30am-7:30pm and Saturday 9am-2pm. There are spacious parking lots outside the walls, such as at Portas de Lagoa, near the aqueduct, north of the city center. It is within walking distance of the center, with no steep hills or stairs. Parking outside the city walls is usually free.

Taxi

There are plenty of taxis near places of interest and the train and bus stations. Local company **Associação de Rádio Táxis de Évora** (Rua dos Altos; tel. 266 735 735) provides service anytime.

Bus

Local bus service **TREVO** (tel. 266 106 923; www.trevo.com.pt; Blue Route day ticket €1.15) serves Évora and its immediate fringes. The Blue Route covers the old city continuously weekdays 8am-8pm and Saturday 8am-2pm. The bus leaves the main terminal (Avenida Tulio Espanca) every 15 minutes.

Essentials

Transportation

GETTING THERE

Traveling to Portugal from anywhere in Europe is quick and easy, with regular direct flights from many European cities as well as from Asia, the Middle East, North and South America, and Africa. Even better, flights can be pretty cheap within Europe, thanks to the growing number of low-cost airlines.

Lisbon Airport is the country's biggest and busiest. Most flights from outside Europe are to Lisbon, with direct flights from the United States, Canada, Brazil, Morocco, Tunisia, Turkey, Russia, Dubai in the United Arab Emirates, Angola, Mozambique, and China. Porto also has regular direct flights from Newark in the United States, Luanda in Angola, and Rio de Janeiro and São Paulo in Brazil, although far fewer than Lisbon. Faro has almost exclusively European flights, the vast majority from the United Kingdom, Germany, and France.

It is easy to travel to Portugal within Europe, with bus and train services connecting Portugal with Spain, France, Belgium, the Netherlands, and the United Kingdom. Driving to Portugal is also possible thanks to a good international road network and the EU (European Union) open-borders policy.

From North America

Some transatlantic cruises include Lisbon, generally just for a short day trip, but the easiest, quickest, cheapest, and most convenient way to travel between the United States and Portugal is without doubt by air. Flights take approximately 7 hours eastbound from the Northeast, and 9 hours westbound.

Portugal's national carrier, **TAP Air Portugal** (www.flytap.pt), has regular direct flights between mainland Portugal and New York (JFK and Newark), Boston, Miami, Chicago, San Francisco, and Washington. US airline **United** (www.united.com) also has direct flights to Portugal.

TAP has invested heavily in the US market, increasing the number of destinations it serves, and has also created the **Portugal Stopover** (www.portugalstopover.flytap. com) program, where US travelers on TAP to other destinations can spend a few days in Portugal before continuing onward. Portugal's national flag carrier also operates onward connecting flights from Lisbon to Porto, Faro, and the islands.

Regional Azores airline **SATA Azores Airlines** (www. azoresairlines.pt) and **Air Canada** (www.aircanada.com) operate direct flights between Portugal and Canada, including a stop in the Azores archipelago.

From Europe
Air

The vast majority of European flights to Portugal are from the United Kingdom, France, Germany, the Netherlands, and Belgium, all 2.5-3 hours away. Direct flights also operate from Finland as well as Eastern European countries such as Poland, the Czech Republic, and Hungary. Flights from neighboring Spain are only to Lisbon and Porto.

Previous: Lisbon tram.

The ever-expanding availability of European flights includes a number of low-cost airlines such as Ryanair (Ireland), easyJet (UK), Vueling (Spain), Eurowings (Germany), and Transavia (France), meaning travel between two European destinations can cost less than €100 round-trip. Prices within Europe are heavily influenced by school holidays at Easter, summer, and Christmas-New Year's, as well as peak tourist seasons in Portugal, especially July-August; pricing can vary widely.

Train

Getting to Portugal from other European countries by train isn't as straightforward as by air and can sometimes be more expensive. The train is slightly quicker than traveling by bus.

Getting to Portugal by train from most of Europe requires passing through an international terminal such as Paris or Madrid. Getting to Portugal from the United Kingdom takes around 24 hours and involves catching the **Eurostar** (www.eurostar.com) from London to Paris, then a TGV high-speed train from Paris to Hendaye-Irun at the border of southern France and Spain, and from there the overnight Sud Expresso train to Lisbon. There are two overnight sleeper trains from Spain: the **Lusitania Hotel Train** (www.cp.pt), linking Madrid's Chamartin Station to Lisbon in about 10 hours, and the **Sud Expresso** (www.cp.pt), which connects Lisbon to San Sebastian in Spain and Hendaye in southern France in about 11 hours.

The easiest way to get around Portugal—and the rest of Europe—by train is with a **Eurail Pass** (www.eurail.com). This EU-wide rail travel pass for non-EU citizens covers train travel in first or second class. The Eurail pass comes in three options: the Global Pass, covering 5 or more of up to 28 European countries; the Select Pass—covering 2, 3, or 4 bordering countries; or a single-country pass. Prices for Portugal range from €82 for a single-country pass to €307 for a basic Global Pass, although prices vary.

An identical pass is available to EU citizens and official residents: the **Interrail Pass** (www.interrail.eu) ranges from €80 for a single-country pass to €208 for a basic Global Pass, although prices vary.

Bus

The main bus lines offering intercity travel within Europe to Portugal are **Eurolines** (Lisbon tel. 218 957 398; Porto tel. 225 189 303; Bragança tel. 273 327 122; www.eurolines.com), **National Express** (www.nationalexpress.com), and Flixbus (www.flixbus.com). These travel to Lisbon from many European countries. The most popular routes are from the United Kingdom, France, Spain, and the Netherlands. Transfers may be required; from London to Lisbon, for example, a change may be required in Paris. There are at least five buses a week between Paris and

Lisbon. Bus trips from Amsterdam to Lisbon start from €144 one-way and take around 36 hours; London to Lisbon is around €150 and 45 hours, and Paris to Lisbon €85 and 29 hours. Flixbus also operates low-cost services within Portugal.

The main bus companies operating between Portugal and neighboring Spain are **Avanza** (tel. +34 912 722 832; www.avanzabus.com) and **Alsa** (tel. 902 422 242; www.alsa.com). A one-way trip from Madrid to Lisbon costs around €23, Seville to Lisbon €25, and Corunna to Lisbon €38.

Car

Europe is connected by a well-maintained motorway network, meaning international travel is straightforward between EU capital cities. Most of Europe exercises an open-borders policy, with no compulsory inspections at borders. Time-wise, for example, driving nonstop from Paris to Lisbon takes around 16 hours; Madrid to Lisbon is 6 hours; and Berlin to Lisbon is 26 hours. Each country has different speed limits, driver alcohol tolerances, and other traffic laws.

Driving from the United Kingdom to Portugal is slightly more complicated, as it requires a ferry between the UK and mainland Europe. There are no direct ferries between the UK and Portugal, so the more common driving routes are from the UK by ferry to France or Spain. Ferries from the UK to France are quicker and cheaper than those to Spain,

but also make the journey longer due to added driving time. Ferry trips between the UK and France often take just a few hours, while a ferry to Spain can take more than a day. There are many ferry routes between the UK and France, and the website **Direct Ferries** (www.directferries.co.uk) provides a comprehensive map of routes and prices.

Ferry crossings between the United Kingdom and Spain tend to change often, but the main crossings are between Plymouth and Santander, generally once a week, and Portsmouth to Bilbao or Portsmouth to Santander, three times a week. Other good ferry comparison sites are www.aferry.co.uk and www.ferries.co.uk. There are also direct ferries between Ireland and France.

The alternative to the ferry between the United Kingdom and mainland Europe is to take the Channel Tunnel, also known as the **Eurotunnel** (www.eurotunnel.com). Taking just 35 minutes to cross under the channel, the tunnel is cheaper and quicker than a ferry but is not for the claustrophobic. It connects Folkestone in the south of England to Calais in northern France via a 50-km (31-mi) rail tunnel. At its lowest point, it is 75 m (246 ft) below the seabed and 115 m (377 ft) below sea level. Costs start from £30 per car (including up to nine passengers).

It is without doubt cheaper and quicker to fly to Portugal from anywhere in Europe than to drive, and tolls and the cost of gasoline can vary noticeably from country to country. But a road trip is always an adventure, as long as you do your research and mapping in advance, and there's no reason why driving to Portugal can't be an enjoyable—if perhaps costly—experience.

From Australia and New Zealand

There are no direct flights between Portugal and Australia or New Zealand. Connecting flights are generally via Dubai in the United Arab Emirates, with a daily direct flight between Lisbon and Dubai on **Emirates** (www.emirates.com), or via Asia. There is also a direct nonstop flight between Australia and London, from where there are many onward flights to Portugal. Most major European air carriers operate code-share flights to major Asian hubs. Singapore, for example, can be reached with just one connection, from Lisbon to Istanbul on Turkish Airlines, or Dubai on Emirates, or via the United Kingdom or Germany with Singapore Airlines.

From South Africa

There are no direct flights from South Africa to Portugal. TAP flies direct to Maputo in Mozambique and Luanda in Angola, also served by Angolan airline TAAG, and connecting flights can be arranged from there. Major European carriers such as British Airways, Germany's Lufthansa, Swissair,

Spain's Iberia, and Air France fly direct to South Africa with connecting flights to Lisbon.

GETTING AROUND LISBON

Lisbon is a large European city with an efficient system of buses, trams, and Metro trains, along with ferries across the Tagus River. In addition, it's a wonderful city to explore on foot (despite the many hills), and public transportation is supplemented by taxis, ride shares, tuk-tuks, and hop-on hop-off buses geared toward tourists.

Bus

The capital's bus service, **Carris** (www.carris.pt), also manages the city's tram system. It provides good coverage of the city, as well as service to neighboring towns and suburbs, and is inexpensive, with most trips under €2. Most buses run 6am-9pm daily, with the busiest lines running until midnight.

Tram

Carris (www.carris.pt) operates a network of historical trams and funiculars, a unique way to get into the city's backstreets. Five tram routes carry 60 trams, most of which are vintage vehicles. Trams and funiculars generally operate 6am-11pm daily.

Metro

Inaugurated in 1959, Lisbon's **Metro** (www.metrolisboa.pt) has consistently grown, including a stop beneath the airport, making travel fast and easy. The Metro has four main lines—Green, Yellow, Red, and Blue—and is simple to navigate, covering the city's important points. Trains run regularly and reliably.

Car

Getting around Lisbon without a car is easy and convenient thanks to the comprehensive public transport network. A car is only necessary to visit outlying areas.

EXPLORING OUTSIDE LISBON
Train

Portugal's train service **Comboios de Portugal (CP)** (www.cp.pt/passageiros/en) is efficient and cheap but complex. It operates on several tiers, from the painfully slow Urbano train service, which stops in every town and village; to the modern Intercity service between main cities; and the high-speed Alfa-Pendular, which connects Porto to Lisbon and the Algarve with a few stops between.

Despite being comprehensive, the national rail network isn't as direct as bus services, and, oddly, some major cities have no train station, while many cities and towns have their train stations on the outskirts, requiring a taxi ride to the center. On the plus side, Portugal's trains tend to be spacious and well-kept on the inside, and offer cheaper second-class tickets and more privacy and comfort in first class, sometimes in private compartments.

Bus

There are many different bus companies in Portugal, including three major intercity long-distance bus companies, Algarve line **Eva Transportes** (www.eva-bus.com), national **Rede Expressos** (www.rede-expressos.pt), and northern **Rodonorte** (www.rodonorte.pt). Local and regional buses link towns, villages, and parishes within municipalities. In Lisbon the local public transport company is **Carris,** which operates buses, trams, and funiculars. Bus travel in Portugal is cheap but not always the most comfortable, although long-distance express buses are mostly equipped with air-conditioning, TVs, toilets, and even onboard drinks and snacks. Pop into a local ticket office to check for updated timetables. Small discounts are given on round-trip tickets.

Car

Driving in Portugal can, in certain places, require nerves of steel and patience. Lisbon has fast and furious traffic, where delaying at a traffic light will inevitably earn a blast of the horn from behind. There can also be a seeming lack of civility on Portugal's roads, with poor usage of turn signals, and passing seems to be a national sport. For the most part, navigating Portugal's roads is straightforward, and major road surfaces are of a decent standard.

Car Rental

The country's airports host many car rental companies, or ask at your hotel. Vehicles can be dropped off at most holiday lodgings. Use price comparison sites like **Auto Europe** (www.autoeurope.pt) or **Portugal Auto Rentals** (www.portugal-auto-rentals.com) to find the best deals. Booking well in advance will mean better prices. Beware of unexpected surprises by double-checking the opening and closing times of the car rental desk at the airport, fuel fees and excess insurance, and electronic toll payments.

Even though the minimum legal age to drive is 18, most rental companies require drivers to be age 21 or to have held a license for at least five years. Costs can vary greatly, from as little as €10 per day in low season but rising exponentially in high season. If you're just visiting one or two areas, a small car is useful as most town centers, including historical hamlets and large cities, have areas that are a tangle of narrow cobbled streets.

Road System

Portugal's road system is decent and major routes are kept in good condition, although the same cannot be said about smaller regional or municipal roads. Some are in urgent need of repair, particularly in rural areas, and on certain stretches signage could use updating.

Motorways are generally in good condition, although major motorways (autoestradas) have tolls, signaled with a large white V on a green background. Secondary and rural roads can be poorer quality, with potholes and sharp bends. In high-elevation areas, such as the Serra da Estrela, snowfall can close roads for hours or even days.

Roads are categorized as follows:

Motorways (autoestradas) start with an **A** (A1, A22) and are major highways between cities or regions. Most A roads have tolls, paid at booths or electronically. Some motorways, such as the A22, are exclusively electronic and have barriers. Electronic toll payment uses the **Via Verde** (www.viaverde.pt) transponder system. More information on tolls and motorways is available at www.portugaltolls.com. Motorways have service areas with cafés, gas stations, and toilet facilities at regular intervals. Emergency telephones are also found at regular intervals.

Main highways (itinerário principal) start with an **IP** (IP1, IP2). These are major roads that are alternatives to the motorways, although the road conditions are inferior, and generally link main cities.

Secondary highways (itinerário complementar) start with an **IC** (IC1, IC2). These roads complement the IPs by connecting them to big towns and cities.

National roads (estrada nacional) start with an **N** or **EN** (N125, also known as EN125) and are the main roads between towns and cities.

Local municipal roads (estrada municipal) start with an **M** or **EM** and are smaller roads within localities.

Portugal is also connected to the

rest of Europe by an **international E-road system,** a numbering system for pan-Europe roads. The main European routes crossing Portugal are the E01, E80, E82, E90, E801, E802, E805, and E806.

General Road Rules

In Portugal traffic runs on the right side of the road. Drivers must be over age 18, and seat belts are compulsory for all occupants.

National speed limits are easy to remember, although some drivers seem to struggle to abide by them: 50 km/h (31 mph) in residential areas, 90 km/h (56 mph) on rural roads, and 120 km/h (74 mph) on motorways. Cars towing trailers are restricted to 80 km/h (50 mph).

The rule on roundabouts (rotaries, or traffic circles) is that the outer lane should be used only if turning off immediately. In practice, this rarely happens. Make allowances for it.

You must park facing the same direction as the traffic flow. It's also illegal to use a mobile phone while driving (although at times you might wonder), and that applies to talking and texting.

Punishment for drunk driving is harsh, ranging from hefty fines to driving bans. The legal limit is 0.5 gram (0.02 ounce) of alcohol per liter (34 ounces) of blood, or 0.2 gram (0.007 ounce) per liter for commercial drivers.

Driver's Licenses

EU citizens require a valid driver's license with a photo on it, issued by the bearer's home country, to drive in Portugal. Drivers from outside the EU require a license and an International Driving Permit, which must be shown both to rental agencies for renting a car and to the authorities if asked. When you are driving on Portugal's roads, the vehicle's documents must be in the vehicle at all times, and drivers need a valid ID, such as a passport. It is compulsory to have certain items in a vehicle. These are a reflective danger jacket, a reflective warning triangle, spare bulbs, a spare tire, and approved child seats for children under age 12 or 150 cm (5 ft). Check that you have these before driving off, as failure to produce them could result in a fine.

Refueling

Diesel (gasóleo) is cheaper than unleaded gasoline (gasolina sem chumbo) in Portugal, and gas stations can be found in abundance (although this is less the case in rural areas). Many large supermarkets and shopping centers have gas stations that offer low-cost fuel options, and there is almost always a gas station near an airport. The main gas stations in Portugal belong to BP, Galp, and Repsol. Most gas stations are open daily 7am-10pm, but stations at service areas on motorways or on main roads should be open 24 hours. Unleaded gasoline has a 95 or 98 octane rating; although both can be used in gasoline vehicles, the 98 is more expensive. All gas stations accept debit and credit cards as well as cash.

Parking

Parking can be hard to find in town centers given the narrow cobbled streets and tourist demand. Big towns and cities have designated parking lots and parking areas, which charge fees, especially in popular places like Faro, Lisbon, and Porto. The closer to the city center, the more expensive the parking will be.

Automobile Associations

A contact number for breakdowns should be provided by the vehicle's insurer. When collecting a rental car, always clarify what to do or who to call in the event of a breakdown or emergency. The **Auto Club Portugal (ACP)** (tel. 808 222 222; www.acp.pt) is the Portuguese equivalent of the American Automobile Association.

Visas and Officialdom

To enter Portugal, all travelers are required to have a valid ID. Most European citizens need only a valid ID or a passport and can circulate freely within the EU by land, air, or sea. People from other countries must have a passport and may require a visa. Always check with the relevant authorities before traveling or with your travel provider. Here are some basic guidelines.

PASSPORTS AND TOURIST VISAS
EU/Schengen

Portugal is part of the EU and the Schengen area. EU nationals traveling within EU or Schengen states do not require a visa for entering Portugal for any length of stay. They do require a valid passport or official ID card (national citizen's card, driver's license, or residency permit, for example).

European citizens traveling between Schengen countries are not required to present an identity document or passport at border crossings. However, it is recommended that travelers have ID documents with them at all times, as they may be requested at any time by the authorities. In Portugal the law requires everyone to carry a personal ID at all times.

As non-European Economic Area (EAA) nationals, different border checks will apply when UK residents travel to other EU or Schengen-area countries. They may have to use separate lanes from EU, EEA, and Swiss citizens when queuing and may also need to show a return or onward ticket. British passport-holders will need to have at least six months left on their passports, which must have been issued within the last 10 years. UK nationals are able to travel to other Schengen-area countries for up to 90 days in any 180-day period without a visa for purposes such as tourism. Furthermore, travel insurance is required to cover healthcare, and roaming charges may apply on cellphone use. Go to www.abta.com/tips-and-advice/brexit-advice-for-travellers, www.gov.uk/visit-europe-1-january-2021, or https://europa.eu/youreurope/citizens/index_en.htm for more information.

United States, Canada, Australia, and New Zealand

People from non-EU countries always require a passport, valid for at least six months, and some may require a visa. Australian, Canadian, New Zealand, and US travelers require a valid passport but do not need a visa for stays of up to 90 days in any six-month period. While it is not obligatory to have an onward or return ticket, it is advisable to have one.

South Africa

South African nationals need to apply for a Portugal-Schengen visa. This should be done three months before travel. Applicants must have a South African passport valid for six months beyond the date of return with at least three blank pages. They also need a recent passport photo (specify to photographer that it has to meet the Schengen visa requirements), a completed original application form, round-trip tickets from South Africa to Portugal, and proof of prepaid lodging or a letter of invitation if staying with friends or family in Portugal, among other requisites.

ETIAS Registration

Beginning in 2025, most travelers who are visa-exempt for short stays in the Schengen Area will also require ETIAS pre-screening registration. ETIAS is required for visa-exempt travelers to 26 European Schengen countries, including Portugal. The online system verifies travelers' info for security risks. Once approved, it's valid for up to 3 years or until passport expiration. If a new passport is obtained, a new ETIAS application is required.

CUSTOMS

Customs is mandatory for all travelers arriving in or leaving Portugal carrying goods or money, although certain limits apply to what can be brought in or taken out. Aeroportos de Portugal (ANA) states that all passengers traveling without baggage or transporting cash or monetary assets under the equivalent of €10,000 or carrying personal items not intended for commercial purposes and not prohibited should pass through the "Nothing to Declare" channel. Passengers carrying over €10,000 or whose baggage contains tradable goods in quantities greater than those permitted by law and that are not exempt from value-added tax (VAT) or excise duty must pass through the "Goods to Declare" channel.

Passengers age 17 or older can bring in the following:

From EU member states: 800 cigarettes, 400 cigarillos, 200 cigars, 1 kilogram (2.2 pounds) of smoking tobacco, 10 liters (11 quarts) of alcoholic spirits, 20 liters (21 quarts) of beverages with alcoholic content under 22 percent, 90 liters (95 quarts) of wine, 110 liters (116 quarts) of beer, medications in quantities corresponding to need and accompanied by a prescription.

For travelers from outside the EU: 200 cigarettes, 100 cigarillos, 50 cigars, 250 grams (0.6 pound) of smoking tobacco, 1 liter (1 quart) of alcoholic spirits, 2 liters (2 quarts) of beverages with alcoholic content under 22 percent, 4 liters (4 quarts) of wine, 16 liters (17 quarts) of beer, medications in quantities corresponding to need and accompanied by a prescription.

Quantities exceeding these must be declared, and passengers under age 17 don't get an exemption for alcohol or tobacco.

EMBASSIES AND CONSULATES

Australian Embassy: Av. da Liberdade 200, Lisbon; tel. 213 101 500; http://portugal.embassy.gov.au; Mon.-Fri. 10am-4pm

British Embassy: Rua de São Bernardo 33, Lisbon; tel. 213 924 000, emergency tel. 213 924 000; www.gov.uk/world/organisations/british-embassy-lisbon; Mon., Wed., and Fri. 9:30am-2pm

British Vice Consulate: Edifício A Fábrica, Av. Guanaré, Portimão (Algarve); tel. 282 490 750; Mon., Wed., and Fri. 9:30am-2pm

Canadian Embassy: Av. da Liberdade 196, Lisbon; tel. 213 164 600; www.canadainternational.gc.ca/portugal; Mon.-Fri. 9am-noon

French Embassy: Rua Santos-O-Velho 5, Lisbon; tel. 213 939 292; https://pt.ambafrance.org; Mon.-Fri. 8:30am-noon

Irish Embassy: Av. da Liberdade 200, Lisbon; tel. 213 308 200; www.dfa.ie/irish-embassy/portugal; Mon.-Fri. 9:30am-12:30pm

New Zealand Consulate: Rua da Sociedade Farmacêutica 68, 1st Right, Lisbon; tel. 213 140 780; consulado.nz.pt@gmail.com, www.mfat.govt.nz; office hours by appointment only

South African Embassy: Av. Luís Bívar 10, Lisbon; tel. 213 192 200; lisbon.consular@dirco.gov.za; Mon.-Thurs. 8am-12:30pm and 1:15pm-5pm, Fri. 8am-1pm Fri., the Consular Section (Annex) Mon.-Fri. 8:30am-noon

Spanish Embassy: Praça de Espanha 1, Lisbon; tel. 213 472 381; www.exteriores.gob.es; Mon.-Fri. 9am-2pm

US Embassy: Av. das Forças Armadas 133C, Lisbon; tel. 217 273 300; https://pt.usembassy.gov/embassy-consulate/lisbon; Mon.-Fri. 8am-5pm

US Consulate: Príncipe de Mónaco 6-2F, Ponta Delgada (Azores); tel. 296 308 330; conspontadelgada@state.gov; Mon.-Fri. 8:30am-12:30pm and 1:30pm-5:30pm

Food

It's not hard to wax lyrical about Portugal's cuisine: fresh, flavorful, comforting, and generous, it is the soul of an unassuming seafaring nation. Largely Mediterranean, the staples are fresh fish, meat, fruit, and vegetables prepared with olive oil and washed down with excellent national wines. Dishes vary from light and fresh along the coast, with grilled fish and seafood, to hearty meaty stews and roasts in rural inland areas, and colorful cosmopolitan fusions in larger towns and cities.

Each region touts its own take on national staples such as the cozido á Portuguesa (Portuguese stew) and caldeirada (fish stew), as well as typical local sweets—all with a story attached to them. Another staple on most menus and one of Portugal's emblematic gastronomic ingredients is salted codfish, or bacalhau, for which the Portuguese are said to have a different recipe for every day of the year.

PORTUGUESE CUISINE
Fish
It is perhaps unsurprising that Portugal, an audacious seafaring nation, is renowned for its bounty of seafood. Coastal areas generally serve shellfish as an appetizer. One-pot dishes such as caldeiradas and arroz de tamboril (monkfish rice) are not to be missed. Salted codfish is a staple throughout Portugal, and grilled sardines are enjoyed voraciously during summer (sardine fishing is limited in winter to allow stocks to replenish); these, along with dourada (golden bream), robalo (sea bass), and cavalas (mackerel), are among the most common fish on menus. Prawns boiled or fried in olive oil and garlic are enjoyed as a snack or appetizer, while more unusual seafood includes razor clams and sea urchins.

Meats
Most restaurants have grilled meat on the menu, most commonly febras (pork steaks), costeletas de porco (pork chops), entrecosto (pork ribs), entremeada (pork belly), and the ubiquitous frango piripiri (chicken grilled and served with spicy chili sauce). Note that the word "grelhado" (grilled) usually means on charcoal.

Cured and smoked meats, especially the smoky, spicy chouriço sausage, presunto (cured ham), and morcela (black blood sausage), also represent a huge chunk of Portuguese gastronomy. They are often eaten simply as an appetizer, accompanied by fresh rustic bread, olives, and cheese, or added to stews and soups to enhance the flavor.

Soups
Almost all cafés and restaurants

Portugal: A Timeline

5000 BCE	First agricultural societies in the region begin to form
700–300 BCE	Celts invade Portugal region in waves, bringing materials such as iron and other cultural influences
300 BCE–CE 500	Roman occupation of Portugal, starting in the south
500	Iberian Peninsula invaded and conquered by the Visigoths
711	Moors from present-day Morocco and Northern Africa claim and settle the Iberian Peninsula
800–1100	Pockets of Christian armies gradually drive back and reclaim territory from the Moors during an era known as the reconquistas; Moors completely driven out by 12th century
1139	Alfonso Henriques, one of the main leaders of the Christian armies, declares himself the first king of Portugal
1249	Alfonso III conquers the southern city of Faro; signs the Treaty of Windsor with the United Kingdom to protect Portugal from Spanish incursions
1415	Prince Henry the Navigator captures the Muslim outpost of Ceuta
1488	Portuguese navigators round the Cape of Good Hope under the leadership of Bartolomeu Dias
1498	Vasco da Gama reaches India
1500	Pedro Álvares Cabral claims Brazil
1571	Established naval and colonial outposts connect Portugal to the coasts of Africa, the Middle East, India, and South Asia

have a homemade vegetable soup on the menu. Caldo verde, potato and kale soup with hunks of smoky chouriço sausage, is a typical soup served at family tables and traditional festivities.

Bread

It is customary in Portugal, especially in restaurants, for a basket of fresh bread to be brought out before a meal, along with olives and butter and fishy pâtés. Don't be misled:

1578	King Dom Sebastião I is killed in the Battle of Alcácer Quibir; Portuguese throne is claimed by Spanish King Phillip II
1668	After 28 years of the Portuguese Restoration War, Spain officially recognizes Portuguese independence
1755	Portugal is brought to its knees by the massive Lisbon earthquake
1890	Portuguese comply with United Kingdom ultimatum to withdraw all troops from African colonies
1910	Coup d'etat organized by the Portuguese Republican Party deposes the constitutional monarchy and proclaims a republican regime, the Estado Novo (First Republic)
1926	Another coup d'état paves the way for the military to seize power under the Diatdura Nacional (National Dictatorship)
1970	Longtime dictator António de Oliveira Salazar dies after almost half a century of oppressive rule; power is handed to slightly less radical Marcelo Caetano
1974	Marcelo Caetano overthrown in the Carnation Revolution, eradicating dictatorial power
1986	Portugal joins the European Union
1999	Macau, Portugal's last colonial possession, handed over to China
2007-2014	Portugal experiences economic downturn and austerity measures during the Global Economic Crisis, necessitating a bailout from the European Union and International Monetary Fund
2021	Current president of Portugal Marcelo Rebelo de Sousa was re-elected in the Portuguese Presidential Elections

these items are not complimentary, and if you eat them, they will be added to the bill. If you don't want them, ask for them to be taken away. Portugal has amazing bread, almost always freshly made. From rustic hobs to seeded baguettes and pumpkin or carob bread, it's hard not to be sucked in by the amazing carbohydrates on offer, especially to soak up those delicious sauces and juices.

Sweets and Pastries

Portugal is renowned for its range of traditional sweets and pastries. Display cabinets in cafés and pastelarias (cake shops) throughout the country are piled every morning with freshly baked treats. Portugal is home to the unique doces conventuais (convent sweets), generally based on egg yolk and sugar and made to ancient recipes said to originate in the 15th century from the country's convents.

Arroz doce (rice pudding with a sprinkling of cinnamon), bolo de bolacha (biscuit cake), pudim flan (custardy pudding with caramel on top), and tarte de natas (creamy chilled pie made from condensed milk with a ground cookie topping) are typical desserts, but the ever-present pastel de nata (custard tart) is Portugal's iconic sweet.

A particularly traditional and enjoyable treat is the Bola de Berlim (sugary doughnut filled with eggy custard) sold by shouty vendors who pace the beach and in every pastelaria (pastry shop) in the country.

DRINKS

Perhaps not as eminent as France, Italy, or Spain, modest Portugal nonetheless boasts a gamut of acclaimed wines, including rosés and unique fresh and fizzy green wines. Even ordinary table wine tends to be palatable, and a small jug of house wine in a low-key restaurant costs as little as €3. Besides wine, Portugal produces beer, the most famous being Sagres, Cristal, and Super Bock. A growing number of craft beers are also on the market.

Traditional Portuguese tipples include ginja (a sweet cherry liqueur, also called ginjinha), licor beirão (a medicinal-tasting liqueur said to aid digestion, made from a long-guarded secret blend of herbs), aguardente (brain-blowing firewater), and amarguinha (a marzipan-tasting, toothachingly-sweet almond liqueur, often chilled). Besides port and madeira liquor-wines, make sure you try the local poncha in Madeira, a mix of alcohol distilled from sugarcane, honey, orange or lemon juice, or other fruit juices.

The legal age to drink and buy alcohol in Portugal is 18. Nondrinkers won't be disappointed with canned iced teas and Sumol sparkling fruit juices, the traditional flavors being pineapple and orange. The Algarve, especially the city of Silves, is renowned for incredibly sweet oranges, and fresh orange juice served here with plenty of ice is a real treat.

The Portuguese are big coffee drinkers, and the standard is a small, strong, black espresso. To get milk in it, ask for café com leite or meia-de-leite (in a cup and saucer), or galão (served in a tall glass), differing only in presentation. "Having a coffee" is synonymous with "catching up," and cafés are the social glue of neighborhoods.

DINING OUT

Restaurants in Portugal are incredibly varied, from down-to-earth, no-frills spots to high-end Michelin-starred eateries. Touristy areas have a wider range of well-known chains and international cuisines. Vegetarian and vegan restaurants are on the rise, while traditional Portuguese eateries can be found in spades.

For real local flavor, try to find a casa de pasto, literally a "grazing house," basic, cheap, and cheerful little diners found off the beaten track that cater to local laborers with good home-cooked food. These characterful places tout three-course "dish of the day" menus for as little as €10, including a bread basket with butter, pâtés, and olives, a fish or meat entrée, a coffee, dessert, and drinks. If your budget allows, head to a high-end eatery where the menu will be a contemporary take on fresh local products and time-honored recipes. If you have a sweet tooth, find a pastelaria (there seems to be one on almost every street) to enjoy a coffee and freshly made traditional cake or a toasted sandwich for just a few euros.

Tipping

Restaurants tend to be the only places in Portugal where tipping is exercised, and a tip reflects how much patrons have enjoyed the food and service. As a general rule, 10-15 percent of the overall bill is the standard, but in less formal eateries it's okay just to leave any loose change you have, but at least €1.

Gratuities are not included on bills. Waitstaff in Portugal appreciate tips, but they are not compulsory.

PICNIC SUPPLIES AND GROCERIES

A great way to save money is to buy your own food, and Portugal is a veritable buffet of fresh produce. Larger supermarkets have counters for fresh fish, cold meats, cooked meats, and delis, with the likes of olives and slaws, as well as a fresh bread section, baked in-house or supplied by local bakers.

Most towns have a farmers market at least once or twice a month, generally on Saturday morning, piled high with locally grown fruit and vegetables as well as treats like dried nuts, dried fruits, sweets, and eggs. Municipal markets, usually open mornings Monday-Saturday, are also great for fish, meats, vegetables, and fruit. Some municipal markets have ready-to-go food counters and sell jams, liqueurs, cured meats, and preserves.

MEALS AND MEALTIMES

Portugal has three main meals: a good breakfast in the continental style, with cereals, bread, cold meats and cheese, and jam, generally eaten before work or school; lunch at 1pm-3pm; and dinner starting from 7:30pm-8pm. Main meals tend to be hearty, and lunch and dinner are often preceded by a bowl of soup. The Portuguese also enjoy lanche, a light midafternoon snack, as well as a coffee and a pastry midmorning.

Accommodations

Accommodations range from run-of-the-mill hotels and tourist complexes to friendly family-run inns, campsites, budget-friendly hostels, and exclusive luxury retreats. Lisbon currently exercises a **tourist tax (taxa turística),** a surcharge of €2 per night per each guest over the age of 13, up to a maximum of seven nights. This is charged directly at reception on check-in.

ACCOMMODATIONS RATINGS

Portugal's rating system is governed by national law and implemented by the national tourism board, **Turismo de Portugal** (www.turismodeportugal.pt). Ratings are based on fulfilled minimum requisites stipulated for each category. Star ratings are generally indicative of the level of comfort and facilities an establishment provides and not necessarily subjective factors such as view or atmosphere. Hotels are classified one to five stars; a one-star property is a basic budget lodging, while a five-star hotel offers a luxurious experience. Estalagens (inns) rate four to five stars, pensões (guesthouses) one to four stars, and apart-hotels rate two to five stars. Campsites are graded one to four stars.

MAKING RESERVATIONS

Most people nowadays make bookings online via price comparison websites or directly with hotels. It's always wise to follow it up with a phone call to ensure everything is confirmed and any special requests are clear. If planning to travel to Portugal in summer, book well ahead, as hotels sell out fast in peak season. Prices can also be much higher in peak season than in low season.

TYPES OF ACCOMMODATIONS
Hotel

All of Portugal's main towns and cities offer hotels spanning three to five stars. The more popular the destination, the greater the choice. Lisbon is awash with smart hotels, most with their own pools. Prices vary greatly by season and the popularity of the resort.

Among the compulsory criteria, minimum requirements for four- and five-star hotels include air-conditioning, TV, and direct phone lines in all rooms; one- to three-star hotels don't necessarily have to have those features. Three- to five-star hotels must also provide room service, laundry service, and air-conditioning in public areas, whereas one- and two-star hotels don't. All categories except one-star hotels must have an on-site bar, a full bath, 24-hour reception, copy and fax service, and safes in the rooms.

Estalagem (Inn)

Portugal's inns (estalagens) are hotel-type lodgings in traditional buildings that, due to their architectural characteristics, style of fixtures and furnishings, and services provided, reflect the region and its natural environs. Inns are classified four or five stars. As a whole, inns must comply with criteria similar to corresponding hotels (24-hour reception, room service, restaurant, bar, air-con in public areas, etc.); the main differences are found in the actual rooms, which tend to be smaller. Generally speaking, inns are more modest than hotels and often rustic and family-run.

Pensão Residencial

Smaller towns and villages will usually have a pensão residencial, or just residencial, private family-run boardinghouses in shared residential buildings. These provide affordable lodgings in central locations. Pensões usually have a restaurant. The word "residencial" is added when the unit provides breakfast only. Residenciais are simple bed-and-breakfast lodgings.

Apart-Hotel

Apart-hotels are self-contained apartments with the full facilities of hotels. There is no room service.

Pousada

Pousadas are state-owned monuments such as castles, palaces, monasteries, and convents converted into sumptuous accommodations reflecting the region and era of the monument. **Pousadas de Portugal** (www.pousadas.pt) is a brand that has iconic monument-hotels in

exceptional locations, including Pousada Serra da Estrela, a former sanatorium in the snowy Serra da Estrela mountains; Pousada Convento Beja, an ancient convent; and Pousada Castelo Óbidos, a castle-hotel in the heart of the famous medieval town.

Hostel

Portugal is renowned for excellent hostels, regularly earning European awards. That doesn't mean all of the country's hostels are above par. It pays to do some research and read reviews before booking. For outstanding hostels in Portugal, see www.hostelworld.com.

Aldeamento Turístico (Tourist Resort)

Tourist resorts, also known as tourist villages or complexes, are developments comprising different types of independent lodging, such as bungalows, apartments, or villas, in communal spaces. These resorts must also have an on-site four- or five-star hotel, entertainment facilities, and room service.

Camping

Portugal has over 100 campgrounds. Camping sites are classified by stars, from the most luxurious four stars to the minimum basic one star. Privately owned camping sites are classified in the same way, preceded by the letter *P*. Campsites tend to stay open year-round, as Portugal has a growing number of winter motorhome visitors, but prices can double from low to peak season. High-season prices may apply to holidays such as New Year's. Most campsites have on-site toilets and showers as well as facilities such as swimming pools and markets, bungalows, and chalets, which are reflected in the star rating. Some have sanitary facilities for RVs. Not all accept pets. For more on camping in Portugal, see www.campingportugal.org.

Festivals and Events

Most of the country's major events, such as the traditional Popular Saints festivities and local festivals, are held in summer.

SPRING
Carnival
mid-Feb.-early Mar.

Carnival (or Carnaval) festivities take place throughout the country, but Lisbon's is especially spectacular, with colorful floats and concerts, music, masquerade balls, and other street events.

SUMMER
Santo António Festival
June

Lisbon's patron saint, Saint Anthony, is celebrated throughout the city the entire month of June, peaking on June 12 with parades and processions lasting through the night.

Tomar Tray Festival
June-July

This ancient festival takes place every four years and features a procession of local girls wearing tabuleiros, traditional headdresses made from bread, along with other traditional celebrations and ceremonies.

WINTER
Wonderland Lisbon
Dec. 1-Jan. 1

There probably won't be any snow but Christmastime is still magical in Lisbon. Besides the many charming Christmas markets that pop up all over the city—and the biggest tree in Portugal, in Comércio Square—Wonderland Lisbon, the biggest Christmas event in the country, with a Ferris wheel, ice rink, Christmas stalls and Santa's village, takes place in the Eduardo VII park from the beginning of December through till after New Year's Day.

Conduct and Customs

The Portuguese are characteristically warm and welcoming and proud to show off their heritage, although they are also modest and conservative. Striking up a conversation about food or soccer, two of Portugal's best-loved pastimes, is a surefire way of opening communication. Conscious that tourism is a main source of income, the Portuguese are generally friendly and helpful toward visitors, although in rural pockets of the country foreigners are still eyed with curiosity. Staunchly traditional and understated, Portugal is a country where recent acquaintances may be greeted like long-lost friends, but raucous behavior, such as drunken rowdiness, is eschewed. Decorum is much appreciated, which is not to say you can't let your hair down and let loose in the appropriate places. As long as you show courtesy and respect to the locals, you can expect the same back.

GENERAL ETIQUETTE

Typically friendly and humble, the Portuguese love to show off their language skills and impress visitors, and few are the people who don't know at least a few key phrases in English. Likewise, the Portuguese very much appreciate efforts by visitors in learning even just a few words of the national language. Modest and somewhat reserved, the Portuguese tend to be quite formal in greetings among those less well acquainted. Men usually shake hands, while women give air kisses on each cheek; women hardly ever shake hands in Portugal. Children are greeted in the same way as adults. Family is the foundation of Portuguese households and takes precedence over most other social and professional affairs.

COMMUNICATION STYLES

The Portuguese appreciate polite directness. Eye contact, a smile, and a firm handshake are the cornerstones of communication. Saying "Bom dia" (Good day or Hello), "Por favor" (Please), and "Obrigado/a" (Thank you) go a long way. Overtly exuberant or loud behavior is not appreciated. The Portuguese tend to socialize on the weekends rather than after work during the week.

BODY LANGUAGE

A big no-no in Portugal is pointing—especially pointing at someone. While conversations can sound heated and loud, the Portuguese are not overly demonstrative with hand gestures or body language. Finger-snapping to get someone's attention is also frowned upon.

TERMS OF ADDRESS

An overtone of formality is required when addressing people, especially strangers. Men should be addressed as "senhor" (abbreviation Sr.) and women "senhora" (Sra.) at all times. A young girl would be "menina" (miss), and a boy, "menino."

TABLE MANNERS

Table manners are relaxed but courteous. Sharing from a bowl while talking animatedly is a mainstay around a family table, although politeness, such as wishing everyone "Bom apetite" (Bon appétit) before a meal and saying thank you afterward, is expected. Domestic dining begins at the say-so of the head of the table or the cook, and feel free to raise a glass to toast (saúde) everyone. Dining out depends on the type of establishment; laid-back eateries are a family-style affair, while upmarket venues require upmarket manners and dress. Arriving late to a meal with friends is acceptable; arriving late to a dinner reservation is not. If invited to dine at someone's home, take a small gift, such as a bottle of wine or flowers.

PHOTO ETIQUETTE

Places where photos are banned will be signed. Taking photos inside churches during mass is considered disrespectful. If you want to take a picture of a local, Portuguese people are generally happy to collaborate, but always politely seek permission beforehand.

Health and Safety

Overall, travel and health risks in Portugal are relatively low, with food- and water-borne illnesses like traveler's diarrhea, typhoid, and giardia not a concern in Western Europe. Insect-transmitted diseases, such as Lyme disease and tick fever, however, are found in Portugal. A number of precautionary steps can reduce the risk: prevent insect bites with repellents, apply sunscreen, drink plenty of water, avoid overindulging in alcohol, don't approach wild or stray animals, wash your hands regularly, carry hand sanitizer, and avoid sharing bodily fluids.

Basic medications such as ibuprofen and antidiarrheal medication can be bought over-the-counter at any pharmacy in Portugal. For emergency medical assistance, call 112 and ask for an ambulance. If you are taken to a hospital, contact your insurance provider immediately. Portugal also has a 24-hour free health help line (tel. 808 242 424) in Portuguese only. For detailed advice before traveling, consult your country's travel health website: www.fitfortravel.nhs.uk (United Kingdom), wwwnc.cdc.gov/travel (United States), www.travel.gc.ca (Canada), or www.smarttraveller.gov.au (Australia).

VACCINATIONS

There are no compulsory immunization requirements to enter Portugal. The World Health Organization (WHO) recommends all travelers, regardless of destination, are covered for diphtheria, tetanus, measles, mumps, rubella, and polio. See your doctor at least six weeks before departure to ensure your routine vaccinations are up-to-date.

Hepatitis A

Recommended for all travelers over age one and not previously vaccinated against hepatitis A. In 2017 a number of European countries, Portugal included, recorded an outbreak of hepatitis A. It is transmitted through contaminated food and water, as well direct contact with infected individuals via the fecal-oral route.

Hepatitis B

The hepatitis B vaccination is suggested for all nonimmune travelers who may be at risk of acquiring the disease, which is transmitted via infected blood or bodily fluids, such as by sharing needles or unprotected sex.

HEALTH CONSIDERATIONS
Sunstroke and Dehydration

The sun and heat in Portugal can be fierce, especially June-September and particularly July-August. Apply a strong sunblock and use a hat and sunglasses. Avoid physical exertion when the heat is at its peak (noon-3pm) and keep well hydrated by drinking plenty of water or electrolyte-replenishing fluids. Avoid excessive alcohol during the hottest hours or being out in the sun with a hangover.

Undertow

Some beaches, especially along the western coast, which is fully exposed to the Atlantic, can experience strong undercurrents when the sea is roughest, particularly in winter and spring. During summer, generally May-September, the sea is calmer and beaches are staffed by lifeguards; off-season they are not. Always obey flags.

Tap Water

Tap water is consumable throughout Portugal and is safe to brush teeth, wash fruit, or make ice, although many people drink bottled water, as opposed to tap water, even at home.

Stray Animals

Portugal still battles errant and abandoned animals. In some places it's not unusual to see stray dogs and cats, even in packs and colonies. A huge amount of work has been done by private and public entities to sterilize and rehome animals, and things have greatly improved since the 1980s, but more work remains. Travelers are advised to not approach, pet, or feed strays. If you are bitten by a stray animal, wash and disinfect the wound, and seek medical advice promptly.

Sexually Transmitted Diseases

Travelers are at high risk of acquiring sexually transmitted diseases (STDs) if they engage in unprotected sex. According to research, Portugal has one of the poorest control rates of sexually transmitted infections; gonorrhea and syphilis are common.

HEALTH CARE
Medical Services

Portugal's state-funded public health service (SNS, Serviço Nacional de Saúde) provides quality care, particularly in emergency situations and those involving tourists. There are also private hospitals operating throughout Portugal, such as the **Hospital Particular do Algarve** (tel. 707 282 828; www.grupohpa.com) group in the Algarve and the **CUF Hospitals and Health Units** (tel. 210 025 200; www.saudecuf.pt) in Lisbon and the north. For minor illnesses and injuries, head to a pharmacy: most pharmacists speak good English and can suggest treatment. If the problem persists or worsens, seek

a doctor. Portugal has two types of pharmacies: traditional pharmacies (farmácia), identified with a big flashing green cross outside, and parapharmacies (parafarmácia), selling only nonprescription medicines.

Insurance

EU citizens have access to free emergency medical treatment through the European Health Insurance Card (EHIC), which replaces the defunct E111 certificate. Non-EU citizens for whom there is no reciprocal agreement for free medical care between Portugal and the traveler's home country should consider fully comprehensive health insurance for serious illness, accident, or emergency. Opt for a policy that covers the worst-case event, like medical evacuation or repatriation. Find out in advance if your insurance will make payments to providers directly or reimburse you later for overseas health expenditures. Travelers to the Azores and Madeira are advised to acquire wide-ranging travel insurance that provides for medical evacuation in the event of serious illness or injury; serious or complicated problems sometimes require medical evacuation to the mainland.

Prescriptions

A prescription issued by a doctor in one EU country is valid in all EU countries. However, a medicine prescribed in one country may not be authorized for sale or available in another country, or it might be sold under a different name. EU doctors can issue cross-border prescriptions valid in all EU countries. Opt for paper copies of prescriptions as opposed to electronic copies.

If you're traveling from outside the EU, have enough of your prescription medication to cover the trip. Talk to your doctor beforehand and travel with a doctor's note, a copy of any prescriptions, or a printout for the medication. Medications should be carried in labeled original bottles or packaging, although this is not compulsory. Some prescription medicines may require a medical certificate; always check with your doctor. Ask for an extra written prescription with the generic name of the drug in the event of loss or if your stay is extended. Portuguese pharmacies will accept prescriptions from countries outside the EU, but drugs have to be paid for in full. Even without the state subsidies, drugs are generally cheaper in Portugal than many other EU countries and the United States. Alternatively, visit a Portuguese doctor and obtain a prescription in Portugal.

Many types of medication—including heart medication, antibiotics, asthma and diabetes medicines, codeine, injectable medicines, and cortisone creams—can be acquired in Portugal only with a prescription.

It is illegal to ship medication to Portugal. When traveling, always transport medicines in carry-on luggage.

Birth Control

Birth control is widely available throughout Portugal. Female contraceptive pills, patches, and rings can be bought over the counter in pharmacies, as can the morning-after pill, without a prescription. Condoms are also widely available in pharmacies, supermarkets, gas stations, and some nightlife venues.

SAFETY
Police

Portugal has three police forces: the **PSP (Public Safety Police— Polícia de Segurança Pública)** (tel. 218 111 000; www.psp.pt), in cities and larger towns; the road traffic police **GNR (National Republican Guard—Guarda Nacional Republicana)** (tel. 213 217 000; www.gnr.pt), also responsible for policing smaller towns and villages and investigating crimes against animals or nature; and the **PJ (Judiciary Police—Polícia Judiciária)** (tel. 211 967 000; www. policiajudiciaria.pt), the criminal investigation bureau, responsible for investigating serious crimes.

The common European **emergency number** is tel. **112,** which redirects calls to the appropriate services.

Crime

Portugal has a relatively low serious crime rate, but opportunistic crime is recurrent, particularly in busy places popular among tourists, such as Lisbon and the Algarve. Popular beaches are hot spots for car theft, so keep valuables on your person or at least hidden from view. Don't leave anything of value, such as passports or computers, in vehicles. Pickpocketing is also common, particularly on the busy trams in Lisbon and Porto. Use a concealed cross-body pouch to carry cash and your ID, and keep money and documents separate. Take the same precautions you would at home—keep valuables safe and avoid walking alone at night or on backstreets.

Harassment

Harassment is not something visitors to Portugal will usually have to deal with. Opportunistic petty drug pushers in busy nightspots and overenthusiastic restaurant or bar staff trying to attract clientele are about the extent of the pestering. Saying a polite but firm "No, thanks" and walking away are generally enough to deter unwanted attention.

Drugs

Since 2001, Portugal has a decriminalized drug system, and being caught with a small amount of some recreational drugs, such as marijuana, is no longer a crime but a medical health issue, addressed with rehabilitative action like therapy as opposed to jail. This health-focused legal shift saw drug-related deaths drop dramatically, but that's not to say it's okay to do drugs in Portugal; drug use is prohibited. The law does not differentiate between citizens and visitors, and tourists caught with drugs will be subject to the same process, which could include fines or being brought before a dissuasive committee or a doctor. Producing or dealing drugs in Portugal is a serious criminal offense punishable with lengthy jail terms. The use of recreational drugs is common in the nightlife areas of places such as Lisbon and Albufeira. Beware being approached by people selling drugs.

Practical Details

MONEY
Currency
Since 1999 Portugal's currency has been the euro; before that it was the escudo. There are 100 cents in 1 euro (€1).

Changing Money
The ability to exchange currency varies greatly by location. In tourist-dense Lisbon, Porto, and the Algarve, foreign currency can be exchanged at almost every hotel, currency exchanges, and even some shops. Airports have exchange bureaus, although their commission rates, along with those in hotels, are more expensive. Keep an eye on exchange rates in the months before you travel to see how they fluctuate, and change some cash beforehand when the rates are favorable. In Portugal, hunt around, do some groundwork, and compare rates to choose the best option. It is almost always more favorable for UK travelers with British pounds to change their cash for euros in the United Kingdom; in Portugal the Scottish pound can sometimes be refused. For up-to-date exchange rates, see www.xe.com.

Banks
Banks in Portugal are generally open Monday-Friday 8:30am-4pm. In larger towns and cities, they will stay open during lunch, but in smaller locales, banks close 1pm-2pm. Portugal's banks close Saturday-Sunday and national holidays. Banks rarely offer foreign currency exchange services.

ATMs
ATM cash withdrawal machines (multibanco) can be found widely in most towns and cities. Smaller villages may have just one or two, normally at bank branches, in supermarkets, on main streets and squares, and at major bus and train stations and airports. Charges apply to foreign transactions. There is an option for instructions in English. Maximum withdrawals are €200 a time, but this can be withdrawn several times a day.

Credit Cards
Credit cards are widely accepted in bigger towns and cities, but not so much in smaller locales. Visa, Mastercard, and American Express cards are widely accepted in hotels, shops, and restaurants. Gas stations usually take only debit cards and cash.

Sales Tax
The standard sales tax rate in Portugal is 23 percent. On wine it is 13 percent, and on medications, books, and optical lenses 6 percent. In Madeira the tax is 22 percent, and in the Azores 18 percent. Many stores throughout Portugal have adopted the Europe Tax Free (ETS) system, which allows non-EU shoppers to recover VAT or sales

tax as a refund. Stores adhering to the ETS system have an ETS sign at the entrance. For more information, see www.globalblue.com/tax-free-shopping/portugal.

Bargaining

Haggling is increasingly a thing of the past in Portugal, as standardized retail prices are enforced in municipal markets and farmers markets. However, haggling at a flea market can still be part of the experience.

Special Discounts

Students, seniors (65 and over), and children generally benefit from discounts on state-run services such as monuments, museums, municipal swimming pools, and public transport.

Budgeting

As one of Europe's most affordable countries, Portugal still offers value for money. Far cheaper than London, Paris, or Barcelona, Lisbon doesn't have to be expensive. As with all the sunshine destinations in Southern Europe and the Mediterranean, hotel rates peak in summer and drop in winter, meaning spring and autumn can offer the best value in terms of lodging and weather. Car rental rates fluctuate with the tourist seasons, and airfares are influenced by EU school holidays. Portugal has a range of inns, vacation rentals, and some of the best hostels in Europe, so how much you spend depends on you.

OPENING HOURS

In the past, most shops and services in Portugal would close 1pm-3pm for lunch. This is still in practice in many establishments, although a growing number of state and private entities such as banks, post offices, and pharmacies now remain open during lunch.

Major national monuments like castles, churches, and palaces are open every day of the week, and those that aren't tend to close on Monday. Attractions stay open longer in summer, opening an hour or so earlier than in winter and closing an hour or so later. Theme parks, especially water parks, and even some hotels and restaurants close for a month or two in winter. Smaller museums and monuments also close for lunch.

Almost all close on bank holidays, such as Christmas Day, New Year's Eve, and New Year's Day. Major holidays such as Carnival (late February or early March) and Lisbon's Santo António festivities (June) may result in closures of banks or other state entities, though bars and restaurants are often open and at their busiest.

Public Holidays

- **New Year's Day (Ano Novo):** January 1

- **Good Friday (Sexta-feira Santa):** Friday before Easter Sunday

- **Easter Sunday (Domingo de Páscoa)**

- **Freedom Day (Dia da Liberdade):** April 25
- **Labor Day (Dia do Trabalhador):** May 1
- **Portugal Day (Dia de Portugal):** June 10
- **Corpus Christi (Corpo de Deus):** 60 days after Easter Sunday
- **Assumption Day (Assunção de Nossa Senhora):** August 15
- **Republic Day (Implantação da República):** October 5
- **All Saints' Day (Dia de Todos-os-Santos):** November 1
- **Restoration of Independence (Restauração da Independência):** December 1
- **Immaculate Conception Day (Imaculada Conceição):** December 8
- **Christmas Day (Natal):** December 25

COMMUNICATIONS
Phones and Cell Phones
Making Calls
Portugal's country code is +351 (00351). To call a phone number in Portugal from abroad, first dial the country code. Within Portugal, there are regional prefixes, and all start with 2. Lisbon, for example, is 21, Faro is 289, and Porto is 22. These are incorporated into phone numbers, which are always nine digits. There is no need to dial 0 or 1 before the number. Mobile phone numbers start with 9. Toll-free numbers start with 8. Portugal's main landline provider is **Altice Portugal** (www.altice.pt).

Mobile Phones
The four main mobile providers in Portugal are **Nós** (www.nos.pt), **Meo** (www.meo.pt), **NOWO** (www.nowo.pt), and **Vodafone** (www.vodafone.pt). Mobile phone coverage is decent throughout the country, particularly in major cities and populous areas along the coast, although it can be patchy in rural or high-elevation areas. Foreign handsets that are GSM compatible can be used in Portugal. Using a prepaid SIM card in Portugal is recommended, particularly for non-EU visitors. They are widely available from the stores of the main mobile phone providers, which can be found on retail streets and shopping centers. You will need a copy of your passport or ID to buy one.

In 2017 the EU abolished roaming surcharges for travelers, meaning that people traveling within the EU can call, text, and use data on mobile devices at the same rates they pay at home, but this applies only to EU countries. Surcharges may apply if your consumption exceeds your home usage limits.

Internet Access
Portugal has an up-to-date communications network, with good phone lines and high-speed internet. Wi-Fi is widely available, and most hotels will either have free Wi-Fi throughout or in designated Wi-Fi areas. Elsewhere, major cities offer Wi-Fi hotspots, as do some

public buildings, restaurants, and cafés. Internet cafés can be found throughout Portugal.

Shipping and Postal Service

Portugal's national postal service is **Correios de Portugal** (tel. 707 262 626; www.ctt.pt), with post offices in all population centers. Postal services range from regular correio normal to express correio azul. Shipping costs for a 2-kilogram (4.4-pound) package range from €4.50 sent domestically to €15 sent abroad. Postcards and letters up to 20 grams (0.7 ounce) cost €0.86 within Europe, €0.91 to other countries. Express mail letters cost €2.90.

Other shipping services operate in Portugal, including **FedEx** (tel. 229 436 030; www.fedex.com) and **DHL** (tel. 707 505 606; www.dhl.pt).

WEIGHTS AND MEASURES
Customary Units

Portugal was the second country after France to adopt the metric system, in 1814. Length is in centimeters, meters, and kilometers, and weight is in grams and kilograms. Temperatures are in degrees Celsius.

In addition, shoes and clothing sizes differ from the British and US systems. For example:

• shoe sizes: US men's 7.5, women's 9 = UK men's 7, women's 6.5 = Portugal 40

• women's dresses and suits: US 6, 8, 10 = UK 8, 10, 12 = Portugal 36, 38, 40

• men's suits and overcoats: US and UK 36, 38, 40 = Portugal 46, 48, 50

Time Zone

Mainland Portugal is in the Western European time zone (WET), the same as the United Kingdom and Ireland. Complying with European daylight saving time, clocks move forward 1 hour on the last Sunday in March and fall back 1 hour on the last Sunday in October. The Azores archipelago is always 1 hour earlier than mainland Portugal. Madeira is in the same time zone as the mainland. In relation to the United States, Portugal is 7 or 8 hours ahead of Los Angeles, 4 or 5 hours ahead of Miami and New York, 5 or 6 hours ahead of Chicago, and 10 or 11 hours ahead of Hawaii.

Electricity

Portugal has 230-volt, 50-hertz electricity and type C or F sockets. Type C plugs have two round pins; type F have two round pins with two grounding clips on the side. Travelers from the United Kingdom, Australia, and most of Asia and Africa will require only an adapter to make the plugs fit. Visitors from the United States, Canada, and most South American countries require an adapter and for some devices a voltage converter. These are available in airports, luggage shops, and most electrical shops. Universal adapters are a great investment as they can be used anywhere.

WHAT TO PACK

Key items to pack include mosquito repellent and sunblock (sunblock is expensive in Portugal) plus a hat for May-October, a windbreaker for all seasons (Portugal can be breezy year-round), and warm sweaters, a jacket, and a light raincoat for winter. Comfortable shoes for walking are advised if your trip is more than a beach holiday, and don't forget an electrical adapter for chargers. Pack a concealable pouch to carry documents and cash while out and about exploring, and never carry cash and documents together.

TOURIST INFORMATION

Portugal is a tourism-oriented destination with widely available visitor information. Each region—Porto and the north, central Portugal, Lisbon, the Alentejo, the Algarve, Azores, and Madeira— has its own tourism board to promote the area, while the national **Turismo de Portugal** (www.

turismodeportugal.pt) promotes the country as a whole. Each main town has at least one tourist office, as do popular villages. Most hotels provide good information on what to do and see locally. Portugal's official tourism website, www.visitportugal.com, provides a wealth of information on history, culture, and heritage as well as useful contacts. Lisbon-specific information can be found at www. visitlisboa.com.

Tourist Offices

Tourist offices can be found in every city, town, and village that has a tourist attraction or monument. Major cities and destinations like Lisbon, Porto, and the Algarve have numerous tourist offices where visitors can drop in with questions and get maps, public transport timetables, and excursion information. Tourist office staffers speak good English.

Maps

Download maps of Portugal and its various regions free from www. visitportugal.com. Most hotel reception desks have maps of the vicinity, or ask at tourist offices.

Traveler Advice

ACCESS FOR TRAVELERS WITH DISABILITIES

Portugal prides itself on being an accessible destination for travelers with disabilities, and massive efforts have been made to become inclusive for all. The main airports have services and facilities for wheelchair users, and infrastructure is gradually being modernized to facilitate mobility. There are a number of wheelchair-friendly accessible beaches along the coast, with equipment and facilities for all to enjoy the beach safely and comfortably. Some monuments, however, are not wheelchair friendly, and people with mobility issues might struggle with everyday infrastructures (such as cobbled streets and high sidewalks).

In 2018 the national tourism board launched an interactive app, **TUR4all Portugal,** that contains a wealth of information about facilities and services for those with special needs visiting Portugal. It can be downloaded for free from www.accessibleportugal.com.

TRAVELING WITH CHILDREN

Youngsters in family-friendly Portugal are fawned over and welcomed practically everywhere. It's not unusual to see children dozing on their parents' laps in a café late on a summer night. Restaurants are very accommodating of younger diners, although kids' menus can be limited to the staple chicken nuggets or fish fingers.

Portugal's capital is a fantastic place for a family holiday, with plenty to keep the young ones entertained. Activities in and around Lisbon for children range from Lisbon's zoo and award-winning Oceanarium and riverfront cable cars, to spotting wildlife in the Mafra Royal Hunting Grounds, surfing on some of Portugal's best beaches, riding the beach train in Costa da Caparica, and playgrounds in almost every public park. Kids also benefit from discounts on public transport, at museums, and at most main attractions.

When the weather is warm, tourist trains and ice cream are found throughout towns and villages, while most resorts and hotels have kids' clubs or at least activities and facilities for children. For some grown-up time, ask your hotel to arrange a babysitter.

To enter and leave Portugal, all minors must have their own passport and be with both parents. If children are not traveling with both parents, legal documentation with formalized permission from the other parent is required. Portugal's border and immigration officials will ask for such papers.

Breastfeeding is applauded in Portugal, although it's rarely done in public, and if it is, it's done discreetly.

WOMEN TRAVELING ALONE

Portugal is a great destination for women traveling alone, given that it is one of Europe's safest and most peaceful countries, and people as a whole are respectful and obliging. If you want to share lodging or to meet new people, Portugal has clean and cheap, well-regulated and well-run hostels, a great way to mingle with fellow travelers. Most people speak decent English and are happy to assist. Besides petty crime in major towns and cities, the serious crime rate is low, and lone women travelers should have no problems. As with any place, common sense should prevail, and taking dark backstreets or walking along deserted streets at night should be avoided.

SENIOR TRAVELERS

With a year-round pleasant climate and placid, laid-back lifestyle, Portugal is a magnet for senior travelers and a top destination for Northern European retirees who make it their second home. Compact, peaceful, and well equipped, with medical facilities (providing you have the right insurance coverage), it meets the needs of travelers of all ages. Geographically, Lisbon and Porto are hilly and a challenge on foot; sticking to the flatter downtown and riverside areas and using the plethora of public transport can help travelers avoid issues with aches and pains.

Portugal has discounts for senior travelers (65 and over) with ID on public transport and in museums, and plenty of attractions, like wine-tasting and spa visits, to appeal to the mature tourist.

LGBTQ+ TRAVELERS

LGBTQ+ travelers will find Portugal mostly welcoming; it legalized same-sex marriage in 2010, the eighth country in Europe to do so. Portugal is currently a popular destination for same-sex weddings. Most Portuguese have a laid-back attitude toward LGBTQ+ visitors, although attitudes toward same-sex couples can vary by region. Despite being progressive, Portugal is traditionally a Roman Catholic society, and inhabitants of remote and small towns might raise an eyebrow or scowl at same-sex displays of affection, but rarely will verbal or physical hostility be directed at you.

While the LGBTQ+ scene is still underground in much of Portugal, Lisbon and Porto, and to a lesser extent the Algarve, have a vibrant and inclusive LGBTQ+ scene. Lisbon and Porto host colorful pride marches and have numerous gay bars, nightclubs, and LGBTQ+-friendly accommodations, although tourists being denied a room or a table based on their sexual orientation or gender identity is not unheard of. The **International Gay & Lesbian Travel Association** (IGLTA, www.iglta.org) provides a wealth of information on LGBTQ+ travel in Portugal, including organized trips, tours, tips, and travel advice.

TRAVELERS OF COLOR

Portugal is widely regarded as one of Europe's safest, most peaceful, and most tolerant countries, and allegations of color-motivated discrimination and attacks are rare. However, in recent times there have been sporadic reports of incidents involving racial bias, specifically at the doors of popular nightspots in Lisbon. Management of these venues strongly deny that bouncers discriminate against clubgoers' entry based on their race, but allegations to that effect have made the rounds on social media. That said, Portugal is home to large communities of Africans from the former colonies, and while racially motivated incidents do happen, they are extremely rare. For the most part, travelers and immigrants of all colors are welcomed and accepted in Portugal, which has one of the most integrated immigrant communities in Europe.

DIGITAL NOMADS

Portugal ranks high on the global digital nomad scene. An increasing number of remote, or "location-independent," workers have been flocking to Portugal in recent times, especially since the country was voted in 2022 as the best county in the world for digital nomads to travel and work, by travel sites Momondo. com and Kayak.com. In large part this is not only thanks to its still relatively accessible cost of living, political stability, security, and weather, but also to the newly created **Digital Nomad (D7) Visa,** a special visa that allows foreigners to stay and live legally in Portugal, extending stays for up to a year. Portugal has a well-established infrastructure for digital nomads, with resources like co-working spaces and Wi-Fi coverage continuously growing. It has also developed many groups and activities like Meetups (www.meetup.com/find/portugal) to involve and unite the various digital nomad communities in Lisbon, such as www.lisbondigitalnomads.org. For official information on the D7 visa, see https://vistos.mne.gov.pt.

Portuguese Phrasebook

PRONUNCIATION

Vowels

The pronunciation of **nonnasal vowels** is fairly straightforward:

a pronounced "a" as in "apple," "ah" as in "father," or "uh" as in "addition."

e pronounced "eh" as in "pet." At the end of a word, it is often silent or barely pronounced.

i pronounced "ee" as in "tree."

o pronounced "aw" as in "got." At the end of a word or when it stands alone, it is generally pronounced "oo" as in "zoo."

u pronounced "oo" as in "zoo."

The **nasal vowels** are much more complicated. Nasal vowels are signaled by a tilde accent (~) as in *não* (no), or by the presence of the letters **m** or **n** following the vowel, such as *sim* (yes) or *fonte* (fountain). When pronouncing them, it helps to exaggerate the sound, focus on your nose and not your mouth, and pretend there is a hidden "n" (or even "ng") on the end. Note that the **ão** combination is pronounced like "own" as in "town."

Consonants

Portuguese consonant sounds are easy compared with the nasal vowels. There are, however, a few exceptions to be aware of.

c pronounced "k" as in "kayak." However, when followed by the vowels **e** or **i**, it is pronounced "s" as in "set." When sporting a cedilla accent (**ç**), it is pronounced with a longer "ss" sound as in "passing."

ch pronounced "sh" as in "ship."

g pronounced "g" as in "go." However, when followed by the vowels **e** or **i**, it is pronounced "zh" like the "s" in "measure."

h always silent.

j pronounced "zh" like the "s" in "measure."

l usually pronounced as in English. The exception is when it is followed by **h,** when it acquires a "li" sound similar to "billion."

n usually pronounced as in English. The exception is when it is followed by **h,** when it acquires a "ni" sound similar to "minion."

r pronounced with a trill. When doubled (**rr**), it should be pronounced with a longer roll.

s pronounced "s" as in "set" when found at the beginning of a word. Between vowels, it's pronounced like "z" as in "zap." At the end of a word, it's pronounced like "sh" as in "ship."

x pronounced "sh" as in "ship" when found at the beginning of a word. Between vowels, the pronunciation varies between "sh" as in "ship," "s" as in "set," "z" as in "zap," and "ks" as in "taxi."

z pronounced "z" in "zap" when found at the beginning of a word. In the middle or at the end of a word, it is pronounced "zh" like the "s" in "measure."

Stress

Most Portuguese words carry stress on the second-to-last syllable. There are, however, some exceptions. The stress falls on the last syllable with words that end in **r** as well as words ending in nasal vowels. Vowels with accents over them (~, ´, `, ^) generally indicate that the stress falls on the syllable containing the vowel.

PLURAL NOUNS AND ADJECTIVES

In Portuguese, the general rule for making a noun or adjective plural is to simply add an **s.** But there are various exceptions. For instance, words that end in nasal consonants such as **m** or **l** change to **ns** and **is,** respectively. The plural of *estalagem* (inn) is *estalagens,* while the plural of *pastel* (pastry) is *pastéis.* Words that end in nasal vowels also undergo changes: **ão** becomes **ãos, ães,** or **ões,** as in the case of *irmão* (brother), which becomes *irmãos,* and *pão* (bread), which becomes *pães.*

GENDER

Like French and Spanish, all Portuguese words have masculine and feminine forms of nouns and adjectives. In general, nouns ending in **o** or consonants are masculine, while those ending in **a** are feminine. Many words have both masculine and feminine versions determined by their **o** or **a** ending, such as *menino* (boy) and *menina* (girl). Nouns are always preceded by articles—*o* and *a* (definite) and *um* and *uma* (indefinite)—that announce their gender. For example, *o menino* means "the boy" while *a menina* means "the girl." *Um menino* is "a boy" while *uma menina* is "a girl."

BRAZILIAN PORTUGUESE

It should be noted that there are significant differences between European Portuguese and Brazilian Portuguese, in many terms, including pronunciation, vocabulary, spelling, and cultural references. Some translation apps may translate to the Brazilian version. That said, speakers of both variations can generally understand each other with little difficulty.

BASIC EXPRESSIONS

Hello *Olá*

Good morning *Bom dia*

Good afternoon *Boa tarde*

Good evening/night *Boa noite*

Goodbye *Tchau, Adeus*

How are you? *Como está?*

Fine, and you? *Tudo bem, e você?*

Nice to meet you. *Um prazer.*

Yes *Sim*

No *Não*

I don't know. *Não sei.*

and *e*

or *ou*

Please *Por favor*

Thank you *Obrigado* (if you're male), *Obrigada* (if you're female)

You're welcome. *De nada.*

Excuse me (to pass) *Com licença*

Sorry/Excuse me (to get attention) *Desculpe* (if you're male), *Desculpa* (if you're female)

Can you help me? *Pode me ajudar?*

Where is the bathroom? *Onde é a casa de banho?*

What's your name? *Como se chama?*

My name is . . . *O meu nome é . . .*

Where are you from? *De onde é que vem?*

I'm from ... *Sou de...*

Do you speak English? *Fala inglês?*

I don't speak Portuguese. *Não falo português.*

I only speak a little Portuguese. *Só falo um pouquinho português.*

I don't understand. *Não entendo.*

Can you please repeat that? *Pode repetir, por favor?*

TERMS OF ADDRESS

I *eu*

you *você* (formal), *tu* (informal)

he *ele*

she *ela*

we *nós*

you (plural) *vocês*

they *eles* (male or mixed gender), *elas* (female)

Mr./Sir *Senhor*

Mrs./Madam *Senhora*

boy/girl *menino/menina*

child *criança*

brother/sister *irmão/irmã*

father/mother *pai/mãe*

son/daughter *filho/filha*

husband/wife *marido/mulher*

uncle/aunt *tio/tia*

friend *amigo* (male), *amiga* (female)

boyfriend/girlfriend *namorado/ namorada*

single *solteiro* (male), *solteira* (female)

divorced *divorciado* (male), *divorciada* (female)

TRANSPORTATION

north *norte*

south *sul*

east *este*

west *oeste*

left/right *esquerda/direita*

Where is ...? *Onde é...?*

How far away is ...? *Qual é a distância até...?*

far/close *longe/perto*

car *carro*

bus *autocarro, camioneta*

bus terminal *terminal das camionetas / terminal rodoviário*

subway *metro*

subway station *estação do metro*

train *comboio*

train station *estação de comboio*

plane *avião*

airport *aeroporto*

boat *barco*

ship *navio*

ferryboat *ferry, balsa*

port *porto*

first *primeiro*

last *último*

next *próximo*

arrival *chegada*

departure *partida*

How much does a ticket cost? *Quanto custa uma passagem?*

one-way *uma ida*

round-trip *ida e volta*

I'd like a round-trip ticket. *Quero uma passagem ida e volta.*

gas station *bomba de gasolina*

parking lot *estacionamento*

toll *portagem*

at the corner *na esquina*

one-way street *sentido único*

Where can I get a taxi? *Onde posso apanhar um táxi?*

Can you take me to this address? *Pode me levar para este endereço?*

Can you stop here, please? *Pode parar aqui, por favor?*

ACCOMMODATIONS

Are there any rooms available? *Tem quartos disponívéis?*

I want to make a reservation. *Quero fazer uma reserva.*

single room *quarto individual / de solteiro*

double room *quarto duplo*

Is there a view? *Tem vista?*

How much does it cost? *Quanto custa?*

Can you give me a discount? *É possivel ter um desconto?*

It's too expensive. *É muito caro.*

Is there something cheaper? *Tem algo mais barato?*

for just one night *para uma noite só*

for three days *para três dias*

Can I see it first? *Posso ver primeiro?*

comfortable *confortável*

change the sheets/towels *trocar os lençóis/as toalhas*

private bathroom *banheiro privado*

shower *chuveiro*

soap *sabão*

toilet paper *papel higiénico*

key *chave*

FOOD

to eat *comer*

to drink *beber*

breakfast *pequeno almoço*

lunch *almoço*

dinner *jantar*

snack *petisco / lanche (mid-afternoon or mid-morning)*

dessert *sobremesa*

menu *ementa*

plate *prato*

glass *copo*

cup *chávena*

utensils *talheres*

fork *garfo*

knife *faca*

spoon *colher*

napkin *guardanapo*

hot *quente*

cold *frio*

sweet *doce*

salty *salgado*

sour *azedo, amargo*

spicy *picante*

I'm a vegetarian. *Sou vegetariano* (if you're male), *Sou vegetariana* (if you're female).

I'm ready to order. *Estou pronto para pedir* (if you're male), *Estou pronta para pedir* (if you're female).

Can you bring the bill please? *Pode trazer a conta, por favor?*

Meat

meat *carne*

beef *carne de vaca, bife*

chicken *frango, galinha*

pork *porco, leitão*

ham *fiambre*

cured ham *presunto*

sausage *salsicha*

Fish and Seafood

fish *peixe*

seafood *frutas do mar, mariscos*

shellfish *marisco*

codfish *bacalhau*

sardines *sardinhas*

tuna *atum*

shrimp *camarão*

crab *caranguejo*

squid *lula*

octopus *polvo*

lobster *lagosta*

Eggs and Dairy
eggs *ovos*
hard-boiled egg *ovo cozido*
scrambled eggs *ovos mexidos*
whole milk *leite gordo*
skim milk *leite desnatado / leite magro*
cream *creme de leite / natas*
butter *manteiga*
cheese *queijo*
yogurt *iogurte*
ice cream *gelado*
sorbet *sorvete*

Vegetables and Legumes
vegetables *verduras, legumes*
salad *salada*
lettuce *alface*
spinach *espinafre*
carrot *cenoura*
tomato *tomate*
potato *batata*
cucumber *pepino*
zucchini *courgette*
eggplant *berinjela*
mushrooms *cogumelos*
olives *azeitonas*
onions *cebolas*
beans *feijões*

Fruits
fruit *fruta*
apple *maçã*
pear *pêra*
grape *uva*
fig *figo*
orange *laranja*
lemon *limão*
pineapple *ananás*
banana *banana*
apricot *damasco, abricó*
cherry *cereja*
peach *pêssego*

raspberry *framboesa*
strawberry *morango*
melon *melão*

Seasoning and Condiments
salt *sal*
black pepper *pimenta*
hot pepper *pimenta picante / piri piri (chili)*
garlic *alho*
oil *óleo*
olive oil *azeite*
mustard *mostarda*
mayonnaise *maionese*
vinegar *vinagre*

Baked Goods and Grains
bread *pão*
pastry (pie) *pastel*
cookies *biscoitos*
cake *bolo, torta*
rice *arroz*

Cooking
roasted, baked *assado*
boiled *cozido*
steamed *cozido no vapor*
grilled *grelhado*
fried *frito*
well done *bem passado*
medium *médio*
rare *mal passado*

Drinks
beverage *bebida*
water *água*
sparkling water *água com gás*
still water *água sem gás*
soda *refrigerante*
juice *sumo*
milk *leite*
coffee *café*

tea *chá*
with/without sugar *com/sem açúcar*
ice *gelo*
beer *cerveja*
wine *vinho*
Do you have wine? *Tem vinho?*
Red or white? *Tinto ou branco?*
Another, please. *Mais um/a, por favor.*

MONEY AND SHOPPING

money *dinheiro*
ATM *multibanco*
credit card *cartão de crédito*
Do you accept credit cards? *Aceita cartões de crédito?*
Can I exchange money? *Posso trocar dinheiro?*
money exchange *câmbio, troca de dinheiro*
It's too expensive. *É muito caro.*
Is there something cheaper? *Tem algo mais barato?*
more *mais*
less *menos*
a good price *Um preço bom.*

HEALTH AND SAFETY

I'm sick. *Estou doente.*
I have nausea. *Tenho nausea.*
I have a headache. *Tenho uma dor de cabeça.*
I have a stomachache. *Tenho dor de estômago.*
Call a doctor! *Chame um doutor!, Chame um médico!*
Call the police! *Chame a polícia!*
Help! *Socorro!*
pain *dor*
fever *febre*

infection *infeção*
cut *corte*
burn *queimadura*
vomit *vómito*
pill *comprimido*
medicine *remédio, medicamento*
antibiotic *antibiótico*
cotton *algodão*
condom *preservativo*
contraceptive pill *pílula*
toothpaste *pasta de dentes*
toothbrush *escova de dentes*

NUMBERS

0 zero
1 *um* (male), *uma* (female)
2 *dois* (male), *duas* (female)
3 *três*
4 *quatro*
5 *cinco*
6 *seis*
7 *sete*
8 *oito*
9 *nove*
10 *dez*
11 *onze*
12 *doze*
13 *treze*
14 catorze, *quatorze*
15 *quinze*
16 *dezesseis*
17 *dezessete*
18 *dezoito*
19 *dezenove*
20 *vinte*
21 *vinte e um*
30 *trinta*
40 *quarenta*
50 *cinquenta*
60 *sessenta*
70 *setenta*
80 *oitenta*
90 *noventa*

100 *cem*
101 *cento e um*
200 *duzentos*
500 *quinhentos*
1,000 *mil*
2,000 *dois mil*
first *primeiro*
second *segundo*
third *terceiro*
once *uma vez*
twice *duas vezes*
half *metade*

TIME

What time is it? *Que horas são?*
It's 3 o'clock in the afternoon. *São três horas da tarde.*
It's 3:15. *São três e quinze.*
It's 3:30. *São três e meia.*
It's 3:45. *São três e quarenta-cinco.*
In half an hour. *Daqui a meia hora.*
In an hour. *Daqui a uma hora.*
In two hours. *Daqui a duas horas.*
noon *meio-dia*
midnight *meia-noite*
early *cedo*
late *tarde*
before *antes*
after *depois*

DAYS AND MONTHS

day *dia*
morning *manhã*
afternoon *tarde*
night *noite*
today *hoje*
yesterday *ontem*
tomorrow *amanhã*

tomorrow morning *amanhã de manhã*
week *semana*
month *mês*
year *ano*
Monday *segunda-feira*
Tuesday *terça-feira*
Wednesday *quarta-feira*
Thursday *quinta-feira*
Friday *sexta-feira*
Saturday *sábado*
Sunday *domingo*
January *janeiro*
February *fevereiro*
March *março*
April *abril*
May *maio*
June *junho*
July *julho*
August *agosto*
September *setembro*
October *outubro*
November *novembro*
December *dezembro*

SEASONS AND WEATHER

season *estação*
spring *primavera*
summer *verão*
autumn *outono*
winter *inverno*
weather *o tempo*
sun *sol*
rain *chuva*
cloudy *nublado*
windy *vento*
hot *quente*
cold *frio*

Index

List of Maps

Photo Credits

MAP SYMBOLS

═══	Expressway	┈┈┈	Unpaved Road	┄┄┄	Railroad	
═══	Primary Road	┄┄┄	Trail	▨▨▨	Pedestrian Walkway
───	Secondary Road	┈┈┈	Ferry	▤▤▤	Stairs

○	City/Town	ⓘ	Information Center	▲	Park
◉	State Capital			⚲	Golf Course
⊛	National Capital	🅟	Parking Area	✦	Unique Feature
✪	Highlight	⛪	Church	🕊	Waterfall
★	Point of Interest	🍇	Winery/Vineyard	◭	Camping
●	Accommodation	🆃	Trailhead	▲	Mountain
▼	Restaurant/Bar	🚉	Train Station	🎿	Ski Area
■	Other Location	✈	Airport	🌀	Glacier
		✗	Airfield		

CONVERSION TABLES

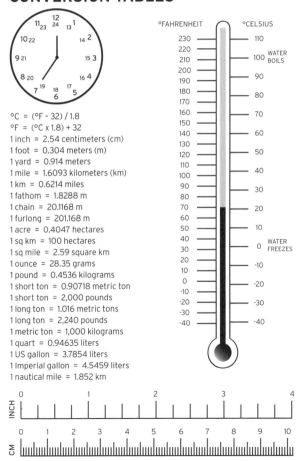

°C = (°F - 32) / 1.8
°F = (°C x 1.8) + 32
1 inch = 2.54 centimeters (cm)
1 foot = 0.304 meters (m)
1 yard = 0.914 meters
1 mile = 1.6093 kilometers (km)
1 km = 0.6214 miles
1 fathom = 1.8288 m
1 chain = 20.1168 m
1 furlong = 201.168 m
1 acre = 0.4047 hectares
1 sq km = 100 hectares
1 sq mile = 2.59 square km
1 ounce = 28.35 grams
1 pound = 0.4536 kilograms
1 short ton = 0.90718 metric ton
1 short ton = 2,000 pounds
1 long ton = 1.016 metric tons
1 long ton = 2,240 pounds
1 metric ton = 1,000 kilograms
1 quart = 0.94635 liters
1 US gallon = 3.7854 liters
1 Imperial gallon = 4.5459 liters
1 nautical mile = 1.852 km

MOON LISBON & BEYOND
Avalon Travel
Hachette Book Group
555 12th Street, Suite 1850
Oakland, CA 94607, USA
www.moon.com

Editor: Devon Lee
Managing Editor: Courtney Packard
Copy Editor: Matt Hoover
Graphics and Production Coordinator: Rue Flaherty
Cover Design: Faceout Studio, Charles Brock
Interior Design: Megan Jones Design
Map Editor: Karin Dahl
Cartographers: John Culp, Erin Greb, Alison Ollivierre
Proofreader: Callie Stoker-Graham
Indexer: Rachel Kuhn

ISBN-13: 9798886470741

Printing History
1st Edition — 2020
2nd Edition — October 2024
5 4 3 2 1

Front cover photo: MAAT - The Museum of Art, Architecture and Technology designed by Amanda Levete Architects © Massimo Ripani / Sime / eStock Photo
Back cover photo: Jerónimos Monastery © Nikolai Sorokin | Dreamstime.com
Back flap photo: Giraldo Square, Evora © Saiko3p | Dreamstime.com

Printed in Malaysia, APS